3 98

D0856268

STEIMATZKY
SHAPOLSKY
JERUSALEM • TEL AVIV
NEW YORK

Most Steimatzky books are available at special discounts for: large purchases, sales promotions, premiums or fund raising activities. Special books or reprinted editions can also be made available to satisfy specific needs.

For additional information, telephone or write:

Director of Special Marketing Arrangements
Steimatzky Publishing of North America
56 East 11th Street
New York, NY 10003

or call our New York office: (212) 505-2505.

THE FULL EXPOSÉ NO ONE DARED PUBLISH

THE MEDIA'S WAR AGAINST ISRAEL

STEIMATZKY
SHAPOLSKY
NEW YORK • JERUSALEM • TEL AVIV

A Shapolsky Book
Published by Shapolsky Books
a division of
Steimatzky Publishing of North America, Inc.

Copyright © 1986 by Stephen Karetzky.
All rights reserved under International and Pan American Copyright
Conventions. Published and printed in the U.S.A. by Shapolsky Books, a
division of Steimatzky Publishing of North America, Inc. No parts of this
book may be used or reproduced in any manner whatsoever without written
permission of Steimatzky Publishing of North America, Inc., except in the
case of brief quotations embodied in critical articles or reviews.

For any additional information, contact Steimatzky Publishing of
North America, Inc., 56 East 11th Street, NY, NY 10003.

Typography by Type Network (KTN)

10 9 8 7 6 5 4 3 2 1

1st Edition January 1986

ISBN 0-933503-01-6

Library of Congress Cataloging in Publication Data
Karetzky, Stephen—1986
    The Media's Propaganda War Against Israel

Dedicated to Harry Karetzky,

whose integrity, intelligence and kindness have earned him the respect and affection of his family, friends and co-workers.

"Swords are in their lips"

—*Psalm 59*

CONTENTS

James Carville

INTRODUCTION
by Congressman Jack Kemp

No country has fought terrorism longer and harder than the State of Israel. For over a quarter of a century before the official birth of the state in 1948, and without letup ever since, the people of Israel have had to fend off terrorist onslaughts. It is a difficult, treacherous and exhausting war, requiring constant vigilance and un-wavering resolve.

Now the advent of highly mobile, satellite-beamed television journalism has added a new dimension to this war. Much of what terrorists do—whether in a sustained campaign, as in Lebanon, or in the unfolding of a hijack-ing, as in the recent TWA drama—is geared to the use of television as theater and a platform for propaganda. In the terrorists' calculations, the impact of TV cover-age on public opinion and on political and military deci-sion-making is paramount.

During the war in Lebanon, administration offi-cials, senators and congressman formed opinions and

Congressman Jack Kemp (Republican—New York) is Chairman of the House Republican Conference, the Senior Republican on the House Foreign Operations Subcommittee and a member of the House Budget Committee.

3

often made public pronouncements based on TV coverage. During the TWA crisis there is no doubt that the way the networks projected the events on the screen influenced millions of viewers' attitudes on terrorism and terrorists.

It is still a relatively new experience for us, and it may be too early to assess the effect of TV journalism on the course of history. But there is no escaping the fact that in recent years the two most successful and least controversial wars were the Grenada and the Falklands campaigns. Both were "off limits" to television.

Nothing can match the impact of the visual. Regrettably, what the screen in our living room has done is to turn the saying "seeing is believing" on its ear. By using movie techniques designed to create illusions (scene-staging, editing, voice-overs, juxtaposition of images, close-ups, etc.) television has transformed news programs into theatrical episodes and mini-dramas, thus making their potential to mislead infinitely greater than that of the written word.

As a theatrical medium, TV lends itself to terrorist theater. To successfully combat terrorists we must recognize this vulnerability as one of the weapons they can and do use against us. Only an open and frank discussion of these problems and potential abuses, and of ways to overcome them, can bring us closer to victory over terrorism.

Foreword

Rael Jean Isaac

The issue of media bias toward Israel came to the fore in the summer of 1982. In reporting the war in Lebanon, the media behaved like a lynch mob, with print and TV reporters, columnists and cartoonists vying with each other in misstatement and calumny. The analogy of Israel to Nazi Germany became a familiar one.

The media performance was so execrable that several studies were published in response, documenting the pattern of misrepresentation. A most detailed account which analyzed the specific performance of major newspapers (*The New York Times* and *Washington Post*), the newsmagazines, and each major network was Joshua Muravchik's "Misreporting Lebanon." It appeared in *Policy Review.* *Commentary's* editor, Norman Podhoretz, titled his essay "J'accuse," evoking the powerful echo of Emile Zola's indictment of anti-Semitism in the Dreyfus affair. Similarly, the title of Edward Alexander's essay in the English journal *Encounter* summed up his theme: "The Journalists' War Against Israel: Techniques of Distortion, Disorientation and Disinformation." Martin Peretz, editor of *The New Republic*, went to Lebanon during the war and indignantly contrasted the media's portrait of massive destruction in

Rael Jean Isaac is the author of *Israel Divided* (Johns Hopkins) and *Parties and Politics of Israel* (Longmans), and is a member of the Executive Committee of Americans For A Safe Israel.

southern Lebanon with his own eyewitness testimony.

There were also studies focussing on specific performances. There was agreement that NBC had been seized by an even higher degree of anti-Israel fervor than CBS and ABC. A film, "NBC in Lebanon," and a pamphlet, "NBC's War in Lebanon" by Edward Alexander, were sponsored by Americans For A Safe Israel. And because the *Washington Post* was more poisonous than the *Times*, Leonore Siegelman analyzed the *Post's* coverage in "Did the Washington Post Tell It?" a pamphlet published by the Zionist Organization of America.

To be sure, disapproval of the media's performance was not universal. The media was well pleased with itself. The influential *Columbia Journalism Review* assessed the media's product during the war and concluded that American journalism

> "reported what it saw for the most part fairly and accurately and sometimes brilliantly, provided balanced comment, and provoked and absorbed controversy. For performance under fire, readers and viewers could have asked for little more."

Most American Jews were taken aback by the virulence of the media attack on Israel. There was a vague sense among Jews that media support for Israel had slipped considerably after the Yom Kippur War of 1973. *Time's* bias was so glaring that it drew particular attention. Jews were shocked in 1977 when *Time* introduced Menachem Begin, the newly elected Prime Minister of Israel, with the words "rhymes with Fagin." (There were no lack of other " rhymes"

6

Time might have used—how about "rhymes with Reagan?")
Martin Peretz was sufficiently disturbed by *Time*'s pattern
of distortion that in 1980, two years before the war in
Lebanon, he asked this writer to do an analysis of *Time*'s
coverage. This was duly published in *The New Republic* as
"'*Time* Against Israel." In analyzing *Time*'s coverage over
a twenty year period, I found that coverage was reasonably
balanced until 1970, tilted against Israel after 1973, and
became venomous after Begin's election in 1977. While the
post-1973 tilt was leavened with a certain disarming
frankness about the impact of the oil weapon on changing
the views of Israel's "friends," *Time*'s reporting after 1977
was equally distant from fairness and reality. Indeed, I devoted a section of the article to "*Time* vs. Reality" showing how frequently and blatantly *Time* departed from the
facts in a randomly selected five week period. The depar-
tures from fact were in a consistent direction, designed to
convince the reader that the PLO wanted peace and that
Israel blocked a settlement.

If the American Jewish community had been less liberal politically, it might have been better prepared for the
media onslaught in 1982. While little had been written
about media bias specifically toward Israel, considerable
attention had earlier been focussed on the media's bias
toward the left. The Media Institute had chronicled the pattern of media bias against business and nuclear energy.
Since 1972 Accuracy in Media has been publishing a
bimonthly newsletter, *AIM Report*, documenting media
misreporting on both domestic and foreign issues. The

most detailed single study of media distortion was Peter Braestrup's massive two volume study *Big Story*, published in 1977. It dealt with the way the American press and television reported and interpreted the 1968 Tet offensive in Vietnam, converting a decisive defeat for the Communists into an American defeat.

Relatively few Jews were interested in these matters. Had the media misreported the Vietnam War? The war was long over and most Jews had been opposed to it anyway. The conservative outlook of most media critics prevented many Jews from taking the criticism seriously. And there was another factor. Conservative groups concerned with media bias had neglected the subject of media bias against Israel. Indeed, the first time Accuracy in Media paid attention to this problem was during the Lebanon war when, to its credit, it came out with a hardhitting issue titled "Lies About Lebanon."

The upshot then was that for many Jews the media assault on Israel in 1982 seemed to come out of nowhere. Unaware of the pattern of hostility that had been developing over the years, many Jews initially accepted what they were being told in their newspapers and on their TV screens and blamed Israel.

The importance of Stephen Karetzky's study is multifold. First, it covers the months of February, March and April of 1982, in other words, a period *before* the war in Lebanon. This enables us to see how the pattern of distortion characteristic of news coverage prior to the war, determined the way the war would be covered (and, one might

8

add, how Israel has been covered since the war). Second, this study spotlights *The New York Times*, the most important and influential source of news in the United States. The *Times* is familiarly referred to as the bible of the media and it sets the news agenda of the electronic as well as the print media. (Russ Braley, a longtime foreign correspondent for the *New York Daily News*, reports his dismay when he was reassigned to New York and discovered that the night editor was required to listen to the New York Times radio station WQXR, at 9 p.m., when the next day's headlines are revealed, and then match every story on the *Times'* front page in at least a paragraph or two.)

The *Times* was treated too lightly in the exposés of media coverage of the Lebanon war. Joshua Muravchik wrote that the *Times* "notwithstanding some notable lapses, maintained higher standards of journalistic objectivity than did any of the other news outlets covered by this study." But as Muravchik himself documents, the lapses were indeed notable. Bias was not merely apparent on the editorial page, where a stand against the war was legitimate, but on the Op-Ed page (where seventeen of the first nineteen essays on the war were hostile to Israel), and, most significantly, on the news pages. There were the familiar wildly exaggerated casualty figures and a lengthy tribute to Yassir Arafat by Thomas Friedman which contained not a whisper of criticism. There was an endless stream of stories by Marvine Howe, many of them based on nothing but mere speculation: "growing fears" that Israel was planning a drive against Tripoli after it was through with Beirut, "fears" that

9

the rights of PLO prisoners were not properly guaranteed, etc.

Muravchik dryly remarks that "Ms. Howe's reports gave the impression that she had travelled Lebanon looking for stories with an anti-Israel twist." In his hostility to Begin, the *Times'* Bernard Nossiter actually doctored his words. When Begin at the UN praised the "*right* of self-defense as the noblest concept of the human mind," Nossiter reported in the *Times* that Begin had called "*wars* of self-defense the noblest concept of the human mind." This made Begin sound wholly ridiculous. Far from correcting the statement, the *Times* repeated it the following day.

Professor Karetzky is forced to compare the *Times* with a range of other papers that were less biased on specific stories. For example Karetzky finds that the *Washington Post* did a better job than the *Times* in reporting the slaying of two Arabs at the Dome of the Rock by a crazed Jewish gunman. Yet, overall, the *Post*'s coverage of Israel is abominable, with some of the most anti-Israel reporters in the business employed there, including Loren Jenkins (who compared Israel to the Nazis in a *Rolling Stone* interview) and Jonathan Randal (whose animus led him to make such bizarre claims as that Sharon and Begin "gloried in the polarization of Israeli society produced by the Lebanese War"). Since the *Post* makes no effort to separate fact from opinion, the attitudes of its journalists strongly color its stories, even if its anti-Israel reporters make some of their most outrageous statements in other forums. In taking on the influential *New York Times* Dr. Karetzky has made the right choice. He shows how poorly the best of our newspapers serves us.

Finally, Professor Karetzky's study is important because it provides a model that can be used in studying other newspapers. He analyzes the ways in which papers can distort material: misuse of photographs, inappropriate use of sources, false analogies, misleading terminology, and so on. The reader can use these categories as a means of evaluating how a given newspaper performs on a specific issue.

What emerges from Karetzky's study, as from the studies of media coverage of the war in Lebanon, is that Israel is judged by a double standard. Occasionally a reporter or columnist will be frank about this. For example, Anthony Lewis has written: "Yes, there is a double standard. From its birth Israel asked to be judged as a light among the nations." (To Anthony Lewis it is plain that the only light Israel emits is a hellish glare.) Or there is the ever-censorious (of Israel) Nick Thimmesch: "The media employs high standards to measure Israel . . . because Israel always claimed high standards for itself." It is true that Israel sets for itself a high standard of behavior. But this does not entitle journalists to set wholly different standards as *appropriate* to Israel and the Arab states, and to give Israel an "F" on the basis of one standard and Arab states an implied "A" on the basis of a totally different one, or worse yet to apply *no* standard to Arab states. For example, just because brutality is to be expected from the Syria of Hafez al-Assad, does not mean that journalists should shrug off as of no

11

interest or consequence repeated demonstrations of that brutality like the slaughter of thousands of civilians at Hama. In his book *Double Vision,* Ze'ev Chafets, former director of the Israeli Government Press Office, notes that what is really at work is a *double* "double standard." Israel is not simply judged on a basis that is inapplicable to her Arab neighbors. Israel is judged by standards more exacting than those applied to other democracies. Surrounded, beleaguered, attacked—Israel is expected to behave like democracies *at peace.*

Karetzky documents the mechanisms of the double standard; he does not address the fascinating, if necessarily speculative question "Why?" In the case of the *Times* there are specific historical factors that may have some bearing. The *Times* has remained the property of the Ochs family, which is of German Jewish Reform background, assimilated, and self-conscious regarding its Jewish origins. (Some of the family now style themselves "Oakes.") Both the German Reform background and the assimilationist attitudes have shaped the *Times'* views and attitudes toward Israel over the years.

As Russ Braley observes in *Bad News,* the first major study of the *Times'* misreporting of foreign events since the Suez Crisis of 1956, the Ochs family were so opposed to Zionism that when Truman, in 1946, advocated that 100,000 survivors of the death camps be permitted to immigrate to Palestine, a *Times* editorial condemned Truman's interference in Britain's affairs. In a commentary, James Reston dismissed the plight of Jewish survivors: "It is

12

generally conceded in the capital that the plight of the Jews in Europe is only one aspect of the melancholy story of the displaced persons of Europe, of whom the Jews are a minority." Apparently it never occurred to Reston that the murder of six million Jews had something to do with their being a minority of the survivors and that this might entitle them to special attention in the "broader" context of displaced persons.

The anti-Zionism of the *Times* faded as Israel became an increasingly well-established fact, but the uneasiness with Israel remained, manifested, for example, in the care the *Times* took to avoid sending a Jewish correspondent to report from Israel. Chafets relates how, in 1979, *Times* executive editor A. M. Rosenthal proudly informed a meeting of *Times* editors that the paper had assigned a new man to Jerusalem, and he was glad to report that the *Times* had become mature enough to send a Jew. The "Jew" was David Shipler—a WASP. Shipler's replacement, Thomas Friedman, *is* a Jew, "seasoned," to be sure, by his five-year stint in Beirut. (Of course, being Jewish has done nothing to mitigate hostility toward Israel; for example, second to none in his antagonism is Jonathan Randal, whose mother is Jewish.)

More significant in the long run, certainly for the tenor of the editorial page, is the tradition of liberal Jewish reform which still gives the *Times* its distinctive stamp. Daniel Patrick Moynihan attributes to that tradition the "universalist, even deracinated air" that marks the *Times* editorial page. It has been observed that if the United States had consistently followed the advice of the *Times,* it would probably no longer exist. But even if the U.S. could have weathered the almost consistently bad advice of the *Times,* there can be little doubt that Israel would no longer exist had she shown the perennial restraint and readiness to accommodate Arab demands urged upon her by the *Times* over the years. In the world of *Times* editorials, there are no irreconcilable conflicts or savage animosities. If the Arabs show fanatical hatred of Israel, then it is up to Israel, by undeviating good will, generous territorial and other concessions, and the saintly turning of cheeks, to set an example of reasonable behavior that the Arabs will feel impelled to emulate.

That the media performed so poorly during the war in Lebanon was owing to a set of specific circumstances. Since Israel swept quickly through southern Lebanon but remained for so long outside Beirut, (intent on forcing PLO forces to leave the city), the focus of media attention for many weeks was the siege of Beirut.

Israel was inflicting death and destruction on the television screen, with all the suffering made immediately accessible to viewers. This inevitably worked against Israel. The PLO refused to leave the city and refused to allow civilians to leave, using them as hostages in the "media war" precisely because civilian bombing casualties made Israel look bad. But the Beirut-based reporters, who dominated coverage in this period, did not explain this to the American public. To understand why, one must understand that the reporters in Beirut were, on the whole, a special group.

14

Chafetz documents in *Double Vision* that reporters in Beirut were subject to a pattern of intimidation since the civil war of 1975. Murder and the threat of murder taught reporters to practice self-censorship and not send home stories unacceptable to either Syria or the PLO. Reporters uncomfortable with self-censorship found Lebanon an uncongenial post and were glad to find another assignment. Those who thrived in this atmosphere did not need to be intimidated because they identified with the PLO, seeing them as "progressive" heroes whose cause deserved support. These newsmen congregated at the Commodore Hotel in Moslem West Beirut. (Chafets reports the dismay at the ABC bureau in Beirut when it was learned that former ABC producer Barbara Newman, who had come to Lebanon in 1980 to film a documentary, was planning to stay at the Christian-run Alexandre Hotel in East Beirut. To ease the situation, the documentary's correspondent, Geraldo Rivera, booked rooms in both places and commuted from one side of the city to the other.) At the Commodore, newsmen interacted with one another, learning to practice "group think."

Newsweek's Tony Clifton authored *God Cried,* perhaps the single most venomous book to be published by a U.S. newsman following the war. He throws considerable light on the process by which the news consensus was formed during the war. When the Israeli invasion began, the media rushed to the scene whatever hands they had available. Clifton, who has openly referred to the PLO as "our side," complains that reporters swallowed Christian "propaganda" and

15

dispensed it as news. He notes that it took a few weeks before the "old hands," i.e. those who had covered the civil war, were sent to Beirut. The "old hands" of course were the pro-PLO hands.

One exception was Kenneth Timmerman, whose failure to toe the PLO line led to his "arrest" (French consular authorities eventually arranged a trade for his release). In an article in *Commentary* in January 1983, he observes that the PLO carefully screened journalists who were sent and "no newspaper or other medium would commit the error of sending in to West Beirut someone who had adversely reported in the past on the activities of the PLO or the Syrians, for fear of him simply disappearing." Ironically, the Western reporters in Beirut became actors in the drama, prolonging the siege and destruction. By acting as a PLO sounding board, the media fanned Arafat's hopes that Israel could be stopped by the pressure of public opinion, and that PLO forces needn't leave the city.

The peculiar mind-set of the *Times* and the special circumstances in Beirut do not explain the pattern of anti-Israel bias that made itself felt after the 1967 war, growing worse after 1973 and worse yet after Begin's accession to power in 1977. Moreover, events in Israel, which these years demarcate, merely reinforced attitudes in the media whose source had nothing to do with Israel, its wars or its choice of Prime Minister.

The real explanation lies in intellectual trends in the West which led many—including a majority of the media elite—to elevate the Third World to a position of moral

16

authority and to see Western democracies, especially the powerful United States, as colonialist-imperialist oppressors. Countries like Israel (that identified with Western political values) were seen as extensions of Western imperialism, while Third World countries (or groups within such countries) that struggled against the West were *ipso facto* virtuous freedom fighters. Moreover, an aura of inevitable success rested upon the insurgents, while the Goliaths of the West were doomed to military helplessness before those on the side of both morality and history, the Davids of destiny.

The conflict between Israel and the Arab states was reconceptualized in terms of these attitudes. Israel was seen as an extension of iniquitous Western power. The central role of the Arab states in the conflict, long taken for granted by the media, was now minimized. The PLO assumed center stage. Once defined as a terrorist organization, it was reinterpreted as a progressive movement of third world liberation. The PLO was guilty of occasional "excesses" perhaps, but its goal of "national self-determination" and anti-Western credentials definitely put it on the moral side of history. (The media dismissed as rhetoric the problem posed by the PLO's repeated insistence that Palestinian self-determination could only be built on the ashes of Jewish self-determination, effectively pretending that the PLO didn't really mean what it said).

That transferring the role of "good guy" from Israel to the PLO gave freshness to reporting a stale conflict was no doubt a welcome plus. But beyond the attraction of fresh news copy, Israel and the PLO changed roles to conform to a broad new agenda that many in the media had embraced.

As the media increasingly assumed an adversarial posture on a host of issues, it began to see itself as a high court, sitting in judgment on the political realm. The publication of the Pentagon Papers by the *Times* was a watershed in the confrontation between the media and the political realm, changing the relations of power between them. As Harrison Salisbury put it: "The *Times* has come to fulfill a new function; it has become that Fourth Estate, that fourth co-equal branch of government of which men like Thomas Carlyle spoke." As Braley notes in *Bad News,* the Pentagon Papers were but a prelude to the media's exercise of more formidable muscle. To quote Salisbury again: "One can imagine the Watergate break-in without the Pentagon Papers affair; one cannot imagine the Watergate exposé, the whole debacle of the Nixon presidency, without the Pentagon Papers."

This adversarial stance toward the political sphere, with the assumption of superior moral virtue and the taste of power, produced an immense arrogance in the media. Reed Irvine, who founded Accuracy in Media, told me that when he started the organization in 1969, he was convinced that research on media inaccuracies would force those responsible to admit errors, issue corrections, and be more careful in the future. Irvine ruefully observed that it did not work out that way. The media refuse to admit the most egregious mistakes. For if they have become a fourth branch of government, it is a branch which, unlike the others, is subject to no checks and balances, one which can behave irresponsibly without fear of consequences.

Increasingly, injured individuals, seeing no other recourse, have turned to the libel suit in the hope of forcing media accountability. The most dramatic recent suits have been those brought by General William Westmoreland against CBS and by General Ariel Sharon against *Time*. But U.S. libel law is so stringent as to make libel extremely difficult to prove. In *The New York Times v. Sullivan*, twenty years ago, the Supreme Court ruled that for a public figure to be "libeled" he or she must prove not only that the material published was defamatory and false, but also that the paper *knew* that it was false or published it with "reckless disregard" as to its truth. "Intent to defame" turns out to be almost impossible to prove conclusively. As a result, when juries have ruled that there was malicious intent, their verdicts have mostly been overturned on appeal. Indeed, barely one in four jury verdicts establishing libel have survived on appeal, judges ruling the jurors did not properly understand the law.

Given the often multi-million dollar price tags and the extremely remote chances of victory, why do cases continue to be brought? It is because the libel suit at least offers the opportunity to hold the media accountable in the court of public opinion. In the absence of any other mechanism to make the media accountable, only the libel suit forces the media to disclose for public scrutiny the way it collects information, the way it verifies it, and the way

19

it edits—and edits out—what it gathers.

The Sharon case revealed that the much vaunted *Time* editorial procedures were a humbug. Steven Brill, editor of *The American Lawyer* and a civil libertarian who opposes all libel suits on constitutional grounds, has provided a long, detailed and devastating analysis of what the trial revealed of *Time*'s procedures. In an "open letter" to *Time* editor-in-chief Henry Grunwald, Brill acidly observes that "it seems from the testimony of your own people that *Time* made up its story—that's right, simply made it up." Brill studied not only the trial but the pre-trial record as well. (*Time* had tried to persuade the judge to dismiss the case prior to trial on a number of grounds, including the ploy that Sharon's reputation was so bad that he was "libel-proof.") On the basis of both studies Brill concluded that the record "reveals an arrogant, bloated bureaucracy in which the reporter of the paragraph that Sharon is suing about is biased to the point of being a near-fanatic, your chief of correspondents isn't much of a chief and has a suspiciously selective memory when he's under oath, your managing editor (the supposed boss of *Time)* doesn't know much of anything about what goes on in his shop, your much-vaunted research department is a sham, and your system for weeding out unreliable reporters is nil." Brill wryly noted that "nobody ever admits a mistake about anything" during the whole sorry process.

Even if *Time* printed the story believing it was true, a few days after publication *Time*'s bureau chief in Israel, Harry Kelly, was told by Knesset member Ehud Olmert (at a dinner party) that *Time*'s story was false. Olmert had seen the secret appendix to the Kahan commission report investigating the massacres at Sabra and Shatilla. (It was this document which *Time* claimed had details concerning Sharon's visit to the Gemayel family where he "discussed" the need "for revenge" for Bashir Gemayel's assassination.) Kelly asked Olmert to confirm this and make sure. Olmert did so and testified that he called Kelly and told him, "There is nothing in this that resembles your story." Kelly did not deny that these events took place, but in his deposition said he did not consider this to be "news." In other words, a false story was "news." Indeed, *Time*'s public relations department felt it had such a "scoop" that it circulated a press release to accompany the story. It claimed that Sharon had "urged" the Lebanese to send Phalangists into the camps. But evidence that a *Time* feature story was false was "not news" and Kelly never even bothered to file a story. Brill, in preparing his *American Lawyer* article, asked Louis Slovinsky, the chief *Time* spokesman, why Time did not acknowledge and correct facts that it discovered to be wrong on its own. He was told: "You sound like a total ass just to ask a question like that. Why should we do that? We don't have to, and we haven't had to for sixty-two years."

So much for journalistic responsibility at *Time*.

Brill contrasts *Time*'s behavior with the behavior it would expect of a president or governor or corporate president in similar circumstances. If *Time* were covering the story it would expect a politician to admit the mistake and fire those responsible. On the contrary, *Time* has cast itself

21

as a hero under fire, protecting free speech against a menacing onslaught. The judge in the case, Abraham Sofaer, has a comment to make about this posture. In denying *Time*'s request that Sharon's case be summarily dismissed without trial, Sofaer stated: "Time has refused to issue any correction or to print plaintiff's denial. Only through the litigation process has plaintiff been able to uncover and publish the evidence from which Time claimed to have learned the contents of the Commission's secret appendix . . .*it would be pure fantasy to treat Time in this case like some struggling champion of free expression, defending at great risk to itself the right to publish its view of the truth."* [Italics added.]

Time "won" the trial in the sense that the jury failed to find intent to tell a lie. CBS won the Westmoreland case in that General Westmoreland withdrew from the case before it reached the jury. The danger then is that while these trials deservedly undermine the media's credibility with the public, they can reinforce the media's sense of invulnerability. (The "cost" of a trial, it is sometimes argued, will have a "chilling effect" on smaller papers and TV stations, which will be afraid to publish articles critical of public figures. But by the same token, the "cost" of a trial will seem prohibitive to an injured party if it is clear that damages cannot be ultimately collected. The Sharon case cost the firm of Shea and Gould over a million dollars, only a third of which has been covered through fund-raising appeals. Organizations like *Time* and CBS have libel insurance: the worst they have to anticipate is higher premiums.)

22

Certainly, the reaction of *Time* to the suit's conclusion is not encouraging. The jury took the unusual step, in announcing its verdict, of issuing an amplifying statement that declared the jury had found certain *Time* employees had acted "negligently and carelessly." *Time*'s managing editor, Ray Cave, subsequently dismissed the jury's criticism, saying he "disagreed" with it. In an official statement on behalf of *Time* he reaffirmed the truth of the story that the jury had found to be false and stated, "We are totally confident that the story is substantially true" and professed "the utmost confidence in our editorial staff and our editorial procedures."* *Time* editor Henry Grunwald, interviewed on the David Brinkley program on ABC on January 27, even announced that *Time* planned to keep David Halevy on its staff. This was despite the fact that Halevy had previously been suspended by *Time* for filing a false story and had been singled out by name in the jury's statement as guilty of negligent and careless reporting.

---

*Judging from a 1969 book, *Evidence* by Robert and Dale Newman (Houghton Mifflin), *Time*'s editorial procedures have not changed much over the years. The study notes that while on a typical newspaper the story is basically a product of the man at the scene, at *Time* "copy filed from reporters in the field is primarily stimulus to editorial imagination. Testimony on this point from defectors from the magazine is unanimous." After chronicling the account of a former *Time* writer on what was done to his story on Marilyn Monroe, the authors note that if such changes "are made in stories where the ideological impact would be minor, one can only imagine what happens when the magazine's biases are touched."

Of course in the Sharon case, the reporter's biases and the editorial biases were in the same direction. Thus Halevy's report that Sharon had given the Gemayel family "the feeling" that he understood their need for revenge was changed by the editor to become Sharon's "discussing" the need for revenge. Both were wrong, but the editor's version made Sharon's supposed behavior even worse.

23

While day-to-day reporting on Israel is rife with the subtle kinds of distortions that Dr. Karetzky analyzes in this book, the media's negative underlying attitudes against Israel persist, ready to surface at any crisis.

Just such an opportunity arose in March 1985, when CBS unjustifiably attacked Israel in the world press. When two Lebanese cameramen working for CBS were killed in a shelling incident, the company's response was all too familiar. Within hours of the incident CBS News President Edward M. Joyce fired off a telegram to Israeli Prime Minister Shimon Peres accusing Israeli forces of "outrageous behavior." A subsequent telegram spoke of "deliberate fire" on "unarmed and neutral journalists." CBS promptly announced that as a "matter of principle" it was cancelling plans for a weeklong Eastern television broadcast from Israel on the CBS Morning News. Not to be outdone, ABC News President Roone Arledge fired off his own telegram to Peres, calling the killings "an appalling act."

Once Israel had been roasted in the court of public opinion for the deliberate murder of journalists by the three major networks, CBS belatedly decided to send someone to investigate what had actually happened. An embarrassed vice president of CBS News in Jerusalem, Ernest Leiser, was then forced to admit that the tank which fired the fatal shell was more than a mile away and that the Israeli action "was certainly not a deliberate attempt to fire guns against our camera people."

A senior Israeli official remarked caustically: "CBS had a gut reaction. They came to their verdict, called us every name in the book, punished us, and then they said they were sending someone over to investigate what happened." The hasty, hysterical attack on Israel must be contrasted with the simultaneous failure of any of the networks to use their Beirut-based reporters for an exploration of the Syrian-Lebanese role in the kidnapping of Americans and others in Beirut.

Needless to say CBS did not apologize for its earlier unfounded attacks on Israel. Indeed, Joyce managed to substitute a new attack for an apology. He expressed "regret" that Peres planned "no measure which could prevent a recurrence of last week's tragedy." CBS gave no indication that it planned to take any steps to safeguard the lives of its freelance Lebanese crewmen by keeping them out of combat areas that Israel had explicitly warned were dangerous and should be entered only with Israeli military escorts. By permitting their unescorted employees to enter this active combat zone it was more accurately CBS who was responsible for the reckless endangerment of their lives.

The CBS cameramen fiasco notwithstanding, Central America has distracted some of the media's attention. The media elite's Third World enthusiasms have been transferred to the Sandinistas and, to a lesser extent, the guerrillas in El Salvador. (The election of Napoleon Duarte as President seems to have dampened media enthusiasm for the guerrillas.) Arafat, temporarily at least, is out of favor as a heroic figure. Although his forces left Tripoli, as they had left Beirut, with a victory sign, his exit this time did not go down triumphantly with the press. This may have been because he was forced out by other Arabs. In any event, outrage is focussed once again on the supposed malice of the U.S. Government in supporting repression and counter-revolution in Central America.

Israel can derive little encouragement from this. As long as those who set journalistic standards retain their self-righteous, adversarial elitism, any respite Israel enjoys from media obloquy will be brief. The process of misrepresentation goes on, which, in the long run, may do more to undermine support for Israel than concentrated bursts of outrageous reporting, such as accompanied the war in Lebanon. The drop of water technique can be more effective than crasser methods.

While there are no easy solutions to the problem of media distortion of the news, this brief survey would not be complete without mention of one encouraging development. That is a new willingness on the part of the media to criticize one another. Although still rare, it is no longer taboo for one newspaper to attack another for inaccurate and distorted reporting. To take one example, in February 1985 the *New York Times* ran a series of front page articles alleging malfeasance on the part of the chief medical examiner of New York City. Only a short time ago the *Times* could have been confident that other newspapers would simply echo its story, while the author of the series would comfortably await his Pulitzer Prize. Elliot Gross, the medical examiner accused of falsifying results, would have been assured of public disgrace whether or not he were found guilty after a prolonged investigation. Gross' chief recourse was a libel suit in which he would have to prove the *Times'* reporter *intentionally* defamed him. But, remarkably, the ink had hardly dried on the *Times'* series when the *New York Post* produced its own investigative study. The *Post's* series was an investigation of the *Times* report! The *Post's* reporter, in fact, found that the *Times* had distorted and misrepresented the views of a number of those it had quoted.

Whatever the merit—or lack of merit—the *Times'* charges are ultimately shown to have, it is an enormously healthy development when the media look skeptically at each other rather than hunt in a pack. What if ABC's *20/20* had decided to do its own study of CBS after CBS had aired its documentary on the alleged "conspiracy" by General Westmoreland to deceive the President? What if *Newsweek* were to reexamine questionable stories published by *Time* and vice versa? There would then be no question of a "chilling effect" on free speech, but rather a genuine exercise of press freedoms and responsibilities. No one likes to be exposed by his peers, and the prospect should help journalists to achieve balance and accuracy in reporting. If the media act to monitor one another, the need both for libel suits and for media monitoring organizations like Accuracy in Media would be reduced.

Without the barrage of criticism that the media have experienced in the last few years, there would not even be the small harbingers of change now visible. Stephen Karetzky's study is a valuable contribution that hopefully will bring about some much needed reform.

THE NEW YORK TIMES
PROPAGANDA WAR AGAINST ISRAEL

INTRODUCTION
I

The most prestigious and influential newspaper in the United States has been presenting an inaccurate, tendentious picture of developments in Israel and its neighboring territories. These developments comprise the most significant foreign news story in the world open to relatively easy coverage by the Western media. This low quality coverage increases the chances of major war in the Middle East, with another disruption of Western oil supplies and another major confrontation with the Soviet Union. It threatens the continued existence of the only Western, democratic, stable, reliable American ally in that strategically important region, the only country there of any significant value to the United States in a military confrontation. The present coverage also exacerbates the widespread anti-Americanism overseas—especially in Arab countries—because of its negative attitude towards Israel: Israel is often erroneously considered to be a client state of the United States for whose actions America is ultimately responsible.

The impact of Times news stories is great. There is a widespread assumption that they are objective, intelligent, complete reports of the most significant developments; and they are read by a large number of the influential and educated in the United States. People of significance in other countries also read them. In addition to the relatively widespread and strategic national and international distribution of the Times itself, its stories are also featured in the International Herald Tribune and in the hundreds of newspapers and broadcasting agencies which subscribe to the New York Times Information Service. On microfilm and computer print-out, the Times will be a prime source for future historians, and of course it is now widely used by contemporary researchers. The quality of the Times reporting is also important because it is the most respected American newspaper, and one *expects* that it adheres to the canons of the journalism profession. It sets a standard for the entire journalistic community, a major component of the nation's democratic system.

The major, interrelated elements in the Times'

distorted news coverage and analysis have been the following:

1. The unbalanced and prejudicial use of personal and written sources.
2. Misperception and misconception of phenomena. A gross incapacity to evaluate sources and data.
3. Phantasy.
4. The use of biased and incompetent sources for news accounts and opinions.
5. Factual errors.
6. Misrepresentation.
7. Distortion through false analogies, playful and inaccurate inversions, and spurious ironies.
8. The use of inaccurate, misleading and prejudicial terminology.
9. Inaccurate labelling of people and phenomena.
10. Manipulative wording and phrasing of sentences.
11. Misleading headlines.
12. The use of photographs to confirm a biased view through the selection of subject matter, the frequency of themes, the size of the photographs, and their placement in the newspaper.
13. The selective cropping of original photographs.

31

14. Inaccurate and biased photo captions.
15. Biased foci: the unreasonably intense scrutiny of particular subjects, and the omission or under-coverage of others.
16. The selective repetition of particular themes, words and stories.
17. The biased emphasis or deemphasis of particular stories by their physical placement in the newspaper.
18. The selective substitution of melodrama and pathos for objective analysis.
19. The selective substitution of subjective, glib discussions of the psychological and/or near-spiritual for concrete, factual analyses.
20. The intrusion of moral judgments. The unfounded nature of these judgments.

An accurate picture of the Times news coverage requires the close analysis which follows. The focus is on the news stories of February, March and April, 1982. (The stories examined appeared in the early edition of the Times. They rarely varied in later editions.) Several noteworthy events occurred during this period (which received much world attention); e.g.: rioting on the West Bank, an armed attack in the Dome of the Rock Mosque, and the final withdrawal of Israeli troops and civilians from Sinai in accordance with the Camp David accords. These developments were the focus of attention in newspapers throughout the Western world. Some warranted the attention accorded them, others did not. Nevertheless, they dominated the front pages until the conflict in the Falkland Islands. The reporting before and after this period appears to use the same methods and has the same general thrust. During the summer 1982 war in Lebanon and its aftermath the quality of the journalism declined further.

2

THE PORTRAYAL OF ISRAEL AS A SUPPRESSOR OF INNOCENT ARABS

One of the major elements of the Times news reports during these months was the presentation of Arabs as helpless, innocent victims; civilians who were in the middle of a terrible situation they bore no responsibility for creating; people being brutalized by calculating, cruel, anti-democratic, voracious Israelis. The Arabs, one is led to believe, used force only when compelled to by the Israelis. An interesting element accompanying this portrayal was the unstated assumption that both the New York Times journalists and the Arabs could look into the minds of the Israelis, discern their innermost thoughts, and foresee their complicated, long-range, nefarious plans.

In "The West Bank Occupation Now Resembles Annexation" (3/28, p. E3) by David Shipler, head of the Times news bureau in Israel, he discussed the "tough handling of stone-throwing Arabs, who were protesting the Government's replacement of elected local officials with Israelis." This was a perverted version of events. In actuality, the Arabs were killing and maiming people, and to characterize the Israeli response as "tough" was a distorted, subjective judgment rather than objective news reporting. (This subject is dealt with at length later.) He noted that six Palestinians had been "shot to death" by soldiers, while "one soldier died when his jeep was hit by a grenade." The very wording here misrepresented the situation. Palestinians were "shot to death" but the blowing up of an Israeli was presented as incidental to the denouement of an almost non-violent occurrence—the effect of a grenade on a jeep, rather than an attack by an Arab on an Israeli. In this, as in most other Times reports, Shipler failed to explain or describe the events surrounding the shootings of the Arabs, e.g., the menacing of vastly outnumbered Israeli soldiers who had shown a great deal of restraint. The actions of the Palestinians were made to appear virtuous compared to those of the Israelis: they were "protesting the replacement of elected local officials with Israelis." The reasons for the dismissal of the mayors were not given here, and the *Arabs* were presented as people who were fighting for democracy.

In Shipler's article, the New York Times correspondent adopted the Arabs' claims concerning the Israelis' activities and aims on the West Bank (note the headline), although it would seem to have been unwarranted to take such a position given the limited evidence available on this complicated, ever-changing situation. The article stated: "From the perspective of the Arabs in their stone villages amid vineyards and olive groves, the Israeli takeover is self-evident and relentless. Not only are Jewish settlements seizing and purchasing tracts of land...." In the second sentence here, the journalist had overtly assumed the distorted perspective of the people he was describing, and the view was presented as the accurate one. It would seem that the claim that the Israelis were "seizing" land, i.e., taking land forcefully (and by implication, illegally), would have required some evidence. None was presented in this piece or in any other in the Times during the period under consideration here.

Shipler's unrestrained story went on to describe some of the Jewish settlers as terrorists, and claimed that "these vigilantes have brought a frightening spirit of lawlessness to the West Bank." This was an unusually harsh condemnation, and it was unsupported. It was mentioned that settlers were "vandalizing electric-generators," but no evidence was pro-

37

vided for even this relatively minor charge. (It was later repeated—as a fact—in one of the many anti-Israeli contributions by the regular Times columnist Anthony Lewis.) In contrast, the Times did not confront the undeniable, tangible facts of Arab violence and riots on the West Bank, and their relationship to any possible "frightening spirit of lawlessness." These are blatant examples of selective perception and the application of a double standard.

Explanations or justifications for the settlers' presence on non-religious grounds (e.g., military, social) were rarely printed in the New York Times in this three-month period. Mention was sometimes made that such settlements in the West Bank were first put up when the secular, socialist Labor Party was in power. It was not pointed out that the settlement policy (and the democratically elected government) was supported by a public which is perhaps only 20-25% religious, a far smaller percentage of "believers," incidentally, than one finds in the United States. Nevertheless, the focus of the Times was on the fundamentalist, religious impulses for West Bank settlements which could easily be misinterpreted by secular Times readers as being merely a Jewish version of Middle Eastern religious fanaticism. A pretence of objective news gathering and "going to the sources" was made by having the religious reasons come out of the settlers' own mouths. Thus we are provided (Shipler, 4/1, p. A3) with declarations such as: "We're acting under orders here. We have the Bible and the Bible says that this is our land; and it commands the Jews to settle the land of Israel."

It was not mentioned in Times articles that vital Jewish settlements existed for the past several centuries on what is now sometimes called the West Bank (such as in Hebron), in addition to those in ancient times. These were evacuated due to massacres bv Arabs in the 1920's and 1930's, and in the voluntary—albeit painful—exodus brought about by the 1948 U.N. partition plan for "Palestine." (Many Israelis, such as the former Prime Minister Yitzhak Rabin, were born and brought up on the West Bank.)

The Jews on the West Bank were consistently presented to Times readers as merely being recent interlopers. In news stories, it was always mentioned when one of them formerly resided in the United States, and the name of the American city he or she came from was given. The sly attempt here was to heighten the contrast between that far-off Middle Eastern territory and the well-known American place to make it appear incongruous that a person (albeit a

Jew) who has been here is now there. Since it is difficult for American Times readers to imagine themselves moving to the Middle East, they might naturally assume that these settlers also do not belong there, and that their presence there is absurd and wrong. There was a brief interview with "Ezra Rappoport, 37 years old, a native of the East Flatbush section of Brooklyn." (Shipler, 3/22, p. A3. It was *not* reported that Rappoport had moved to Israel *eleven years ago.*) Shipler wrote of "Yorucham Leavitt, a lanky 41-year-old who came to Israel from Cleveland three years ago," (4/11, p. A3), but in the same article Shlomo and Orna Shkedi and Jacqueline Elliaz were also interviewed, and no mention was made of where they came from or when. Apparently, noting that a settler orignally came from Jerusalem, Morocco or even the West Bank, or that he had immigrated many years ago, was not useful to the general thrust of the stories and was thus omitted. The use of this technique for propagandistic distortion becomes even clearer when one sees that the man responsible for killing many Arabs at the Dome of the Rock in Jerusalem, who had emigrated from America to Israel a few years ago and was in the Israeli army for only ten days, was usually identified in the Times as an "Israeli soldier." (This will be dealt with later.)

The myths of Arab innocence and of Arab persecution by Jews who desire to force them from their land were extended in the Times back to 1948. The reader was apparently supposed to believe that there was a parallel between the recent developments and the events of that time. Shipler wrote: "Some Palestinians think they [the Israelis] are laying the groundwork for the expulsion of the Arabs or the flight of the Arabs in a future war, as occurred during Israel's 1948 war of independence." (3/28, p. E3.) In a melodramatic news report one month earlier, "Boys on the West Bank Arrested at Night for Weeks of Questioning by Israelis," (2/27, p. 5) he had presented the same view, which is the very same, self-serving, paranoid one generally put forth by the Arabs. He reported that in 1948 "many Arabs were driven out by the Israelis or fled to escape the battle." It was not indicated that many of the Arabs within Israel—some of whom now live on the West Bank and Gaza strip— were the frontline fighters of the Arab armies in 1948. The men were well-armed by the departing English and the surrounding Arab countries, and often had excellent strategic positions close to the Jewish areas, sometimes in the very same towns and cities. The Jews in cities like Jerusalem and Haifa were almost entirely surrounded. It was the Arabs who were confident and armed-to-the-teeth. One percent of the Jewish population was killed in this long, bloody war. The Arabs were not driven out, but rather had been asked to stay and live in peace in the new country. Most who left did so on the orders of the surrounding Arab countries to facilitate the envisaged massacre of the Jews.

Another Times story (Shipler, 3/22, p. A3) reported the Arab claim that Israelis on the West Bank were trying to set up the same psychological atmosphere that allegedly existed in 1948, an atmosphere designed to drive them out. This claim received no critical evaluation, and tended to be supported by the other elements put forth in this report. As I note briefly elsewhere, Times opinion columns and editorials were umbilically connected to such news stories. Thus, Anthony Lewis (4/5, p. A23) repeated a statement by "Elias Freij, the gentle moderate who is Mayor of Bethlehem," which had been quoted a few days before in a David Shipler news article (3/31, p. A16): "The rate of settlement in the area is driving people crazy, and the heavy hand, the censorship, the arrests. People are ready to explode, they feel so oppressed."

As already mentioned, David Shipler's news article of February 27, 1982 had the damning headline: "Boys in the West Bank Arrested at Night for Weeks of Questioning by Israelis." The article was later complimented as objective reporting in an Anthony Lewis column, and referred to in a major Times editorial. In truth, the so-called "boys" were actually teenagers or young adults: *all* were fourteen years or older according to David Shipler and Anthony Lewis. (A careful reading of another Shipler story headlined "West Bank Boy Dies as Israeli Forces Fire on Arab Protesters" [3/21, pp. 1,12] uncovers the fact that this "boy" was seventeen. Incidentally, Israelis—male and female—are drafted into the army after high school and some undoubtedly were serving on the West Bank during this period. No attention was paid to *their* difficulties in the Times.) The news story was a manipulative, melodramatic piece calculated to evoke sympathy for the teenagers and their families. We were presented with a picture of sensitive "boys" who struggled to hold back their tears when relating their stories to a Western newsman. The piece was an attempt to evoke disgust for authorities who, the reader was supposed to believe, arrested ("at night," no less, with its "knock on the door" connotations) and incarcerated teenagers indiscriminately. Shipler described in detail some of these teenagers and their arrests. He chose as his final sentence the words of a mother whose son had been arrested: "All these soldiers for taking a child?" Thus, the Times ended its article by implying an unneeded and irrational brutality against *children.*

The possibility that some of these "boys" may have actually been guilty of some of the violent acts by Arabs so common on the West Bank—and which were *occasionally* reported by the New York Times— appears to have been inconceivable to Shipler and Lewis. This was in spite of the fact that a recent series in the Times had shown that a great deal of the murders, rapes and other violent crimes in America are committed by teenagers. Shipler blamed the *Israelis* for any extremism which existed among the Arabs. He said that the situation "indicates that boys are being forced by harassment to become radicals."

Shipler claimed (3/30, p. A12) in another article that "Israeli military censorship, based on the 1945 emergency regulations of the British mandate in Palestine, is always stricter with the Arab press than with the Israeli or foreign press, officials explain. Arabic papers must submit all material to the censor." Stories for Israeli and foreign newspapers, he affirmed, are inspected only if they concern military matters. Here, as elsewhere, Shipler did not mention who these "official" sources were. The nature of the censorship regulations were made to appear sinister and ridiculous by claiming that they are based on the emergency regulations dating from the British mandate. For some reason, this minor historical sidelight was stated often in the Times, and one wonders whether it was done to imply that while the Jews were once oppressed by a colonial, military rule in this area, they have now adopted a position analogous to their former oppressors. (Such false analogies, inaccurate inversions, and wild attempts to portray spurious ironies have become popular recently among political commentators to the point where Israelis, i.e., Jews, have been put forth as the modern-day Nazis.) It should be explained that when Israel became independent in 1948, it was sensibly declared by the government that all laws and regulations then in force would remain in effect unless rescinded. Thus a great number of the laws now in force are British in origin, and many even date from the time Turkey ruled the area. In addition, the particular Times report in question erroneously distinguished between the "Arab" press and the "Israeli" press: Arabs in Israel are full-fledged Israeli citizens with the same rights of freedom of speech and press. The *radical* Arab press, geared largely towards West Bank residents but distributed throughout Israel too, are published in Jerusalem and are protected by Israeli law. Charges against them must usually follow a lengthy, tortuous route through the court system. The worst fate that any of them has ever faced (Al-Fajr) has been a one month suspension. (In an article in the Columbia Journalism Review by an American observer, Milton Viorst, he expressed great surprise at what he found was allowed to be printed in these newspapers, which are, he pointed out, the freest, least-censored Arabic-language newspapers in the Middle East.)

The Times article was incorrect when it claimed a great difference in the procedures in the censorship of the Arabic-language press and the "Israeli" (i.e., Jewish) and foreign ones. The contents of the Hebrew language papers are *also* closely scrutinized, in part because many seemingly harmless stories have military implications. It is known that the Israeli press is closely examined by Israel's enemies. Thus, a seemingly innocuous story shortly before the 1973 war about the sending of holiday cakes to Israeli soldiers on the Golan Heights indirectly and inadvertently signaled to the Syrians how many soldiers were there.

During this period, a highly significant story was made public to the world press by the Israeli government. It revealed that reporters from Western media had been physically intimidated in Lebanon and elsewhere by the P.L.O. in an attempt to make them report more sympathetically on Arab activities. (See Shipler, 2/14, p. 9.) However, Shipler's Times article on this revelation left out the fact that New York Times reporters had been involved. (See "Special to the N.Y. Times," 2/18, p. A4. This information had not been censored from the Times story appearing in the European-based International Herald Tribune.) When this omission was pointed out by the Israeli government, the Times denied that a P.L.O. kidnapping of its reporters and the direct threats made in this and other instances had had any effect on the work of its journalists. Craig R. Whitney, the deputy foreign editor and soon-to-be chief foreign editor, made the absurd claim that the facts had never been published in the Times because they had never been considered newsworthy! John Kifner, one of the Times journalists in Beirut who had been kidnapped, then publicly shrugged off the incident as a mere "mistake" by the P.L.O. (See his Times story 2/22, p. A4). Thus, any fear, error, dishonesty, censorship or secret agreements were never admitted to by the Times. (See also Shipler, 2/24, p. A3.)

In contrast, reports concerning Israeli censorship were common in the Times. (See, for example, "Special to the N.Y. Times," 2/26, p. A11.) The temporary banning of reporters from the Golan Heights—part of the successful attempt by the Israeli government to avoid precipitating violent clashes—received a good deal of attention. (For example, 3/24, pp. 1, A6.) The reasons for these restrictions were not generally reported. No comparisons of these policies with those in other countries in comparable circumstances were made.

The Arab population within Israel has thrived since 1948, and their villages, towns and cities are vital. Yet in a description of Israel (3/21, sec. 10, pp. 14, 20) David Shipler neglected to mention these places but instead noted that there are "Arab refugee camps." Of course there are no such camps—they exist only in Shipler's head. He has a fixed and distorted picture of the area in his mind, and it appears that he is unable to see anything that does not fit into this phantasm.

A common practice in the Times during this period was to portray the mayors of the towns on the West Bank and Gaza strip as "moderates." Among these were the mayors who were dismissed for not cooperating with the moves to change from military to civilian rule. They were held up as heroic, elected officials who were being unfairly victimized. In a news article (Shipler, 3/29, pp. A1, A4) Shipler described Elias Freij of Bethlehem and Rashad al-Shawwa of Gaza as "two relative moderates." (In a column from Paris on March 8, Anthony Lewis had also called Freij and al-Shawwa "moderate.") In another article, Shipler quoted Freij—the least radical of the handful of mayors expelled—at length about the alleged suffering of the Palestinians and about Israeli oppression. He also quoted Freij's description of himself: "I will not be a yes man, and I will not be an extremist. I will continue to follow my line of moderation." (3/31, p. A16) There was no critical evaluation of any of Freij's absurd claims. As previously noted, a few days later Lewis quoted some of the very same statements on Israeli oppression in his column, and described the man as "the gentle moderate." (4/5, p. A23) There were no discussions anywhere in the Times of the other former mayors, like Bassam-al-Shakr, and their very extreme political activities.

Covering the _same_ events concerning the mayors in the Sunday Times of London (3/21), reporter David Bundy mentioned the links between these West Bank (and Gaza) mayors and the National Guidance Committee, the coordinating body of pro-P.L.O. forces in the West Bank and Gaza. Ibrahim

Tawil, one of the dismissed mayors, was most often described in the New York Times as the intended victim of an unsuccessful bomb attack whose perpetrators have never been found by the Israeli authorities. (For example, see Shipler, 3/26, pp. 1, A4.) The implication was always that the act was done by Jewish terrorists whom the government had no sincere desire to catch. (However, it was usually noted that Israeli soldiers alerted Tawil about a possible assassination attempt, that they found a bomb in his car, and that an Israeli soldier was blinded when he tried to defuse it.) The British journalist Bundy noted in his Sunday Times story that Tawil "has close links with a Marxist-Leninist P.L.O. faction, the Democratic Front for the Liberation of Palestine." (The D.F.L.P. is a "rejectionist" group, that is, it rejects *any* intercourse with Israel, including even the arrangement of cease-fires. It is more radical than Yasser Arafat's P.L.O. group, El Fatah.)

While the New York Times correspondents had nothing good to say about the *true* Arab moderates on the West Bank, and gave them little coverage, David Bundy acknowledged their existence and their significance. He noted that in contrast to the urban areas with their radical mayors, the Palestinians who lived in the countryside and constituted 60-65% of the

West Bank population were relatively apolitical. The New York newspaper paid scant attention to these people. It also had nothing positive to say about the Village Leagues the Israeli government and the new civilian governor, Menachem Milson, encouraged in the countryside to offer the residents an alternative to the P.L.O. Although far from impressed with these Leagues, Eric Silver of the British newspaper The Observer noted (3/21, p. 5) that "His [Milson's] policy of sponsoring village leagues has made indisputable headway in the Hebron region, south of Jerusalem, where an authentic local leader, Mustapha Dudeen, was already seeking to cooperate with Israel." The New York Times, however, kept its coverage focused on the urban mayors who were P.L.O. spokesmen. An article by correspondent Henry Kamm, "Pro-Israel West Bank Official Wounded by Bomb," (4/1, p. A3) gave few details of this significant story of truly moderate Arabs and their fate, but focused instead on unrelated Middle Eastern diplomatic issues.

The New York Times view of supposed "moderate" Arabs and alleged Israeli trouble-making was extended to the international sphere—to essential American foreign interests and to the American-Soviet conflict. Shipler reported (3/7, p. E4): "Bitter differences over Jerusalem have helped frustrate Washington's notions of bringing moderate Arabs into an anti-Soviet alliance with Israel." The onus for the frustration of Washington's goal, of course, must lie with Israel since the United States does not recognize Israel's claim to Jerusalem. Furthermore, the use of the word "moderate" here to describe highly immoderate, unstable countries served to obscure the situation. Shipler's statement also ignored the central and indisputable fact that the so-called "moderate" Arabs have repeatedly asserted that the major military threat in the area is Israel rather than the Soviet Union. No mention was made of the frequent and impolite Arab rebuffs of American requests for bases and/or cooperation aimed at fighting back any Soviet military aggression.

Biased coverage of Jewish-Arab relations *within* Israel was common in New York Times news stories during the time period under examination here. (One area—that of alleged unfair censorship of Arab newspapers—has already been described.) Subjective descriptions were readily used in news reports to the detriment of the Jews. For example, in an article attempting to show that the Bedouins in the Negev desert were being brutalized by the Jewish Israelis, a special governmental group (the "Green Patrol") formed to help oversee programs in this wilderness and whose members are akin to American park service rangers, was described as "a squad of tough young Israelis." (Shipler, 3/9, p. A2) It would have been better journalism to refrain from making such a characterization and just objectively present the facts concerning their actions and their work. Readers could then judge whether they were in fact "tough," and indeed whether they *should* have been.

The headline for this particular melodramatic news report by David Shipler was "Israelis Survive Storm over Bedouin Baby's Death." It tried to indicate an Israeli mistreatment of Bedouins which in this case resulted in the death of one sick infant. Several important factors were not dealt with in the story. For example, the physical condition of the baby's dozen brothers and sisters was not mentioned. Also omitted were *facts* concerning the origins and aims of these Bedouins: Did they originate in the Negev? Why had they *chosen* to live there under Israeli rule when there were (and are) alternatives? Ignored too was their general relationship to Israeli society: the efforts of the government to provide them with health care and education, and the generous housing offers Israel's Jewish citizens envy. Instead, Shipler began the news item with "The

Israeli authorities involved in driving seminomadic Bedouins off their ancestral lands...." The Bedouins' roles as spies and large-scale smugglers of drugs and arms were not mentioned. The focus was on the unfortunate fate of one sick infant, in a manipulative attempt to create something from very little. Despite the sensational headline, it does not appear that there was, in fact, much of the proclaimed "storm," and it is no wonder that the "Israelis" managed to "survive" it as the headline proclaimed. Shipler made the claim that "the Green Patrol has intensified a campaign of denigration of the Bedouin's culture and tradition." There was a photograph accompanying the piece which showed the father of the dead baby peacefully squatting and drinking some coffee in the traditional manner

A few weeks later, a very long article by Shipler (4/4) starting on page one and taking up most of page sixteen—a rare occurrence in the New York Times— was a paean to Bedouin culture. Focusing on the Bedouins of the Sinai, it did maintain some balance by at least mentioning that when the area came under Israeli rule the Israelis made great efforts to provide education for the Bedouins, in contrast to the Egyptians when they had governed the territory. It even noted that the Bedouins engage in smuggling, but unfortunately presented this in a romantic light (e.g., there was an interview with a smuggler who writes poems about his way of life), ignoring both the deleterious effects of illegal drugs on Israel's young people as well as the civilian deaths caused by smuggled bombs and weapons. Once again, Arabs were portrayed as impotent, helpless people who are affected by others (mainly the Israelis) or by great social forces (for example, modernization), but who do nothing of their own volition, and do nothing which has any negative consequences for others: they are innocents. Incidentally, it could have been mentioned in these articles on the Bedouins that those living in northern Israel (who are generally ignored by the Times) are on relatively good terms with the Jews and have never had good relations with non-Bedouin Arabs. Many volunteer to serve in the Israeli army.

The Times' treatment of tension between Israelis and the Druze Arabs on the Golan Heights was biased. It was stated in a news article (Shipler, 4/13, p. 2): "Long quiet and devoid of overt anti-Israeli activity, the Golan Heights region has grown tense since its annexation...." References were made elsewhere to the "Pro-Syrian Druzes" (Shipler, 3/24, pp. A1, A6) who began a long strike after the annexation.

Doubtless there were pro-Syrian Druze on the Heights. However, the focus should probably have been on the fact (mentioned only in passing) that a large percentage of these inhabitants had relatives in Syria, and that they feared reprisals against them for any overt gesture of cooperation with the Israelis' announced "extension of Israeli rule" to the Golan Heights. (One can be certain that they were aware of the Syrian army's destruction of one of its own cities, Hama, during this period, with the slaughter of at least twenty thousand of its civilian residents, many of whom did not support the government.) In addition, the Golan Heights has changed hands many times through history, and its inhabitants feared that an Israeli-Syrian bargain of "land for peace" might one day be made with the Golan, similar to that with the Sinai. Israel's stated policy did not preclude such an agreement, although it did seem unlikely. Under a renewal of Syrian rule, those who had agreed to cooperate with Israel—becoming citizens, serving in the army, etc., would face a bleak fate. The Druze on the Heights also knew well that although the area had been held by Israel since 1967, it was quite successfully—albeit temporarily—overrun by the Syrians in 1973.

Perhaps the most significant factor in the reluctance of these Druze to cooperate with an incorporation into Israel was the fear that they would lose the land (through purchase by the Israeli government) that they had seized when a large number of inhabitants fled during the 1967 war. This factor was never mentioned in the Times. Although pictured in the Times as yet another Israeli-oppressed Arab group, many of the inhabitants were in reality thriving squatters.

The treatment of this Israel-Druze conflict was done in such a biased manner by the major Western media that a Druze member of the Israeli parliament who was serving as an unofficial negotiator between the Israeli government and the Golan Druze came to the United States to publicly explain the actual situation. His visit was not reported by the Times. According to this parliamentarian, Zeidan Atashi, the three major fears concerning the Israeli rule expressed to him by the Golan Druze were the fear of being forced to accept Israeli citizenship, of serving in the Israeli army, and losing the land they held. (The Jewish Press of New York covered Atashi's visit adequately. See 4/16, p. 3.) He reported that citizenship was *not* being forced upon them, and that an involuntary draft would be illegal under Israeli laws concerning Druze since they are only conscripted when a Druze town council freely elects to have such a draft. The third great fear would be difficult to allay: all governments retain the right to expropriate and use land for the public good. Atashi noted that the whole affair was being exaggerated by the American media. There were only 9,000 Druze living on the Golan, compared to 45,000 Druze Israeli citizens within the borders established in 1948. Most of the latter opposed the strike by their brethren.

A large percentage of Druze elect to serve in the Israeli army and border police for many years. Traditionally a beleaguered minority in the Middle East, they did not fight alongside the other Arabs in the 1948 War of Independence and have enjoyed great freedom, prosperity and political power in the Jewish state. They dislike other Arab groups. Shipler's statement (4/13, p. 2) that "Many Druze in Israel proper are drafted, and they often serve in the occupied West Bank, putting down demonstrations by Palestinian Arabs, with whom they have no affinity" did not give a clear, vivid picture of the situation. The danger of warfare between the Israeli Bedouins and Israeli Druze in northern Israel—a very significant story during this period—went unreported in the Times.

3

THE COVERAGE OF CLASHES IN THE WEST BANK, GAZA, AND ISRAEL

There was gross distortion in the New York Times coverage of some violence which—rightly or wrongly—was in the spotlight of world attention during this time period: the clashes between Israelis and Palestinians in the West Bank and Gaza, and within the pre-1967 borders of Israel. In this story, the general portrayal of Arabs as the innocent victims of aggression was able to find a focus.

There were weeks of rioting; knifings; the throwing of rocks, pipes and burning torches at Israeli soldiers and civilians (as well as at Western tourists); and the menacing of outnumbered Israelis by Palestinian mobs. The violent aggressors committing these acts were labeled in the New York Times as "protesters" or "demonstrators," and their actions as "demonstrations" or "protests." (See, for example: Shipler, 3/24, pp. A1, A6; 3/25, p. 1; 3/29, pp. A1, A4; 3/31, p. A6.) These words connote an honest and

earnest public display against an injustice. (See
Webster's unabridged New International Diction-
ary.) In contrast, the same events were more accurately called "riots" and "clashes" in the Sunday
Times of London (3/21, p. 1). In the New York Times,
the precise actions of the Arabs were rarely described, although the riots were sometimes called
"violent demonstrations" (such as Shipler, 3/25, pp.
A1, A9; 3/31, p. A6). It is significant, however, that
there were never "violent demonstrators." With the
arrival in the Middle East of the Times correspondent, Henry Kamm, near the middle of the time
period dealt with in this analysis, reporting on the
riots improved slightly, although he too used the
words "demonstrations," "demonstrators," and
"protestors." (For example, see Kamm, 3/28, p.9.)
An Associated Press story printed in the Times on
April 9th used the more appropriate term "clashes."

One article ("Special to the N.Y. Times," 4/17,
p. 3) noted that the use of regular bullets by the Israeli
army, rather than mere tear gas and rubber bullets,
marked a very recent change. The army explained
that the use of real bullets was necessitated by the
threats to soldiers' lives. Statements that the soldiers' orders were to aim for the legs of the Palestinians was reported throughout these months.

Arab violence was rarely explicitly acknowledged, in contrast to the playing up of force used by the Israelis. It was also implied that the Israeli force was unwarranted. Thus, soon after the beginning of the riots Shipler referred to "days of violence in the West Bank in which soldiers, firing into crowds of Palestinian demonstrators, killed 2 teen-age boys and wounded 16." (3/24, pp. A1, A6.) The next day he wrote (pp. 1,9) that a "third Palestinian was killed in a demonstration." Note again the avoidance of attributing violence to the Arabs, and the use of the words "boys" and "demonstrators." (In a column dealing with the Golan Heights [4/5, p. A23], Anthony Lewis noted curtly: "Four Druze demonstrators have now been shot.")

As noted, Arab violence was consistently played down. One method of doing so mentioned earlier was to describe it in passive rather than active sentences. In addition, it was often portrayed as if it had been committed against inanimate objects, rather than people. The example given was in Shipler's article of 3/28, p. E3, which reported that six Palestinians had been "shot to death" by Israeli soldiers, while "one soldier died when his jeep was hit by a grenade."

The size and physical placement of the stories further distorted the truth. Unlike many of the previously-mentioned stories which appeared on page one, a *very* small article on page five ("Special to the N.Y. Times," 4/8) had the headline "Grenade Wounds a Nun in West Bank Town." Thus the headline stated that the brutal act was done by a grenade rather than by an Arab. The story noted that a grenade was thrown into a Greek Orthodox shrine on the West Bank town of Nablus after tourists went inside. Another very small article from the Associated Press two days later was also buried on page five: "Two Israeli Girls Hurt by Rocks in West Bank." It stated that "one girl, Brenda Kamm, suffered a fractured skull and other injuries when Arab demonstrators threw rocks at their bus." It noted that the sources for the story were Israeli military authorities and a spokesman for the Jewish settlement, Kiryat Arba. In yet another story considered low priority by the Times, Shipler noted in a page nine piece (3/25) that "A tourist bus was stoned and its headlights smashed." The Times could have made the shocking truth clear that innocent civilians were being attacked, and that the civilians were both Israelis and Western tourists.

Arab violence was explained and excused, and Israeli force criticized. The usual background picture described earlier of the alleged unfortunate Arab being forced to action out of a desperation caused by oppression was of course brought forward. The specific circumstances of each new event also provided material with which to criticize the Israelis.

Many Israeli soldiers were injured or killed in these numerous "demonstrations." An article by Shipler (3/26, pp. 1A, 4A) was headlined "Israeli Sergeant is Killed in Gaza in Grenade Attack," but only the first two sentences and one at the end concerned the murder of the Israeli. Thus there was almost no information about the killing or the soldier —no interviews with fellow soldiers, friends or family. It was not reported that this thirty-year-old man had a wife and three children. (In contrast, the "human interest" factor was common when the focus was on Arabs.) The story began: "An Israeli Army sergeant was killed and three other soldiers were wounded today, when a grenade was thrown into their jeep in occupied Gaza." It quickly shifted its focus, however. The Times noted that it was the first Israeli death, compared to six Palestinian deaths, in recent days. Again the usual picture was painted: "In the widespread demonstrations set off by Mr. Tawil's dismissal, Israeli soldiers, Jewish settlers and border police have fired into crowds of rock-throwing protesters, killing six. Most of the victims were teenagers; a boy shot in the head Wednesday in the Gaza strip was 13, the Jerusalem Post reported today." The focus was also shifted from the killing of the Israeli by the photograph accompanying the story. It showed a smiling man in a nicely-tailored suit and had the caption "Bassam al-Shaka yesterday after he was removed from office."

The stabbing to death of a Druze Arab soldier in the Israeli army on the West Bank received little attention, despite the possibility here of an interesting "human interest" story as well as a story which could have revealed a good deal about the *actual* situation in this area of the Middle East. There was also no interest shown by the Times in the wounding of a female soldier by a hand grenade hurled by a Palestinian. The woman was riding in a van full of civilians in the Gaza strip when the grenade was thrown in. Thus, this was actually an attack on civilians, not even on military personnel. (The story was reported adequately in the New York-based Jewish Press.) It is telling that there was scant Times coverage when a Palestianian was blown up on the West Bank by an explosive device he was preparing.

Throughout these three months in early 1982, story after story told of an impending invasion of Lebanon which could be touched off by any occurrence. There was not much in the way of explanation of the causes which might make such an invasion necessary for the safety of Israel's citizens. The constant repetition created the image of a country always poised to invade its Arab neighbors, in much the same way it did not hesitate to brutalize the Palestinians under its control.

The application of a perverse double standard and the unjust castigation of the Israelis is made manifest when even comparable actions by Palestinians and Israelis were described differently. For example, Henry Kamm stated in a story (3/28, p. 9) that Israeli police "intimidated" Arab shopkeepers who wanted to close their stores as a show of protest, but he noted that there were "those [Arabs] who wanted to bring pressure on unwilling shopkeepers to join the strike." The actions of the Arab intimidators were dealt with gently: they don't "intimidate," they merely "want to bring pressure."

As noted in the previous section, the substitution of biased judgment for fact was common in Times news stories. A news report by Kamm (3/28, p. 9) referred to "the Government's harsh measures on the West Bank" as if this were a *fact.* The first line of the story was "The Israeli government last week enforced its hard line." On the same day, David

Shipler (3/28, p. E3) presented as *fact* his opinion that the handling of the Arabs by the soldiers (who in truth were being assaulted) was "tough." Similarly, the headline in the Week in Review segment (p. E2) on the situation written by Barbara Slavin and Milt Freudenheim of the Times home office on April 4th was "Hanging Tough on West Bank and Sinai." An objective outside observer might well have found the reactions of the government and the army *lenient*. In sharp contrast to this, there was little attention or analysis in the Times concerning the explicit public threat made by the Jordanian government during this period to kill the Palestinians on the West Bank who did not sever their connections with the moderate Village Leagues. There were, in fact, violent attacks on Arab moderates. (In November 1981 when Yusal al-Khalih of the Leagues had been ambushed and killed by two men, the P.L.O. claimed responsibility.) See the story by Kamm of one bomb attack on the head of a West Bank Village League. (4/1, p. A3)

The Times coverage was not *totally* lacking descriptions of Arab mob violence: "In the Gaza strip, Arab demonstrators in the town of Rafeh threw stones at troops, and soldiers were seen on Israeli television hurling stones back." (Shipler, 3/24, pp. A1, A6). This was an astoundingly mild reaction by a fully-equipped army to a violent provocation, and it was especially telling since this one was being accused of brutality. It is strange that the rather mild reaction of the soldiers was noted to have appeared on Israeli television. If Shipler meant to imply that Israeli television was being used to present a distorted view of the army's activities, he was not being candid. In fact, the one state-run Israeli television station was strongly attacked by the government for being biased against it in its coverage of the West Bank clashes and of the army-Arab violence. The same article by Shipler rather delicately mentioned that "Stones were thrown [by Arabs] at pedestrians in the Old City of Jerusalem."

As mentioned, towards the middle of this three-month period in question the reporting on the clashes became slightly more balanced, in part due to the stories filed by Henry Kamm who had been sent to Israel temporarily to help cover the increased activity. The Times finally began to describe more fully the violent attacks by the Arabs, the moderate reactions of the Israeli soldiers and settlers, and the emotional feelings of the Jews when attacked. Thus one story (Shipler, 3/22, p. A3) reported that "the stone-throwing [at Jews in cars] infuriates settlers," and quoted one man as saying: "You can get killed.

You're traveling at 50, 60 miles per hour, a rock comes, hits you in the face, you lose control of the car." This same man also noted that the settlers' general policy was to react to harassment by their Arab neighbors only after two such incidents. A story by Kamm (3/30, p. A13) noted that an Israeli on the West Bank "was stoned while driving on the Jerusalem-Hebron road. Injured, he retaliated by opening fire, wounding one of his attackers." The story was not given any prominence in the newspaper.

A story on April 17th ("Special to the N.Y. Times," p. 3) was subtitled "13 Wounded While Assaulting Soldiers." Part of it read as follows:

In the Sajiya quarter of Gaza, hundreds of Arab men wielding knives, stones, bottles and sticks tried to assault a detachment of troops, who fired tear gas and then shot into the crowd, the [army] spokesman said.

In the town of Khan Yunis, the army spokesman continued, a group of Palestinian residents surrounded three or four soldiers, who first shot into the air and then at the legs of people in the crowd....

In the Gaza beach refugee camp, about 500 people reportedly attacked a five-man patrol. The soldiers fired tear-gas cannisters and rubber bullets.

[In the West Bank] ... a crowd coming out of a mosque after Friday prayers attacked a small contingent of troops at a checkpoint, the spokesman said. They threw and rolled burning tires toward the soldiers, he reported, and the soldiers responded with gunfire, wounding three Arabs in the legs.

It was reported that an officer was asked why rubber bullets rather than live ammunition were not used in *all* situations, as before, and he replied that the special attachment necessary to fire rubber bullets made it take a dangerously long time to load and reload such bullets. There was no analagous questioning of rioters on the appropriateness of their weapons or tactics.

On April 15th (p. A7) Kamm described the violent actions of rioters:

"...a gasoline bomb was hurled at a military patrol...."
"In the town of Gaza, three Arabs were arrested after they assaulted an Israeli soldier and tried to wrest his weapon from him."
"Arabs were arrested on suspicion of overturning and smashing tombstones in a Jewish cemetery on the Mount of Olives in Jerusalem."

A day of Arab protest and riot within Israel
focusing on the Israeli government's land policy—an
annual event begun in the mid-1970's—took place at
the same time as the West Bank and Gaza riots.
Barbara Slavin and Milt Freudenheim tersely noted
(4/4, p. E2) the "killing of six Arabs by Israeli troops
in 1976 during protests against Government expropriation of Arab land in Galilee." This sentence,
with the usual Times use of the words "killing,"
"protests," and "expropriation," was used to draw
the typical, misleading picture of Israeli aggression
against peaceful Arabs seeking justice. Henry Kamm
stated (3/29, p. A5) that there had been "clashes" on
that particular day in 1976, which did at least indicate
that the Arabs may not have been merely passive
prey. However, in another of Kamm's stories (3/31, p.
A16) he referred to "the killing by security forces of
six Arabs during protests against the Israeli expropriation of Arab-owned land in Galilee." In truth it
was the *Arabs* who instigated the violence on that day
in 1976. The Daily News (New York) noted in its story
of March 31, 1982 (p. 6) that three Israeli police
officers had been hurt in 1976 in the "violent protest"
and "bloody riots." Although the expropriation of
Arab land received attention in the Times, it was not
noted that such expropriation is legal—as it is in

70

other countries—and that *most* land in Israel is government-owned, i.e., "public land." The continuous and wide-spread illegal and immoral appropriation of public land by the Arabs in northern Israel—a grave national problem—was never mentioned.

Kamm's eye-witness account (3/31, p. A16) in the town hosting the major 1982 Land Day demonstration of ten thousand people reported: "Evidently determined to avoid clashes, the police and the army were not visible within miles of this town. The rally passed without incident...." Kamm also noted that a hand grenade had been thrown in an Arab terrorist attack in Jerusalem. On the very same page as Kamm's report was a story filed by David Shipler from Jerusalem about the generally quiet day on the West Bank. It contradicted Kamm's story when it reported: "While the Arab citizens of Israel proper clashed with the police...." Shipler was apparently committed to a particular view of events which was unaffected by the facts. One wonders why the editors assembling the paper in New York did not alter his news story so that it would not contradict Kamm's eye-witness report.

Despite the lack of a significant or eventful story here, the Times seemed committed to keeping Land Day in the public eye and presenting it in a particular light. Thus, there was a front-page photograph concerning the protest, and another one on page sixteen. The latter one was of the main demonstration, and showed a large number of shouting Arab protesters. Many were wearing keffiyas, cloth headwear rarely worn by Israeli Arabs, and using them to cover their faces. This style had become part of the image cultivated by Yasser Arafat and other P.L.O. terrorists, and it was thus a *potentially* telling photograph regarding the affinities of the demonstrators. However, the UPI photograph chosen for the front page was quite different. It showed three people: an Arab youth standing defiantly, a policeman aiming his rifle at him, and another policeman at his colleague's side with his hand on the other's shoulder, obviously urging restraint. The photographer had positioned himself behind the Arab, so the Times reader saw this situation from the point of view of the rioters, with the police rifle aimed at him or her. The caption read: "Violence is minor as Arabs Defy Israelis." This was not inaccurate. The rest of the caption in the early edition of the day's Times read: "Israeli policemen aim weapons at Arab youths who stoned their station." In the later edition this patently incorrect description of the scene was changed to note that one policeman's gun was trained on the Arab and the other policeman was physically and verbally urging control. The same picture was printed on page six of the Daily News (3/31), not page one, and the caption there showed that this paper's journalists were able to see from the very first that both policemen were not aiming their rifles. One must question how the erroneous Times caption came to be used in the first place, and why *this* photograph was chosen for the front page instead of the one on page sixteen which was more appropriate. The latter one was full of activity and emotion. Most importantly, it more accurately presented the central event of this news story.

In this, as in other instances, the Times seems to have been obsessed with Israelis aiming their guns at Arabs. Why was a photograph of the Arabs throwing stones at the policemen not shown? It is extraordinary that during these three months of stone-throwing, not *one* picture of this—or of any other Arab violence—appeared in the New York Times. The main demonstration Kamm witnessed and described was perhaps best shown in a photograph which appeared in the New York weekly, the Jewish Press. It showed a large number of protesters with clenched fists, and young men holding children aloft who were carrying P.L.O. flags.

73

The events related to the Times' front page picture were described by Kamm in his story on page sixteen:

> In the nearby town of Arabe, about 100 youths threw rocks at the police station. The police dispersed the crowd with tear-gas grenades. The police spokesman said the disorder had been set off by the appearance on the scene of a foreign television crew. By mid-afternoon Arabe was quiet.

It is quite probable that a good deal of the Arab activity on the West Bank during this entire period was encouraged by the very presence of the Western media, especially since its coverage of the events was so favorable to the rioters.

The 1982 Land Day demonstration in Israel was considered by many of its supporters to have been primarily a show of support for the West Bank and Gaza rioters. It was significant, therefore, that the major rally drew only 10,000 people. There are over 600,000 Arabs in Israel, most of whom live in the north within twenty miles of the demonstration site. The fact that relatively few of them came *should* have received a good deal of attention in the Times. Kamm did *briefly* note that 31 of the 54 local Arab councils in Israel refused to support the Land Day strike which had been called. Kamm stated that a large number of the groups which did support the strike were communist or communist-influenced, and that the leading role in the demostration was played by the largely Arab, pro-Soviet, Israeli Communist Party. An in-depth analysis of these points was essential for an understanding of the situation which was receiving so much attention. It was never made, however. The focus of the Times coverage was elsewhere.

4

PROPAGANDISTIC PHOTOJOURNALISM AND THE DISTORTED IMAGE

The use of photographs was an effective technique for the Times to present its distorted picture of events. The Land Day photos just described in the last chapter comprise a good example. So too does the previously mentioned picture of a well-dressed friendly-looking Bassam al-Shakr speaking on a telephone. (4/2, p. A3.) This presented a favorable image (that of an American-style, white-collar politician) of this dangerous political extremist. It appeared with the story headlined "Israeli Sergeant Killed in Gaza in Grenade Attack." As was also previously noted, the text of the story itself failed to deal adequately with the murder. The event mandated the headline, but it could not command the attention of the print and photo journalists.

The false view that the day-to-day life of Arabs in and near Israel is a dismal, oppressed existence was conveyed by the photographs appearing in the

Times. For example, on April 6th (p. A2) there was a photograph of some pained-looking Arab children standing behind some barbed wire, looking as if they were in some sort of prison camp. If examined, however, it becomes quite clear that the photograph was staged. Any suspicion of its essential dishonesty is buttressed by the fact that when one looks closely, one can see several Arab men in the background watching the photography session and smiling.

Day after day the photographs of the clashes on the West Bank and Gaza showed only the Israeli response to Arab violence and pictured the Arabs only as victims. On the front page of the paper on March 25th was a photograph of an Israeli soldier leading away an Arab woman with the caption reading: "An Israeli soldier leads away an Arab protester in Ramallah, West Bank." Readers of the Times had no way of knowing that this photograph was actually a doctored version of the original UPI photo: the latter had been cropped at the bottom. The Washington Post of that day showed the full photograph on page twenty. *Recognizable* in the foreground of the complete photo was a burning, smoking tire. These burning tires were used as roadblocks by crowds of Arab rioters, and were sometimes rolled at soldiers at the same time torches, sticks and rocks were thrown.

On aesthetic grounds alone, the original was a better photograph than that in the Times—it was clearer, better composed and more exciting. On purely journalistic criteria the original was much better since it showed what the scene of the riot actually looked like, and at least gave an indication of the Arab violence. The New York Times, however, was apparently not influenced much by these factors and did not give its readers the full picture.

The Washington Post's caption for the photograph was no more sound than that in the Times: "A Palestinian Girl is Led Away by an Israeli Soldier on the Sixth Day of West Bank Demonstrations." The flaming tire and the arrest would indicate to an objective observer that more than a mere "demonstration" took place, and the woman looks far too old to be called a "girl." The full photo was used in the Times' "Late City Edition" with this misleading remark added to the caption: "In foreground is a tire that caught fire...." There was no mention in either the Times or the Washington Post of what the "protester," as the Times called her, did to cause her to be arrested. It is interesting that the Sunday Times of London—overtly opposed to Israel's policies more than the New York Times—did not share the New York paper's aversion to showing or describing the violent actions of the Arabs. For example, on March 28th (p. 9) it printed a photograph (credited to Moshe Milner) with the caption: "Flames on the West Bank: Israeli soldiers shift a blazing oil drum after violent clashes at El Bireh."

The most common photographs concerning Israel that appeared in the New York Times during this period showed an Israeli soldier either arresting and leading away an Arab or committing some violent act against an Arab. Thus, on March 29th (p. A4) an Associated Press photograph showed a soldier grabbing a young Palestinian. Unlike most of the Times captions, however, this one did describe the violent provocation: "In Nablus, occupied West Bank, a Palestinian youth is seized by an Israeli soldier after rocks were hurled at soldiers on patrol." On April 13th, there was a front-page photograph of helmeted soldiers and some young people with the caption: "An Israeli soldier firing tear gas at demonstrators in Jerusalem." It also noted that there was an Arab strike, which "...was called to protest an Israeli soldier's raid Sunday on the Temple Mount." As in other instances, there was no relevant front-page story and its placement thus seems wanton. Accompanying a news story on page three was an AP photograph of an Arab man holding up his hands to protect himself from an Israeli soldier menacing him with a club. The caption described it thusly: "An Israeli soldier raised a stick as he confronted a demonstrator yesterday in Nablus, in the Israeli-occupied West Bank. Protests were in reaction to an Israeli soldier's wild shooting Sunday on the Temple Mount." Thus Times readers were told of a "demonstrator" in a "protest" about something that sounds like a brutal Israeli act which warrants a protest. The violence presented in picture and word was all by Israeli soldiers. The New York Post's caption for the same photograph (4/13, p. 2) was: "Israeli soldier raises a stick against a Palestinian he caught throwing stones in a West Bank demonstration against a Jewish gunman's attack on a Moslem shrine." The latter caption is journalistically better than the one in the Times, since it is more informative, more objective and more accurate. It notes the Arab's actions as well as the Israeli's, and its description of the attacker at the mosque as a "Jewish gunman" is much closer to the truth than the Times' pet term for him.

On April 17th (p. 3) a UPI photo in the Times showed several Israeli soldiers with an Arab man who bore a pitiful look on his face. The striking photo could easily evoke sympathy for the man, although this particular picture did offer an explanation of why he was being arrested: "Israeli soldiers removing an Arab youth from his home in Gaza. They said they were arresting him for throwing rocks during a demonstration." As usual, there was no photo of rock-throwing or other violence by Arabs. One is merely shown one frightened-looking civilian with several armed soldiers.

On April 18th (p. 3) there was a photograph of an Israeli tank in Gaza with the caption heading "Show of Force." There was no accompanying news story and no related news whatsoever—the rioting had ceased. Nevertheless, the Times apparently considered it important to keep the picture of Israeli military force before the eyes of its public. The photo caption also provided an opportunity to again remind its readers of the attack on Arabs at a Jerusalem mosque "by an Israeli soldier."

On April 22nd the New York Times printed its sole photograph in this entire three-month period of a violent attack on Israeli soldiers. In a remarkable action, it placed a huge photograph on the top of its front page which covered one-quarter of the page. The size of the photo and its placement signaled an extraordinary event in the history of this traditionally staid newspaper, and one would have assumed the photo to be of an event of truly mammoth proportions. It was not. The photograph showed _Jewish_ civilians in Sinai who were opposed to Israel's final troop withdrawal on top of a building throwing objects at Israeli soldiers trying to get them down.

5

THE BIASED COVERAGE OF VIOLENCE IN NEARBY COUNTRIES AND AGAINST AMERICANS

While the New York Times was focusing on the violence on the West Bank and in Gaza, there was little coverage of the violence occurring on a much greater scale between Arabs within fifty miles of Israel—in Lebanon and Syria—depite the fact that there were several Times correspondents in Beirut and Damascus. (There was also relatively little attention paid to the bloody Iraq-Iran war, a conflict with potentially great consequences for the region and for the United States.) In the case of Syria it was somewhat more excusable since there were restrictions on newsmen. For Lebanon, even the violent intimidation by the P.L.O. could not have accounted for the lack of significant information dispatched from there. In one news story the accusation of this laxity on the part of the Western press was noted. It was reported that Menachem Begin stated publicly that the Syrians had recently slain thousands of their own civilians in the city of Hama and destroyed dozens of mosques. In addition, the Syrians were guilty of killing thousands of Lebanese Christians. Iraq, Begin said, was still fighting a war of aggression against Iran, and he tried to remind the world that in 1970 Jordan had not hesitated to use heavy artillery on Palestinian refugee camps to drive the P.L.O. out. (Ten Thousand Palestinians had been killed during "Black September.")

In February, March and April 1982 there were merely a few relatively minor news stories in the Times about the above mentioned attack by the Syrian army on the city of Hama, whose Muslim residents opposed the minority Alawite Muslim regime of President Assad. In an article sometime after this period, the Times reported that the city was largely in ruin from the shelling, and that fifteen thousand civilians had been killed. Later estimates raised this to twenty thousand or more.

There was also far more bloodshed in Lebanon than in the West Bank or Gaza during this period, but *this* was not front page material in the Times, and the coverage was rather minimal. The most extensive treatment was presented in one article by John Kifner (4/16, p. A3) of the Times' Beirut office which noted that fighting in Beirut and south Lebanon between Lebanese Muslims and Palestinians had killed forty-two. (This was several times the number of fatalities which occurred in the Arab-Jewish clashes which was the major story in the Western media during these three months.) Kifner reported that the Lebanese Muslims were angry because the Palestinians had taken their land and because they attracted Israel's bombs. There was an AP photograph of a Palestinian girl whose father—a P.L.O. fighter—had been killed. Two days later a one paragraph AP story buried on page eight noted that in six days of fighting in Lebanon the death toll had reached 79, with 194 wounded. As for who was fighting whom and why, this report merely noted that "Rival Moslem militias battled...." A very short Reuters item on the same page noted that an American military attache had been shot by a sniper in Beirut. A rocket attack against the U.S. embassy there (Howe, 4/13, p. A6) was only mentioned in passing. (The failure of the Times to cover Arab attacks on American tourists in Jerusalem will be discussed later.) These stories would seem to have warranted more extensive treatment.

A rather small news article dealt with a significant situation in Lebanon which was related to the violence there ("Special to the New York Times,"

4/5, p. A4). "Prominent delegates" from many countries, from the European Parliament, and from various organizations met with the Christians in Lebanon to call for the withdrawal of Syrian troops and the disarming of the P.L.O. Messages of support were sent by Senator Edward Kennedy, Congressman Jack Kemp, former French President Giscard d'Estaing, and other "prominent individuals." This article made the important point that the Christians in Lebanon comprised almost half of the total population.

When contrasted with the neglect of Arab violence, the Times' gratuitous preoccupation with Israeli counterattacks seems even more absurd and malicious. Israel was alleged to be brutish to Americans as well as to Arabs. A front page story by Richard Halloran (3/25) of the Times' Washington bureau which focused on the subject of American military surveillance ships had as one of its subtitles: "Ship Attacked by Israel in 1967." It is difficult to see any journalistically valid reason for this subtitle, since the unfair, one-sided treatment of the subject—a tragic accident in the midst of the Six Day War which resulted in the deaths of many American sailors—was a very small part of the story.

Another news report ("Special to the N.Y.

Times," 3/31, p. A15) which did not deal directly with policy ended with this statement: "Some State Department officials oppose allowing Israel to dictate policy towards friendly Arab countries, asserting that this polarizes the area." The Times was accepting the absurd charge and the absurd phrase which had been gaining currency among American government officials and among critics of Israel that Israel had in fact "dictated policy" or tried to. (Charges of Israeli control over Washington should certainly have ceased after that country's failure to stop the sale of AWACS to Saudi Arabia. However, being based on fantasies, the accusations were immune to such facts.) This attack was in strong contrast to the reference to "friendly Arab countries." No evidence of such "friendship" was provided. Indeed, it would have been impossible to do.

6

THE INJUDICIOUS USE OF
ARAB AND ISRAELI
ANTI-GOVERNMENT SOURCES

New York Times reporters uncritically used the information and opinions provided by Arab and Israeli anti-government (anti-Begin) sources to present their negative picture of Israel. The reliance on such stories was injudicious, and their utilization in stories often propagandistic. Henry Kamm referred in a news story (4/22, p. A3) to the "Palestinian sources [for newsmen] here who gather information throughout the occupied territory." News reports *occasionally* noted when the sources were Palestinian (such as Shipler's story, 3/23, pp. A1, A7), but they *often* did so when the source was a spokesman for the army. (Usually, the stories were from an Arab perspective but of course were not identified as such.) Reports of an incident were sometimes given from both official Israeli sources and from Palestinian sources. This gave a false appearance of reportorial objectivity. Equating the two in this way gave the unidentified Palestinian sources a recognition and weight they may well not have deserved, while derogating the official government statement from a person accountable for his remarks to the status of being merely another version. One example of this was in the very brief treatment ("Special to the N.Y. Times," 4/6, p. A3) about the finding of a dead Palestinian. It reported that an Israeli army official claimed that the dead man had accidentally blown himself up while preparing an explosive device, while "Palestinian sources quoted local Arab residents as contending that he had been killed by settlers." Some relatively simple investigation by the Times could have determined with some certainty which version was correct, and very possibly revealed some significant facts about the violent Arab activities on the West Bank. It could also have revealed something important about the relative reliability of Israeli and Palestinian sources. Such an investigation of trustworthiness—essential to good coverage in the area— was apparently never made.

Many stories were one-sided, giving only the Arab version and perspective. (As noted, the general outlook of the reporters on the decades-old Jewish-Arab conflict seemed to coincide with that of the Palestinian Arabs.) One such report on the confrontations (Barbara Slavin and Milt Freudenheim, 4/4, p. E2) quoted Arab shopkeepers and West Bank mayors for their views, but neglected to give any Israeli opinions concerning the situation. Since it was not the expressed intention of this piece to give the Arab view, but rather objectively describe the situation, this was clearly an example of biased reporting.

Israel was also made to appear culpable through the use of damaging statements made by *unnamed* Israeli "officials." One was often told nothing about these "officials," even whether they were in the army or the government or whether they held positions of some importance. This was done, for example, in the previously mentioned news article by David Shipler on censorship (3/30, p. A12). The content of the statements chosen for quotation would have made a very well-informed Times reader question the knowledge of this "official" on the subject. Since such statements by "officials" were often damaging to the Israeli position, the critical reader might have wondered about either the common sense or the political party affiliation of those quoted (that is, whether they opposed the government in power). The critical reader should have wondered how such "officials" were selected for quoting, and how such absurd statements were elicited. The use of such quotes should make one question the ability, judgment, objectivity and aims of the Times reporters.

One technique of the Times journalists for having others state what they themselves believed was to quote from the editorials of Israel's anti-government newspapers. Thus again, under the guise of "going to the sources," they quoted liberally from the *editorials* of the Jerusalem Post, an English-language organ which strongly supported the opposition Labor Party; Haaretz, a liberal, highbrow newspaper; and even al-Hamishmar, the paper of a small, extremist, left-wing group. (One should note that Haaretz and the Jerusalem Post were able, to a large degree, to keep the opinions expressed in their editorial pages and columns separate from their objective news reporting. Although they often opposed the government's policies, it was difficult to detect this solely from their news stories.) It is significant that the readership of these newspapers was, and is, relatively small. To the discredit of the Times, the opinions expressed in the large circulation newspapers, Maariv and Yediot Aharonot, which were much more in tune with the general Israeli public opinion than the foregoing newspapers, were not reported. The pro-government daily Hatzofeh, geared primarily for the twenty percent of the population which is religious, was similarly ignored.

Opposition in Israel to the government's policies—real opposition and fabricated opposition—was focused on and played up, but popular support for the democratically elected government was ignored. Thus, David Shipler noted (3/23, pp. 1, A7) that the Begin government had been the object of increasing condemnation by "liberal-minded Israelis." On the subject of the West Bank he quoted from the Jerusalem Post to indicate that what he termed "extreme" statements of the Defense Minister, Ariel Sharon, had served to widen the gap between social groups. In the same story he also quoted from Haaretz. In another news story (3/28, p. E3) his source for a relevant quotation was al-Hamishmar, which he chose to describe as "socialist."

In a manipulative attempt to make Menachem Milson—the newly-appointed civilian governor of the West Bank and the architect of the new policies there—appear to be unreasonable, Shipler quoted a brief exchange between Milson and a news correspondent from Sweden. The journalist, Shipler noted, had been in a concentration camp, had been a foreign correspondent in Israel for several years, and had a son who was about to enter the Israeli army. The reader seems expected to interpret Milson's critical words to her in only the most simplistic way, and to assume the journalist's sagacity concerning Israel's security because of her background. Milson was, in fact, questioning her wisdom, although the newswoman's reply made it clear that (1) she did not understand this, (2) she believed her background made her beyond certain criticisms, and (3) she held that Milson was obviously unfair to her and out of touch with reality.

As stated, the New York Times reports from the Middle East generally gave the impression that there was a widespread and growing public disfavor in Israel with the government's policies, and much unwarranted attention was given to such sentiments. For example, Shipler wrote about protests by some Israelis concerning the treatment of the Bedouins in the Negev (3/9, p. A2), and in another story he stated that a public stir concerning the behavior of the army and the West Bank settlers was created (3/23, pp. A1, A27) in an incident on the West Bank which had been shown on Israeli television. Other Times correspondents did the same. Henry Kamm reported on March 28th (p. 9) that "In Tel Aviv, several thousand Israelis rallied after sundown ended the Sabbath to protest against the Government's harsh measures on the West Bank." (As noted before, the word "harsh" reflected a biased, subjective judgment, and should not have been used.) The next day Shipler mentioned (3/29, p. A4) that there were growing attacks on the government by Labor Party adherents and members of the Peace Now movement. The Times placed no stress where it should have been: on the unquestionable fact that Begin's West Bank policy was popular among the Israeli public (which had a good understanding of the matter). The Sunday Times of London reported on March 29th (p. 9) that Begin's new West Bank policy was approved of in Israeli public opinion polls.

New York Times journalists seemed to believe that they could perceive the true goals underlying the Israeli government's actions. This was despite the fact that the data necessary to support many of their assertions were absent. The accuracy of their glib judgments seems even more unlikely since the situation in the Middle East was extremely complex and fluid, as usual, and the Israeli government's policies seemed to be adjusting to the changing situation. Like other elements of the journalists' views of the past, present and future developments in the area, the alleged goals of the government were the same as those proclaimed by the Palestinians and by a few Israelis. The headline of David Shipler's "news and analysis" piece on March 27th (p. 4) was "Israel in the West Bank: The Goal Becomes Clearer." The supposed goal which Shipler was certain he could perceive was annexation. The next day the story by this pseudo-seer (p. E3) was headlined "The West Bank Occupation Now Resembles Annexation."

7

THE COVERAGE OF THE ATTACK
AT THE MOSQUE

The New York Times coverage of the killings at the Mosque of Omar (The Dome of the Rock) in Jerusalem and the rioting which immediately followed was very misleading. On April 12th it was the primary story of the day (Shipler, pp. 1, A12). The Times stressed that the culprit was an Israeli soldier, and the paper's headline read: "An Israeli Attacks Dome of the Rock, Killing at Least 2; Soldier at Moslem Shrine also Wounds 9 before Capture— Protests Injure Many." The first line of Shipler's story began: "An Israeli soldier with an automatic rifle...." No background on him was given in the story, although it was stated that it was unclear at the time whether he was a reservist or a member of the regular army. (Almost all Israeli men serve in the reserves until the age of 55.) A sub-heading near the beginning of the story proclaimed: "Link to Extremists." This "link" to so-called "extremists" was merely the fact that some literature of the Kach movement had been found where he had been living. Past threats by the Kach movement to take over the Temple Mount were noted. The front page had a photograph of the attacker, and the caption referred to him as "A man identified as Alan Harry Goodman, formerly of Baltimore." On the inside pages were photographs of Arabs injured in the riots which followed the shootings.

The emphasis in other major newspapers was different from that in the Times, treating the culprit *primarily* as a maniac who had come from America, and focusing much attention on the rioting. Other newspapers were generally much more objective and accurate. The Washington Post's headline for that day (4/12) was "Two Killed in Mosque in Israel; Jerusalem Arabs Riot after Shooting by U.S.-Born Jew." There were photos of angry Arabs, the P.L.O. flag being held aloft, and an Arab injured by Israeli security forces. A photo caption referred to the assailant as the "gunman." The story, by William Claiborne (a very strong critic of Israeli government policies) began: "An American-born Jewish gunman wearing an Israeli Army uniform and firing an M16 assault rifle...." The story reported that it appeared that the assailant had done a short stint in the army

100

and was a reservist. (This was not true.) It stated that the United States State Department declared that the act was "obviously the work of a deranged individual."

The headline in the New York Post (4/12) was "Easter Sunday Mayhem." Featured on the front page was a photograph of an injured Arab and the explanation: "A wounded Arab is carried off by fellow Palestinians during the worst day of rioting in Israel's history following a shooting spree by a crazed American Jew." Inside the paper (pp. 2, 32, 33) were photographs of Goodman, of a woman who had been shot, and of an angry mob with a youth holding a P.L.O. flag aloft. The main story was written by a New York Post correspondent in Israel and entitled "Jerusalem Mayhem as Gunman Slays Two." Its lead sentence was "A crazed American-born Jew opened fire inside a sacred mosque...." It noted that he was wearing an Israeli army uniform and claimed that he had been called up to do reserve duty two weeks earlier. It added that "Police initially suspected that Goodman was a member of an extremist organization [the Kach movement] that is an offshoot of Rabbi Meir Kahane's Jewish Defense League. But officials later denied there was any involvement with the Jewish extremists."

The major Daily News story (4/12, pp. 2, 25), written from "combined dispatches," began with "An American-born Jew wearing an Israeli army uniform shot his way...." It said that he was apparently an army reservist. The news story provided background information on Goodman which showed that he was clearly mentally disturbed. There were photographs of an injured Arab, angry Arab crowds chanting, the P.L.O. flag being waved, and Alan Goodman.

The New York Times' identification and description of Goodman was generally erroneous, propagandistic and malicious. On April 13th, a day after its major story on the mosque attack, the Times had an article dealing with Goodman's background which indicated that he was not sane. As already shown, this highly significant information had been included in the main stories of the attack sent from Israel which had appeared in other newspapers the previous day, and the man's insanity was an essential and obvious element in their many subsequent stories. In the Times, however, his apparent insanity was almost entirely confined to this one article appearing a day after the major story.

In the days following the attack, the Times continued to refer to the assailant in the same terms it had in its first major story. Thus, a report from Israel on the following day ("Special to the N.Y. Times," 4/13, p. A3) referred to him *three times* in the first sentence as an "Israeli soldier," and gave the same identification two more times in the report. His name was mentioned once—in the seventh paragraph. A photo caption on page one also referred to "Israel soldiers" (*sic*). A Times Week in Review synopsis (Barbara Slavin and Milt Freudenheim, 4/18, p. E2) similarly referred to the shooting rampage by an "Israeli soldier." The primary designation in the news stories of Henry Kamm in Israel (4/15, p. A7) and Beirut correspondents John Kifner (4/15, p. A6) and Marvin Howe (4/14, p. 1) was "American-born Israeli soldier," although he was often simply referred to as "an Israeli soldier" ("Special to the N.Y. Times," 4/13, p. A3; Kamm, 4/17, p. 2). As already noted, the designations used by such newspapers as the Washington Post, the Daily News and the New York Post gave a very different (and more accurate) picture. The caption for an AP photograph which appeared in the New York Times (4/13, p. A3) referred to the assailant as an "Israeli soldier." The same photograph in the New York Post (4/13, p. 2) had the term "Jewish gunman" in its caption. An AP story the New York Post printed on the same page referred to Alan Harry Goodman, an "immigrant from the U.S.," and a

UPI story described him solely as a "Gunman" in its title. Another news report in the New York Post referred to "American-Born Alan Harry Goodman."

The New York Times terminology was also incorporated into its coverage of the riots in the days following the assault. For example, one story ("Special to the N.Y. Times," 4/13, p. A3) began: "Violent protests erupted throughout the Israeli-occupied West Bank and Gaza Strip today over the rifle attack by an Israeli soldier on Moslems in the Dome of the Rock. Sixteen Arabs were reported shot by soldiers breaking up the demonstrations." (See also "Special to the N.Y. Times," 4/17, p. 3 for a similar statement.)

The Times version of the events at the Dome of the Rock was inaccurate and incomplete. As with other stories, such things were never explicitly corrected in later days, and thus the facts did not appear in the Times even after their publication in other newspapers. In the main story on the attack by Shipler, he incorrectly asserted of the gunman: "In uniform, he had no trouble carrying his weapon through the two checkpoints leading to the [Temple] mount, where even handbags are usually searched for guns and explosives." In contrast, the Washington Post and other newspapers accurately reported in their first stories of the incident how Goodman had

had to shoot his way to the Mount, and that his first two victims were two police guards—one Arab, one Jewish.

In reaction to the shooting, Arabs began to crowd onto the Mount as well as elsewhere in Jerusalem and rioted. The Times reported that the Arabs waved sticks and shook their fists, and that "Stone-throwing youths injured at least 27 Israelis and foreigners on the Mount of Olives, and two of the injured were hospitalized." The Washington Post reported that the Israeli troops were called in "to disperse angry rock-throwing crowds" of Palestinians brandishing knives and clubs who filled the thirty-five acre Temple Mount. It noted that many Israeli police and troops, as well as foreign tourists, had been hurt by stones and had been sent to the hospital. It added that the Israeli news agency (ITIM) had reported that some of the tourists were Americans. The Daily News noted in the *first* paragraph of its report on this story that several of the tourists who were injured were Americans and that many other foreigners and Israelis were hurt. The New York Post also reported that American tourists were injured. As I have noted, the Times paid little attention to the Arab violence and described the injured tourists primarily as "foreigners."

The vocal enunciations of the rioting Arabs reported in the Times were much milder than those reported in other newspapers. The Times stated that the Arab mobs yelled what it termed "nationalist slogans": "Palestine is Arab," "Jews Out," and "God is Great." The Washington Post reported that the crowds chanted "P.L.O., P.L.O., Palestine is Arab," and "We will avenge with blood and spirit the [mosque's] honor." They vowed to "redeem in blood" the honor of the mosque. The New York Post correspondent reported that the rioters were screaming "God is Great" and "Death to the Jews."

A small incident which received some attention in the Times, and was apparently *supposed* to be telling, concerned the fact that when the Israeli troops were leaving at the end of the clashes one Israeli soldier threw a tear gas cannister near the mosque entrance, and that—according to the reporter—it was perfectly placed since a wind carried the tear gas directly into the mosque. In contrast, an action mentioned in the New York Post may have better characterized the general attitude and approach of the Israeli army: before entering the mosque to go after the gunman, the Israeli soldiers removed their boots out of consideration for Muslim tradition and sensitivity.

It has already been mentioned that indications that Goodman may well have been connected with the Kach movement were made in the Times. The early stories noted that those in this movement had made threats in the past, and that the Arabs believe there is a plan by the Israeli government to ban Muslims from this mosque on the Temple Mount. I should add that those in the Kach movement (the so-called "extremists") want the Great Jewish Temple—first erected by King Solomon on this spot—rebuilt, and are bitter about the fact that the Arabs constructed a mosque on this Jewish holy ground. They demand the right to pray on the site. The mosque was correctly identified in the Times as the third holiest place in Islam, after those in Mecca and Medina in Saudi Arabia. (Medina, or Yathrib, had been a Jewish city for five hundred years until the Jews were expelled by Mohammed.) The Times also reported that The Temple was destroyed by the Romans in 70 A.D., and that "There has been no Jewish presence on the mount since then, although it is one of the holiest places in Judaism." This and other statements concerning the Temple Mount were inaccurate, incomplete and misleading. The reason for the lack of a Jewish presence on the Mount should have been noted: Jews were forbidden to set foot on it by the successive conquerors of Jerusalem, who have primarily been Muslims. It is not "one of the holiest places in Judaism," but has been the only true Jewish holy place for thousands of years. The Washington Post correctly noted that it is the traditional site of the Holy of the Holies. Both the Washington Post and the Daily News reported that the Israeli government had placed the Temple Mount off limits to Jewish worshippers as a conciliatory gesture to the Arabs, who vehemently oppose their presence.

In all Times news stories during this period, in its maps and even in its Sunday travel section, the "Western Wall" of the Temple Mount was called the "Wailing Wall." (See, for example: Shipler, 3/17, p. A3; 4/12, pp. 1, A12; 4/11, pp. 1, 15, 19; "Special to the N.Y. Times," 4/13, p. A3.) This was the name given it in the past because Jews came there for almost two thousand years to bemoan the destruction of the Temple and the forced dispersion of the Jewish people, as well as to pray. After its repossession in the 1967 war it was formally renamed the Western Wall since wailing was no longer relevant. It was insensitive and insulting to call it by its former name because of its associations, and the Times reporters should have known this and acted with some decency, especially those in the Jerusalem bureau (like Shipler) who have lived in Israel for years. The Washington Post called it the Western Wall in all of its stories and its maps. (See, for example, 4/12, pp. A1, A17.)

Two days after the attack at the mosque, the Washington Post noted that when Goodman was being led to court to be formally charged, he made a senseless attempt to escape. (See the photo caption.) The New York Post headlined its story of the day (4/13, p. 2) on the subject "Court Outburst by Temple Gunman." The New York Times story of the arraignment, "Israeli Arraigned in Mosque Raid" ("Special to the N.Y. Times," 4/14, p. A6), did not even mention his wild actions described in the New York Post. Unlike the Washington Post and other newspapers, it did not carry a photograph of his being brought to court by the police, that is, of his being brought to justice by the Israeli state. The story did report that police spokesmen stated that Goodman had been on leave from basic training when he carried out his attack, and that he had been in the army for only two weeks. However, this important story of the arraignment was relegated to page six of the Times and it was not noted in either the paper's detailed daily index or in its "News Summary" section of important items. The other stories that day concerning Israel which *were* included in the index were:

"Boy, 8 years old, Killed in Gaza Strip"; "Moslem Nations Denounce Israel at the U.N."; and "Brinkmanship Strategy on Peace with Egypt and War with P.L.O.," which was an analysis of Menachem Begin's policies by David Shipler.

A headline in the New York Post (4/13) used a quote by Alan Goodman in its story of the arraignment: 'My Mosque Murder Spree was Act of Revenge against Arabs." It focused on the man and his stated motives. It indicated that he was insane, but that he did have a political ideology. The story began:

> A self-described "Zionist fanatic" told police here he joined the Israeli military reserves so he could get an automatic weapon and kill Arabs, the Post has learned. In a bizarre confession to Jerusalem police, American-born Alan Harry Goodman said he had decided "years ago" to "take revenge against Arabs for terrorist operations."

It goes on to report that he claimed to be taking vengeance for the March 1978 P.L.O. killing of 36 Israeli civilians and the wounding of 70 more when terrorists commandeered a bus in Israel." 'The terri-

110

fying pictures of that massacre were chasing me,' the gunman said. 'I felt myself obligated to take vengeance.' "

In its many stories related to the Mosque incident and its aftermath, the Times mentioned several important items rather briefly which should have been reported in full and with some analysis. This would have revealed significant elements of Arab psychology as well as political policies which were of central importance to (1) the stories being covered, (2) the entire situation in the Middle East, and (3) American interests in the area. The Times quoted (4/13, p. A3, "Special to the N.Y. Times," "30 Injured in West Bank Violence") the wild claims of the Supreme Islamic Council that "it was absurd of the Prime Minister's [Begin's] office to describe the assailant as deranged because all regular soldiers were supposed to undergo physical examination. Moreover, the council contended the prisoner had not been alone. It said he had been covered during his attack by fire from many sides." The next day ("Special to the N.Y. Times," 4/14, p. A6) the Times repeated the accusation of the Council that more than one person was involved in the shooting. Another story by its U.N. correspondent (Nossiter, 4/14, p. A11) indicated that King Hassan of Morocco said

through his envoy at the UN Security Council that
Israel bore responsibility for the Mosque attack, and
accused Israel of 'passivity if not collusion' with
'Zionist-terrorist groups.' A piece in the Times' Week
in Review section (Barbara Slavin and Milt Freudenheim, 4/12, p. E2) noted that the Arabs were trying
to place the blame for the attack on Israel as a whole.
It was never reported in the Times, or any other major
American newspaper, that some Arab countries were
broadcasting that the assailant was actually an American agent working for the Israeli government. It has
already been noted that the first article on the
Mosque attack reported the Arab belief that there is
a plot by the Israeli government to take over the
Muslim holy sites. (The fact is that the holy places
have been left in the hands of Muslim officials, and
such a belief is true paranoia.)

8

COVERAGE OF THE IMPENDING ISRAELI WITHDRAWAL FROM SINAI

During these same three months in 1982, the Times' treatment of Israeli fears concerning their return of the remaining part of Sinai to Egypt (in accordance with the Camp David agreements) tended to belittle the apprehensions of the Israelis concerning the real, tangible threat this posed to their security. The reluctance of many Israelis to giving back Sinai was not usually attributed by the Times to their valid strategic concerns, but rather to religious impulses or to alleged psychological and near-spiritual elements embedded in the Israeli psyche. (This was in sharp contrast to the usual absence of any psychological analysis of the Arabs.) Thus Shipler claimed (4/1, p. A3) concerning the traumatic abandonment of the settlements in Sinai that for the Jews in Palestine and Israel "settlement has been a nearly-sacred precept since early in the century."

Related to this was the repeated minimization in

the Times of the charges by Israel that Egypt was violating the recent treaty in the areas of Sinai already evacuated. One news story (Shipler, 4/6, pp. 1, A4) noted that Israel had "charged" that Egypt had allowed Bedouins to smuggle five hundred weapons through the area Egypt already controlled, and that Israel "claimed" to have intercepted them before they reached their proximate destination—Palestinians in Gaza. Concerning Egyptian troop violations, Shipler wrote that "they have been characterized by some officials as minor." It was not made clear whether these "officials" were Israeli, Egyptian or American. He continued: "Some [alleged violations] apparently involve the deployment of units that provide the capability of rapid expansion into a wartime posture, Israelis say, and this is worrisome for officials in Jerusalem." The Egyptians, it was reported, agreed to withdraw the troops Israel "says" exceeded the allowable limit. Subsequent Times reports clearly showed that the Egyptians had indeed exceeded these limits, but the significance of such transgressions was consistently minimized.

Another front-page Times story (Shipler, 4/14, pp. 1, A10) subjected Israelis and their leaders to psychoanalysis, and proclaimed Begin guilty of "Brinkmanship Strategy" in its headline because of his government's threat to not carry out the rest of the withdrawal agreement because of Egyptian violations. (It did at least mention that the Israelis "claimed to have captured guns, grenades and explosives in Gaza which had been brought from Egypt through the area of Sinai already returned to Egypt.") A story filed by Henry Tanner in Cairo the same day (p. A10) was headlined "Egypt Denies any Violations of Peace Accords with Israel." An article summarizing the developments before the final Israeli withdrawal (Shipler, 4/18, p. E2) attributed Israeli actions primarily to irresponsible guile: "Prime Minister Menachem Begin and his cabinet ministers led Israel and the rest of the world on a roller coaster of apprehension last week about the peace process with Egypt." He continued: "The rapid shift in Jerusalem's official mood appeared to be part manipulation, part authentic change." The very real and specific Egyptian violations of the treaty agreements to police the Sinai and adhere to certain numbers of troops equipped with specific arms were again minimized. It offered the incredible justification that "Egypt regards the limits as flexible." Shipler maintained that Egyptian President Mubarak's less-than-friendly actions and statements in recent weeks, which had caused great worry among

115

Israelis, were made merely to please other Arab countries and were thus not significant. Back in March Shipler had stated: "For its part, Israel has shown little appreciation for Mr. Mubarak's political problems." (3/7, p. E4. In March [3/25, p. A2] the columnist Anthony Lewis, who was touring the Middle East, was permitted to file a "news" story from Egypt. It was a lengthy presentation of Mubarak's views.)

One of Henry Tanner's stories which complemented Shipler's April 18th article and was printed on the same page dealt with the Israeli "claims" of unwarranted Egyptian troop levels and Israel's repeated protests about the smuggling of arms into Gaza. This article was headlined "Why Egypt Regards the Withdrawal as Overdue" and indicated that Egypt had no desire to confront or menace Israel. In one of the rare instances in the Times of analysis of the Arab psyche, Tanner focused on the supposed positive aspects of Egypt's concern for its "dignity" and "pride," and failed to discuss the bloody results of the neurotic Arab obsession with these matters.

9

AFTERWORD: THE TREATMENT OF ISRAEL IN TIMES EDITORIALS, OPINION COLUMNS, AND OP. ED. ESSAYS

The focus in this analysis has been on the New York Times' news stories, although a few words have been said about its opinion columns and editorials. Some brief comments should be added concerning these as well as the guest columns on the "Op. Ed." ("Opposite the Editorial") page. In general, these presented a view not very different from that in the news reports, and Times news stories were often referred to for evidence. The contributions of the staff columnist Anthony Lewis—which leaned heavily on the news stories of David Shipler—have received widespread criticism (in Commentary and The New Republic, for example) for their wild claims and gross inaccuracies, as well as the unreliability of Lewis' sources. Although more leeway can be expected in such opinion pieces than straight news reports, some standards of evidence and fairness should be maintained.

Needless to say, the news stories and columns were generated and presented within a common social and intellectual context produced, in part, not only by the reporters and columnists, but the editors and the publisher.

The editor of the Op. Ed. page for several years, including this period, was Charlotte Curtis, a former society reporter. Curtis is the author of two books—one on Jacqueline Kennedy and the other on life among the "jet set." According to the Times, the purpose of the Op. Ed. page "is to give readers a broad range of opinion and analysis of current issues," and the Times' publisher Arthur Ochs Sulzberger stated publicly that "Charlotte Curtis has fulfilled that mission with great distinction." (4/15, p. C28.) The fact is, however, that the great preponderance of the opinion pieces by both the regular columnists as well as the guest writers during these months was strongly anti-Israeli.

J'ACCUSE
by Norman Podhoretz

The war in Lebanon triggered an explosion of invective against Israel that in its fury and its reach was unprecedented in the public discourse of this country. In the past, unambiguously venomous attacks on Israel had been confined to marginal sectors of American political culture like the *Village Voice* and the *Nation* on the far Left and their counterparts in such publications of the far Right as the Liberty Lobby's *Spotlight*. Even when, as began happening with greater and greater frequency after the Six-Day War of 1967, Israel was attacked in more respectable quarters, care was often taken to mute the language or modulate the tone. Usually the attack would be delivered more in sorrow than in anger, and it would be accompanied by sweet protestations of sympathy. The writer would claim to be telling the Israelis harsh truths for their own good as a real friend should, on

Norman Podhoretz is the editor of *COMMENTARY* and the author of five books, the latest of which is *Why We Were in Vietnam*. Among his contributions to these pages [*COMMENTARY*, September 1982] is *"The Abandonment of Israel"* (July 1976).
Reprinted by permission of COMMENTARY, (c)1982 The American Jewish Committee.

the evident assumption that he had a better idea than they did of how to insure their security, and even survival. In perhaps the most notable such piece, George W. Ball explained to the readers of *Foreign Affairs* "How to Save Israel in Spite of Herself." No matter that Ball warned the Israelis that unless they adopted policies they themselves considered too dangerous, he for one would recommend the adoption of other policies by the United States that would leave them naked unto their enemies; no matter that he thereby gave the Israelis a choice, as they saw it, between committing suicide and being murdered; he still represented himself as their loyal friend.

And so it was with a host of other commentators, including prominent columnists like Anthony Lewis of the *New York Times*, academic pundits like Stanley Hoffmann of Harvard, and former diplomatic functionaries like Harold Saunders. To others it might seem that their persistent hectoring of Israel was making a considerable contribution to the undermining of Israel's case for American support and thereby endangering Israel's very existence. Nevertheless, they would have all the world know that they yielded to no one in their commitment to the survival of Israel. Indeed, it was they, and not Israel's "uncritical" supporters, who were Israel's best friends in this country. As a matter of fact, they were even better friends to Israel than most Israelis themselves who, alas, were their "own worst enemies" (an idea which recently prompted Conor Cruise O'Brien, the former editor of the London *Observer,* to remark: "Well, I suppose Israelis may be their own worst enemies, but if they are, they have had to overcome some pretty stiff competition for that coveted title").

This kind of thing by no means disappeared from the public prints with the Israeli move into Lebanon. In the thick file of clippings I have before me there are many expressions of "anguish" and "sadness" over the damage Israel was doing to its "image" and to its "good name." In a fairly typical effusion, Alfred Friendly wrote in the *Washington Post* (of which he was formerly the managing editor):

> Perhaps it was expecting more than was possible—that Israel should remain the country with a conscience, a home for honor, a treasury for the values of mind and soul. At any rate, it is so no longer but merely a nation like any other, its unique splendor lost...its slaughters are on a par with...Trujillo's Dominican Republic or Papa Doc's Haiti. Still absent are the jackboots, the shoulder boards, and the bemedalled chests, but one can see them, figuratively, on the minister of defense. No doubt Israel is still an interesting country. But not for the reasons, the happy reasons,

that made it such for me.

In addition to lamenting Israel's loss of moral stature as a result of Lebanon, these great friends of Israel condemned the resort to "unselective and disproportionate violence" (Anthony Lewis) on the ground that it "cannot serve the spirit of Israel, or its true security."

But the sympathetic protestations of this particular species of friend—including even Lewis, perhaps the most unctuous of them all—became more perfunctory and more mechanical in the weeks after the war began. One got the feeling that they were offered mainly for the record or to fend off criticism. And in any case, the preponderant emphasis was no longer on the putative damage Israel was doing to itself by its wicked or stupid policies. The focus was now unmistakably on the evils Israel was committing against others, as in this passage from a column by Richard Cohen in the *Washington Post*:

> Maybe the ultimate tragedy of the seemingly nonstop war in the Middle East is that Israel has adopted the morality of its hostile neighbors. Now it bombs cities, killing combatants and non-combatants alike—men as well as women, women as well as children, Palestinians as well as Lebanese.

Israel's "true friends," then, were liberated by Lebanon to say much more straightforwardly and in more intemperate terms than before what they had all along felt: that Israeli intransigence and/or aggressiveness and/or expansionism are the main (and for some, the only) source of the Arab-Israeli conflict and therefore the main (or only) obstacle to a peaceful resolution of that conflict.

Even if this were all, it would have increased the volume and intensity of the attacks on Israel to an unprecedented level. But what made matters much worse was the proportionate escalation and increasing respectability of the attacks from quarters that had never pretended to friendly concern with Israel.

To be sure, apologists for the PLO who had always been ugly about Israel—Edward Said, Alexander Cockburn, and Nicholas von Hoffman, to mention three prominent names—had been getting a more and more deferential hearing in recent years. Books by Said like *The Question of Palestine* had been widely and sympathetically reviewed in the very media he indiscriminately denounces for being anti-Arab; Cockburn, whose weekly pieces in the *Village Voice* have set a new standard of gutter journalism in this country (and not merely in dealing with Israel), has been rewarded with regular columns in *Harper's* and the *Wall Street Journal* (where in exchange for access to a respectable middle-class audience he

123

watches his literary manners); and von Hoffman, who is only slightly less scurrilous than Cockburn, has also found a hospitable welcome in *Harper's* and a host of other mainstream periodicals both here and abroad (not to mention the television networks). Writing to a British audience in the London *Spectator* (for which he does a regular column), von Hoffman exulted openly about this change:

> Where before it was difficult to print or say something that was critical of Israeli policies and practices, the barriers are now coming down. Some writers used to believe —rightly or wrongly—that to expound a Palestinian point of view was to risk blacklisting. Now many have become emboldened. . .

But if they were becoming "emboldened" before Lebanon, their tongues now lost all restraint. Von Hoffman himself is a case in point, having been emboldened in another piece in the *Spectator* to compare Lebanon to Lidice and the Israelis to the Nazis: "Incident by incident, atrocity by atrocity, Americans are coming to see the Israel government as pounding the Star of David into a swastika."

Whether von Hoffman published these words in the United States, I do not know, but by his own account he could easily have found an outlet. "Where once, among the daily press, only the *Boston Globe* could be counted on to print other points of view as a matter of consistent policy...now other voices are becoming somewhat more audible.''

Somewhat? According to one estimate, of the first 19 pieces on the war in Lebanon to appear on the *New York Times* Op-Ed page, 17 were hostile to Israel and only two (one of them by me) were sympathetic. I have not made a statistical survey of the *Washington Post* Op-Ed page, but my impression is that the balance there was roughly the same. In short, not only did the kind of virulent pieces formerly confined to the *Village Voice* and other yellow journals of the Left and Right increase in number and intensity; such pieces now also began appearing regularly in reputable papers and magazines.

Thus no sooner had the Israelis set foot in Lebanon than Edward Said was to be found on the Op-Ed page of the *New York Times* declaring Sidon and Tyre had been ''laid waste, their civilian inhabitants killed or made destitute by Israeli carpet bombing,'' and accusing Israel of pursuing ''an apocalyptic logic of exterminism.'' The comparison of Israel with the Nazis here was less brazen than in von Hoffman's piece, but William Pfaff more than made up for it in the *International Herald Tribune:* ''Hitler's work goes on,'' he began, and concluded with the prediction that Hitler might soon ''find rest in Hell' through "the knowledge that the Jews themselves, in Israel, have finally...accepted his own way of looking at things." The famous spy novelist John le Carré was imported from England by the *Boston Globe* to deliver himself of similar sentiments:

> Too many Israelis, in their claustrophobia, have persuaded themselves that every Palestinian man and woman and child is by definition a military target, and that Israel will not be safe until the pack of them are swept away. It is the most savage irony that Begin and his generals cannot see how close they are to inflicting upon another people the disgraceful criteria once inflicted upon themselves.

Finally, the syndicated cartoonist Oliphant, like Cockburn in the *Wall Street Journal*, portrayed besieged west Beirut as another Warsaw ghetto, with the PLO in the role of the Jews and the Israelis in the role of the Nazis.

Many other writers were also "emboldened" by Lebanon, but not quite enough to compare the Israelis with the Nazis. Alfred Friendly, in the passage quoted above, only compared them to Trujillo and Duvalier. Hodding Carter, in the *Wall Street Journal,* invoked Sparta (though his use of language like "Several Lebanese towns have been pulverized by the tactics of total war [and] tens of thousands of Lebanese have been killed or injured since the blitzkrieg was launched" suggested that Sparta was not really the state he had in mind). And Joseph C. Harsch, in the *Christian Science Monitor*, brought up Communist Vietnam: "Vietnam is imperial. It dominate[s] its neighbors Laos and Cambodia. In that same sense Israel is now the dominant power in its own area." Extending this ingenious comparison, Harsch wrote:

> Israel's major weapons come from the U.S. Israel's economy is sustained by subsidies from the U.S.... It depends on Washington, just as Vietnam depends for major arms and for economic survival on Moscow. Neither Israel nor Vietnam could dominate their neighborhoods if the support of their major patrons were withdrawn.

But the prize for the most startling comparison of all goes to Mary McGrory of the *Washington Post,* who was reminded of the dropping of atomic bombs on Hiroshima and Nagasaki. More startling still, Miss McGrory said that in her opinion what the Israelis were doing in Lebanon was worse. Addressing Begin directly she wrote:

> You were trying to save your own troops.

127

We understand that. We are, after all, the country that dropped atomic bombs on Hiroshima and Nagasaki. . . . But grant us that we were up against a mighty, if weakened, war machine and a totally mobilized nation. You were punishing a wretched country that reluctantly shelters factions, which, while hostile to you, could not wipe you off the face of the earth, however much they might want to.

What are we to make of words and images like these? How are we to explain them? How are we to understand what they portend?

There are well-wishers of Israel, among them a number of Jews, who recoil in horror from the idea that the Israelis are no better than Nazis, but who believe that Israel under Menachem Begin and Ariel Sharon has brought all this violent abuse on itself. Even though the degree of condemnation is excessive, say these anxious well-wishers, the Israelis have only themselves to blame for besmirching their "good name." Yet I would suggest that the beginning of wisdom in thinking about this issue is to recognize that the vilification of Israel is the phenomenon to be addressed, and not the Israeli behavior that supposedly provoked it. I say supposedly because when a reaction is as wildly disproportionate to an event as this one was, it is clearly being fed by sources other than the event itself.

But what am I or anyone else to say to those for whom there is nothing obvious about the assertion that in this particular case the reaction was disproportionate? From such people one is tempted to turn away in disgust. Yet difficult as it may be to entertain, even for as long as it takes to refute it, the loathsome idea that Israel is to the Palestinians as the Nazis were to the Jews, the world evidently still needs to be reminded of the differences.

To begin with, then, the Nazis set out to murder every Jew on the face of the earth, and wherever they had the power to do so, they systematically pursued this objective. Is this what the Israelis have tried to do to the Palestinians? If so, they have gone about it in a most peculiar way.

In Germany under the Nazis, the Jews were first stripped of their civil and political rights and then sent to concentration camps where virtually all of them were put to death. For more than thirty-five years, by contrast, Palestinian Arabs living in the state of Israel have enjoyed Israeli citizenship and along with it a degree of civil and political liberty, not to mention prosperity, unknown to Arabs living in any country under Arab sovereignty.

For fifteen years, moreover, about a million Palestinians on the West Bank and Gaza have been in the power of Israel under military occupation. Have squads of gunmen been dispatched to shoot them

129

down in the fashion of the *Einsatzgruppen* who murdered an approximately equal number of Jews in those parts of the Soviet Union occupied by the Nazis? Have the West Bank Palestinians been rounded up and deported to concentration camps in preparation for being gassed, as happened to some three million Jews living in other countries occupied by Nazi Germany? The Nazis in less than six years managed to kill more than five million Jews in occupied territory. How many Palestinian Arabs have been killed by the Israelis in fifteen years? A hundred? And if even that many, has a single civilian been killed as a matter of policy? Again, the fact is that the Palestinians living even under Israeli military occupation, and even since the recent political offensive against PLO influence on the West Bank, have enjoyed a greater degree of civil and political liberty than any of their brother Arabs living anywhere else *except* in Israel as Israeli citizens.

It is or ought to be obvious, then, that any comparison between the way Israel has treated the Palestinians and the way the Nazis dealt with the Jews is from a rational perspective, let alone morally, disproportionate to a monstrous degree. Anyone who makes such a comparison cannot possibly be responding to the facts of the case and must be driven by some other impulse.

But what about the comparisons of Israel with Sparta, or Haiti, or Communist Vietnam? Are they

130

any the less disproportionate? If so, it is only because nothing could match the intellectual and moral excess of equating Jews with Nazis. Still, these comparisons are sufficiently outlandish in their own right.

Sparta, to start with the least repellent of them, was a police state so dedicated to war and so single-mindedly devoted to the martial values that any male child deemed unfit to become a soldier was taken to the mountains and abandoned to his death. Israel is a democracy with an army made up largely of civilian reservists to whom nothing is more distasteful than going to war and to whom peace is the highest value. As for Haiti or the Dominican Republic under Trujillo, they have so little in common with Israel in any respect that bringing their names into the discussion can only be seen as an effort to sneak by with the absurd charge that Israel is no longer a democratic country.

Apparently, though, not even this charge was too absurd to surface openly in the public prints. Thus, Douglas S. Crow, Professor of Religion, no less, at Columbia University, wrote in a letter to the *New York Times* of Israel's "posturing as a bastion of democracy." But if Israel, where all citizens, including Arabs, have the right to vote and where all individuals and parties, including the Communists, enjoy a full range of liberties—speech, press, assembly, and so on—is not a bastion of democracy, where shall such a bastion be found?

The same point can be made of the analogy with Communist Vietnam, where there is even greater repression than in Trujillo's Dominican Republic and perhaps even greater economic misery than in Haiti. To compare Israel—which can indeed be described as a bastion of democracy—with what is by all accounts one of the most Stalinist regimes in the entire Communist world, is a sufficiently gross travesty. But is the comparison Joseph C. Harsch makes between the behavior of the two states toward their respective neighbors any more justifiable?

Both, says Mr. Harsch, are "imperial" states using military forces to dominate the countries of the region. That this is an apt characterization of Communist Vietnam very few will nowadays contest. Two years after signing a peace treaty with South Vietnam, the Communist regime of the North invaded and conquered the South. Not content with that, Vietnam proceeded to invade Cambodia where it installed another puppet regime, while keeping some 40,000 troops in Laos to insure its domination over the Communist regime there. Nor could Vietnam claim to be acting defensively: neither South Vietnam nor Cambodia nor Laos posed any threat to Hanoi.

If we now ask what this set of relationships has in common with the relations between Israel and its neighbors, the answer can only be: nothing whatever. One grows weary of reciting the facts of the Arab-

Israeli conflict over and over again. But the controversy generated by Lebanon demonstrates that far from being tiresomely familiar, they are still unknown by some and forgotten or deliberately ignored by others for whom they are politically inconvenient.

In 1947, then, the United Nations adopted a partition plan for Palestine, dividing it into a Jewish state and a Palestinian one. The Jews accepted the plan; the Arabs rejected it. The form this rejection took was a war against the new Jewish state of Israel launched by the armies of five neighboring Arab states, with the aid and encouragement of all the others. Israel successfully fended off this assault and begged its neighbors to make peace with it. But they all refused, rededicating themselves instead to the elimination of any trace of a sovereign Jewish state from the region.

Living in consequence under siege, with a coalition of nineteen nations pledged to its destruction, Israel maneuvered as best it could. In 1956, it joined forces with the British and the French in an attack on Egypt which left the Israelis in control of a stretch of the Sinai desert. But in response to American pressure, all three parties soon withdrew, and Israel in particular returned the Sinai to Egypt (without any *quid pro quo*). So much for the first instance of Israeli "expansionism" or "imperialism" and the only one to which these epithets have so much as a remotely plausible claim.

The next episode occurred in 1967, when Egypt took a series of actions clearly spelling an intention to resort once again to military force whose explicit objective was—as its then leader, Nasser, put it—"the destruction of Israel." After waiting for about two weeks while the United States and others worked unsuccessfully to avert a war in which they might be "wiped off the map" (Nasser's language again) if the Arabs struck the first blow, the Israelis launched a preemptive attack. Six days later, thanks to a brilliant campaign, they found themselves in possession of territory formerly belonging to or occupied by Egypt (the Sinai), Syria (the Golan Heights), and Jordan (the West Bank).

To the Arabs and their apologists, this was another instance of expansionism and imperialism. But since virtually no one doubts that Nasser provoked the 1967 war or believes that there would have been a war at all if not for his closing of the Straits of Tiran (among other actions he took), how can it be regarded as an imperialistic operation by Israel? In any case, Israel begged King Hussein of Jordan to stay out of the war once it started, and if he had agreed, the Israelis would not have been obliged to respond to his attack and they would not have ended the war in control of the West Bank.

Even so, Israel once again, as it had been doing since the day of its birth, asked only for recognition

and face-to-face negotiations with its Arab neighbors. Such negotiations would have resulted in the return of occupied territories with whatever minor
boundary adjustments security might dictate. Yet
once again, as they had from the beginning, the Arab
states refused, responding this time with the famous
three No's of Khartoum: No recognition. No negotiation. No peace.

Finally, seven years later and after yet another
war—this one unambiguously started by Egypt in a
surprise attack—Anwar Sadat (Nasser's successor)
called what had been universally regarded in the Arab
world as Israel's "bluff" by offering recognition and
face-to-face negotiations. Almost overnight, Israel
responded by agreeing to return every inch of Egyptian territory and then honored the agreement. So
much for imperialism.

Now comes Lebanon. To show that Israel is be-
having toward Lebanon as Vietnam has behaved toward Cambodia, Joseph C. Harsch writes:

> Israel has now decreed that there must be
> no more "foreign" military forces in Leba-
> non. That means that Israel wants all Pal-
> estinian and Syrian armed units out of
> Lebanon, leaving Lebanon in the hands of
> elements which would be sympathetic to
> Israel and to its interests.

There are so many astonishing features in these two sentences that one hardly knows where to begin. In the first place, why the quotation marks around the word foreign? Is Harsch trying to suggest that the "Palestinian and Syrian armed units" are indigenous or native to Lebanon? In the second place, what is illegitimate about Israel's desire to leave Lebanon "in the hands of elements which would be sympathetic to Israel and its interests"? In view of the fact that those "elements" would be the Lebanese people themselves, there can be nothing wrong in leaving Lebanon in their hands; and in view of the fact that before Lebanon was taken over by the PLO and the Syrians it was sufficiently "sympathetic to Israel and its interests" to live peacefully alongside Israel, a more accurate way of putting the case would be to say that Israel hopes to free Lebanon from the domination of foreign forces who have turned an unwilling Lebanon into a battlefield of their war against Israel.

But of course putting it that way would defeat the purpose of portraying Israel as an imperialistic power imposing its will upon a helpless neighbor. And it would also show the falsity of describing the war as an invasion of Lebanon. Yes, the Israelis did invade Lebanon in the sense of sending military forces across the Lebanese border. But if we are looking for analogies, a better one than any fished up in recent weeks would be the invasion of France by allied troops in World War II. The purpose was not to

136

conquer France but to liberate it from its German conquerors, just as the purpose of the Israelis in 1982 was to liberate Lebanon from the PLO.

Harsch and many of his colleagues may not know this, but the Lebanese people do. In spite of the sufferings inflicted upon them by the war, and in spite of the fact that they have no love for Israel, they have greeted the Israelis as liberators. Representative Charles Wilson, a Texas Democrat who is so far from being reflexively pro-Israel that he voted for the AWACS sale and intends to vote for the Jordanian arms sale, testified after a visit to Lebanon in July to

> the universal enthusiasm with which the Lebanese welcomed the Israeli army. . . . I mean it's almost like a liberating army. . . . It was astonishing. I expected this, somewhat, from the Christian population. But I didn't expect it from the Muslim population. . . . And in talking to a group of people, some of whom had lost their homes, some of whom had lost relatives, they said it was awful. But they said that all in all, to be free of the PLO it was worth it.

One can see why. According to a news story by David K. Shipler in the *New York Times,* the PLO, whose "major tool of persuasion was the gun," ruled

over a large part of Lebanon, terrifying and terrorizing the local populace, Christian and Muslim alike. It
took over land and houses, it confiscated automo-
biles, it stole at will from the shops, and anyone who
complained was likely to be shot. Operating as a state
within a state, the PLO humiliated local Lebanese officials and displaced them with its own police and
"people's committees."

On top of all this, writes Shipler, the PLO
"brought mercenaries in from Bangladesh, Sri
Lanka, Pakistan, and North African countries. By all
accounts the outsiders were crude, undisciplined
thugs." And then there were the killings. "Before the
PLO," one Lebanese woman told Shipler, "we used
to be pro-Palestinian. . . . [But] when we saw the Palestinians were killing us and threatening us and having barricades and shooting innocent people, then
came the hatred."

Rowland Evans and Robert Novak, whose column has always been notorious for its pro-Arab bias,
arrived at the same assessment: "Once incorruptible,
its extraordinary success in accumulating arms and
money...had made the PLO itself an occupying
power...permeated by thugs and adventurers."

If this disposes of the idea that a Vietnam-like Israel was imposing its imperial will upon Lebanon, it
does not dispose of the charge that the war in Lebanon
was imperialistic in a different sense—that Israel's
purpose, as Anthony Lewis (among many others)

138

charges, was "to exterminate Palestinian nationalism" in preparation for annexing the West Bank.

Here again, before taking up the substance, one
is forced to begin by pointing to the form in which the
charge is expressed. By using the word "exterminate"
—a word which is inescapably associated with what
the Nazis did to the Jews—Lewis contrives to evoke
the comparison while covering himself by designating
"Palestinian nationalism" rather than the Palestinian
people as the victim. But even in this form the charge
is an outlandish misrepresentation. For the *maximum*
objective of the Begin government is to establish
Israeli sovereignty in the West Bank while allowing to
the Palestinians living there a degree of control over
their own civil and political affairs far greater—once
more the point must be stressed—than they have ever
enjoyed in the past, or than Arabs enjoy in any country under Arab sovereignty. This is "to exterminate
Palestinian nationalism"?

And even this—to repeat, Begin's *maximum* objective—is subject by Begin's own commitment to
negotiation. That is, in signing the Camp David
agreement, Begin has obligated the state of Israel to
settle the question of sovereignty after five years by
negotiations among all the interested parties, including the West Bank Palestinians. This means that
whether Begin and Sharon like it or not, they or their
successors might well find themselves turning over the
West Bank to Jordan or to a new Palestinian leader-

139

ship willing, unlike the PLO, to live in peace both with Israel and Jordan.

It is precisely the hope of encouraging such a leadership to emerge that lies behind the two-sided strategy of destroying the PLO as a military force in Lebanon and as a political force on the West Bank. I urge anyone who doubts this to read "How to Make Peace with the Palestinians" by Menahem Milson.* In that article Milson said that Israeli policy on the West Bank had in the past inadvertently led to the strengthening of the PLO's influence there. He therefore advocated a new policy aimed at weakening the PLO so that the "silenced majority"—which in his judgment wished to live in peace with Israel—could make itself heard. The end result was to be a demand by the Palestinians on the West Bank that King Hussein repudiate the PLO as "the sole representative of the Palestinian people" and resume his old role of their spokesman.

After reading that article, Begin and Sharon appointed Milson (then a professor of Arabic literature at the Hebrew University) to the post of civil administrator of the West Bank, from which position he has been putting the policy outlined in the article into practice. The PLO and its apologists have naturally done everything in their power to sabotage and discredit Milson. But the political war against the PLO

---

*COMMENTARY, May 1981.

was proceeding on the West Bank as the military campaign against the PLO in Lebanon was being launched.

No one can say what the eventual disposition of the West Bank will be. What one can say with complete assurance, however, is that so long as the only alternative to Israeli occupation is a Palestinian state ruled over by radical forces pledged to the destruction of Israel, then no Israeli government—no matter who might be its prime minister—will be permitted by Israeli public opinion to withdraw. But one can also say, though with less assurance, that if an alternative should present itself, then no Israeli government, including one headed by Ariel Sharon, would be permitted by Israeli public opinion to absorb the West Bank.

Israelis have different reasons for wanting to rid themselves of the West Bank. Some fear the effects of continued occupation on the character of Israel as a democratic society; others fear the effects on the character of Israel as a Jewish state of adding so many Arabs to its demographic mix; still others are convinced that continued occupation is a formula for continued war.

But whatever their motives, many or (as I read Israeli public opinion) most Israelis would favor a withdrawal from the West Bank provided they were reasonably confident that the successor regime would be willing to live in peace with a neighboring Jewish state (and provided also, probably, that Jews who wished to go on living in Judea and Samaria would have the same right to do so as Arabs have in Israel). Elimination of the radical rejectionist Palestinians—whether or not they call themselves the PLO—is a precondition for any such resolution of the Palestinian problem. Consequently if Begin and Sharon succeed in their objective of destroying the PLO, they may well make it impossibly difficult for Israel to annex or absorb the West Bank—not because of pressures coming from Washington but because of pressures coming from within Israel itself.

All this, however, is for the future. Returning to the present and to the war in Lebanon, we still have to face the charge that Israel was waging a wanton and indiscriminate campaign against defenseless civilians.

In the early days of the war, words like "holocaust" and even "genocide" freely circulated in the media, along with horrendous estimates of the number of civilians killed or rendered homeless by Israeli arms. At first it was said that 10,000 people had been "slaughtered" in southern Lebanon and 600,000 turned into refugees. But no sooner had these figures been imprinted on the public mind than it was revealed that the local Lebanese authorities themselves put the *total* population of the area in question at 510,000—almost 100,000 fewer than were supposedly driven out of their homes. Israel claimed that there were 20,000 refugees and perhaps 2,000 casualties, of whom more than half were only wounded. Correspondents and other visitors to Lebanon soon confirmed that the original figures were "extreme exaggerations" (Shipler), while casting evenhanded doubt on the much lower Israeli figures. Even though "discussions with local officials and residents of the cities tend to reinforce the Israeli estimates of casualties there," wrote Shipler, "the Israeli figures exclude a lot."

Thus arose what came to be called "the numbers game." But the damage to Israel had already been done. In any case, what did it matter, asked Mary McGrory, what the exact figures were? Whatever the precise number, "it is already too many." In her open letter to Begin, she asked:

Does Israel's security have to be purchased by the slaughter of innocents?... We have been seeing every night pictures of wounded babies and old men. We read about people standing outside devastated apartment buildings, wearing masks against the stench of corpses, waiting to go in to claim their dead. They were a threat to you? Yes, we know, your planes dropped leaflets before they dropped the bombs. But why did you have to bomb their cities at all? People in apartment buildings may be PLO sympathizers or even devoted adherents of Yasir Arafat. But they were unarmed civilians.

Indeed they were, but Miss McGrory's letter might better have been directed to Arafat than to Begin. For (in Shipler's words):

> The huge sums of money the PLO received from Saudi Arabia and other Arab countries seem to have been spent primarily on weapons and ammunition, which were placed strategically in densely populated civilian areas in the hope that this would either deter Israeli attacks or exact a price from Israel in world opinion for killing civilians. Towns and camps were turned into vast armories as crates of ammunition were stacked in underground shelters and antiaircraft guns were emplaced in schoolyards, among apartment houses, next to churches and hospitals. The remains could be seen soon after the fighting, and Palestinians and Lebanese can still point out the sites.

This strategy of hiding behind civilians was entirely natural for the terrorist organization whose greatest exploits in the past invariably involved hijackings and the killing of innocent bystanders. Having held airplanes and buildings hostage, the PLO—as the American Lebanese League declared in a newspaper advertisement—was now holding much of Lebanon itself hostage, and especially west Beirut. Who, the League asked, gave "the PLO authority to insist that Lebanese civilians die with them?" Certainly not the Lebanese civilians themselves.

It is also important to note that under international law (specifically Article 28 of the Geneva Convention of 1948), "the presence of a protected person may not be used to render certain points or areas immune from military operations," and the responsibility for civilian casualties or damage rests on the party, in this case the PLO, who thus uses protected persons or areas. What the other side, in this instance Israel, is required to do is exactly the kind of thing Miss McGrory derides in her reference to the dropping of leaflets: that is, warn the civilians so that they have a chance to leave the area or otherwise protect themselves.

While scrupulously observing this requirement, the Israelis also took other steps to minimize civilian casualties, some of which led to an increase in their own casualties. This is why Miss McGrory's citation of the bombing of Hiroshima and Nagasaki is so bizarre. As it happens, I myself agree with her in thinking that the United States was justified in that action (because the result was to shorten the war and to save many more lives than were lost in the two raids). But the whole point of the bombing of Hiroshima and Nagasaki was to wreak indiscriminate damage which would terrorize the Japanese into surrendering. The Israelis were doing almost exactly the opposite in Lebanon. Their strikes were so careful and discriminating that whole areas of southern Lebanon were left untouched. If they really had been carpet bombing, both the levels of destruction and the number of casualties would have been far greater.

That a left-wing liberal like Mary McGrory should be driven into comparing Israel's military tactics in Lebanon with the dropping of the atom bomb on Hiroshima and Nagasaki is demented enough. But that she should go on to defend the use of the atom bomb by the United States (which in any other context she would surely condemn) in order to score an invidious point against Israel is a measure of how far her animus extends. It literally knows no bounds.

Obviously a reaction like this can no more have been provoked by the facts of Israel's behavior than the comparisons of Israel with Nazi Germany. Nor can the relatively milder denunciations of Israel as comparable to Sparta or Haiti or Vietnam be taken as a rational response to what Israel has done. What then can explain them?

In thinking about this question while reading through dozens of vitriolic attacks on Israel, I have resisted the answer that nevertheless leaps irresistibly into the mind. This answer, of course, is that we are dealing here with an eruption of anti-Semitism. I have resisted because I believe that loose or promiscuous use of the term anti-Semitism can only rob it of force and meaning (which is what has happened to the term racism). In my judgment, therefore, it should be invoked only when the case for doing so is clear and precise. When that condition is met, however, I also believe that one has a duty to call the offending idea by its proper name.

Not everyone agrees, not even Meg Greenfield, who in *Newsweek* happily endorses "plain talk about Israel" and who as editor of the *Washington Post* editorial page has certainly done a lot of plain talking herself. Miss Greenfield sees it as a "good thing" that the "resentful, frustrated, expedient silences" Americans have maintained over Israel have now been "interrupted by outraged, emotional condemnation of what Israel is doing." Some of this, she acknowledges, is excessive: "The comparison [of the Israeli invasion] to Nazi policy, for instance, has been as disproportionate in its way as the military violence it complains of." But the rest is understandable, and is anyway not to be confused with being anti-Israel or anti-Semitic. Indeed these very accusations have intensified the pent-up resentments which are now exploding into what Miss Greenfield calls "no-holds-barred attacks on the Israeli action."

In other words, though we are to have "plain talk about Israel," and though such talk is healthy when directed against Israel, we are not to have equally plain talk about the attacks on Israel. To say that such "no-holds-barred attacks on Israel" are anti-Israel is unhealthy, and to say that they are anti-Semitic is even worse.

George W. Ball also rules out any use of the term anti-Semitism:

> I long ago made it a practice not to answer any letter questioning my position on Middle East problems that contains the assertion or implication that I have said or written anything anti-Semitic. That accusation, in my view, is a denial—I might even say an evasion—of rational argument.

Yet when he goes on to explain why it is absurd to accuse him of anti-Semitism, he brings forth so shallow a conception of what the term means that it can only be described as historically illiterate. Anti-Semitism, according to Ball, is the dislike of Jews; it is therefore a sufficient refutation to point out that some of his best friends are Jewish, and that all his life he has admired the Jews for their contribution to the arts, to intellectual life, and to liberal political causes.

That a man of George Ball's experience and education should regard this as an adequate account of

148

anti-Semitism reveals an astonishing blind spot. But this blindness is an advantage, enabling Ball to accuse American Jews of dual loyalty—a classic anti-Semitic canard that also surfaced in the debate over the AWACS—and then indignantly and self-righteously to deny that this makes him an anti-Semite.

Unlike Ball, Conor Cruise O'Brien, who has a habit of speaking plainly on all subjects, does believe that some critics of Israel are "motivated by some kind of anti-Semitic feeling, possibly unconscious." In some instances, he concedes, it may be that what is at work is "genuine compassion for suffering Arabs, expressing itself in terms of a generous hyperbole." But in most others "there are indications to the contrary." These indications include the absence of any concern for the civilian casualties in the war between Iraq and Iran, and the silence that greeted the killing of an estimated 20,000 Sunni Muslims recently by President Assad of Syria in the city of Hama. (To O'Brien's examples may be added the indifference to the 100,000 people killed in internecine strife in Lebanon since 1975 on the part of virtually all those who have wept over the civilian casualties in Lebanon since the Israelis went in.) O'Brien suggests, however, that a term other than anti-Semitic is needed because "the people in question are...extravagantly *philo*-Semitic these days, in their feelings for the Arabic-speaking branch of the Semitic linguistic family." He proposes "anti-Jewism," and he offers a test by which it can be detected in the discussion of Israel: "If your interlocutor can't keep Hitler out of the conversation,...feverishly turning Jews into Nazis and Arabs into Jews—why then, I think, you may well be talking to an anti-Jewist."

The trouble is that the term "anti-Jewist" cannot be applied to those like George Ball who are loud in their protestations of friendship for the Jewish people, and who might even agree that comparing the Israelis with the Nazis deserves to be called anti-Semitic.

Let me therefore propose that we retain the historically sanctioned term anti-Semitism and let me outline a more general criterion for identifying it than the one O'Brien suggests. Historically anti-Semitism has taken the form of labeling certain vices and failings as specifically Jewish when they are in fact common to all humanity: Jews are greedy, Jews are tricky, Jews are ambitious, Jews are clannish—as though Jews were uniquely or disproportionately guilty of all those sins. Correlatively, Jews are condemned when they claim or exercise the right to do things that all other people are accorded an unchallengeable right to do.

As applied to the Jewish state, this tradition has been transmuted into the double standard by which Israel is invariably judged. The most egregious illustration is the UN resolution condemning Zionism as a form of racism. According to the thinking of this resolution, all other people are entitled to national self-determination, but when the Jews exercise this right, they are committing the crimes of racism and imperialism. Similarly, all other nations have a right to insure the security of their borders; when Israel exercises this right, it is committing the crime of aggression. So too, only Israel of all the states in the world is required to prove that its very existence—not merely its interests or the security of its borders, but its very existence—is in immediate peril before it can justify the resort to force. For example, whereas the possibility of a future threat to its borders was (rightly in my opinion) deemed a sufficient justification by the United States under John F. Kennedy to go to the brink of nuclear war in the Cuban missile crisis of 1962, the immense caches of arms discovered in PLO dumps in southern Lebanon have not persuaded many of the very people who participated in or applauded Kennedy's decision that the Israelis were at least equally justified in taking action against the PLO in Lebanon.

Criticisms of Israel based on a double standard deserve to be called anti-Semitic. Conversely, criticisms of Israel based on universally applied principles and tempered by a sense of balance in the distribution of blame cannot and should not be stigmatized as anti-Semitic, however mistaken or dangerous to Israel one might consider them to be. A good example can be found in the editorials published in the

New York Times on Lebanon. Unlike the consistently superb editorials on Lebanon in the *Wall Street Journal,* the ones in the *Times* have been harsh on Israel, they have often been unfair, and they have pointed toward policies that would jeopardize Israel's security. But they have not been guided by the usual double standard, and therefore cannot and should not be stigmatized as anti-Semitic.

Criticisms of Israel that *are* informed by a double standard on the other hand, deserve to be called anti-Semitic even when they are mouthed by Jews or, for that matter, Israelis. That being Jewish or possessing Israeli citizenship guarantees immunity from anti-Semitic ideas may seem a plausible proposition, but it is not, alas, borne out by experience. Like all other human beings, Jews are influenced by the currents of thought around them; and like all other minority groups, they often come to see themselves through the eyes of an unsympathetic or hostile majority. Jews are of course the majority in Israel, but the state itself is isolated among the nations, and subjected to a constant barrage of moral abuse aimed at its delegitimation. This seems finally to be taking the inevitable psychological toll in the appearance among Israelis of the term fascist in talking about their own society, when by any universal standard it is among the two or three countries in the world least deserving of this epithet.

To be sure, very few Israelis have reached the

152

point of blaming the Arab-Israeli conflict largely on Israel or Menachem Begin or Ariel Sharon. But a number of American Jews have been adding their own special note to the whining chorus of anti-Israel columnists, State Department Arabists, and corporate sycophants of Saudi Arabia which has grown more raucous over Lebanon than ever before. The misleading impression has been created that these "dissenters" reveal a serious split within the American Jewish community over Israel. In fact, however, with a few notable exceptions they represent the same minority of roughly 10 or 15 percent which has all along either opposed Israel (because as socialists they considered Zionism a form of reactionary bourgeois nationalism or because as Reform Jews they disliked nationalism for other reasons), or else came to support Israel grudgingly and only on condition that it comport itself in accordance with their political ideas. It is these people who have lately been congratulating themselves on their courage in "speaking out" against Israel. A few of them—those who live and work within the Jewish community—are actually dissenting. But most of the rest live in milieux like the university or work in professions like journalism in which defending Israel takes far more courage than attacking it.

Not only do these people invoke a double standard in judging Israel: they proudly proclaim that they do. "Yes, there is a double standard. From its birth

Israel asked to be judged as a light among the nations." These words come from one of the endless
series of columns Anthony Lewis has written on the
war in Lebanon. Lewis is Jewish, and even though he
makes no public point of it, I single him out here because his thinking is typical of the way Jewish "dissenters" who have been signing ads and giving interviews see not only the war in Lebanon but the Arab-
Israeli conflict as a whole.

Thus while he usually pays his rhetorical respects
to the Arab refusal to recognize Isael, Lewis's emphasis is always on the sins of Israel, whether real or
imaginary.* And while piously proclaiming his great
friendship for Israel, he harasses it relentlessly and
obsessively, justifying himself in this by hiding behind
the political opposition in Israel or behind Zionist
heroes of the past like Justice Brandeis. (Others use
the Bible for these purposes, humbly comparing
themselves to the prophets of old: "[The] biblical tradition of criticism and dissent should now guide public practice," two young Jewish academics declared
on the Op-Ed page of the *Times*. "Jeremiah's polem-
ics indicate that a government's foreign and security
policies, as well as societal inequity and immorality,

---

*For an example of the latter, see Ruth R. Wise's discussion in "The
Delegitimation of Israel," in the July COMMENTARY. The case in
point was a false allegation of censorship against the Israeli authorities
on the West Bank, combined with complete silence about the repression
of free speech on the East Bank—that is, in Jordan.

are grounds for legitimate dissent.'')

But is it true that ''From its birth Israel asked to be judged as a light among the nations,'' or even as the socialist paradise dreamed of by so many of Israel's Jewish ''friends'' on the Left? No doubt there have been Zionist enthusiasts who indulged in such rhetoric, but it is a historical travesty to claim that this was the animating idea behind the Jewish state. If perfection had been the requirement, it would have been tantamount to saying that an imperfect Israel had no right to exist; and since imperfection in human beings is unavoidable, Israel would have been sentencing itself to an early death from the day of its birth.

In any event, the opposite is more nearly true: that the purpose of Israel was to *normalize* the Jewish people, not to perfect them. The Jewish state was to create not a utopia but a refuge from persecution and a haven of security in which Jews who chose or were forced to settle there could live a peaceful and normal life. Thanks to the refusal of the Arab world to agree to this, the Jews of Israel have instead had to live in a constant state of siege. It would have been fully understandable if under those conditions Israel had become a garrison state or a military dictatorship. Yet no such development occurred. Founded as a democracy, it has remained a democracy, a particularly vital variant of the species—the only one in the Middle East and one of the few on the face of the earth.

In reminding ourselves of that enormous and wondrous fact, we come to the greatest irony of this entire debate. Although Israel is no more required than any other state to justify its existence through what Anthony Lewis or anyone else, myself included, considers good behavior; and although elementary fairness dictates that Israel not be condemned for doing things that all other nations are permitted to do as a matter of course; even so, even judged by the higher standard that Lewis and his ilk demand, the truth is that Israel *has* become a light unto the nations.

Thus, in remaining a free democratic society while surrounded by enemies and forced to devote an enormous share of its resources to defense, Israel has demonstrated that external threats do not necessarily justify the repression of internal liberties. For casting this light, in whose glare the majority of the nations of the world stand exposed, Israel not surprisingly wins no friends at the UN.

If its persistence in democratic ways under the most unpromising circumstances has helped win Israel the enmity of the Third World, the fierceness of its will to live is what has made it a scandal and a reproach to its fellow democracies in the Western world. For in the glare of *that* light, the current political complexion of the Western democracies takes on a sickly, sallow, even decadent look. We in the West confront in the Soviet Union a deadly enemy sworn to our destruction, just as Israel does in the Arab world. But whereas the Israelis have faced the reality of their peril and have willingly borne the sacrifices essential to coping with it, we in the West have increasingly fallen into the habit of denial, and we have shown ourselves reluctant to do what the survival of our civilization requires. We tell ourselves that the danger comes from our own misunderstanding and misperception; we castigate ourselves for being the main cause of the conflict; we urge unilateral actions upon ourselves in the hope of appeasing the enemy.

It is a rough rule of thumb that the more deeply this complex of attitudes is rooted in an individual or a group or a nation, the more hostility it will feel toward Israel. I readily admit that other factors also come into play. Anxiety over oil or business connections in the Arab world often turn people against Israel who might otherwise admire it precisely for setting the kind of example of realism and courage they would wish the West to follow. Secretary of Defense Caspar Weinberger is perhaps one such case and there are others scattered through the Defense Department, the State Department and the White House. There are also so-called hardliners where the Soviet Union is concerned (Evans and Novak come to mind) who have always believed that a tilt away from Israel and a more "evenhanded" policy in the Middle East is necessary if we are to contain the spread of Soviet power and influence in that region. This idea dies so hard that it may even survive the tremendous blow it has suffered in Lebanon.

On the other side, one can find many American Jews and liberal politicians concerned about Jewish support who back Israel even though in most other situations they tend to sympathize with forces comparable to the PLO (such as the guerrillas in El Salvador) and even though they are great believers in the idea that all disputes can and should be settled through negotiation.

Even allowing for these complications, however, one can still say that the more committed to appeasement of the Soviet Union a given party is, the more it opposes "military solutions to political problems," and the more hostile it will be to Israel. Thus the West European governments—the very governments which are so eager to prop up the Soviet economy, to ignore Afghanistan and Poland, and to ratify Soviet military superiority in Europe through arms-control negotiations— are far less friendly to Israel than is the American government. And within the United States itself, the people who are most sympathetic to the European point of view on the issue of the Soviet threat are among those least friendly to Israel.

These are the same Americans who also tend to pride themselves on having learned "the lessons of Vietnam"—lessons which, as Terry Krieger points out in a brilliant piece in the *Washington Times*, Israel has now dramatically refuted. For Israel has shown that military force is sometimes necessary; that the use of military force may also be beneficial; and that a Soviet client, "whether it be a guerrilla force or a terrorist organization," can be defeated by an American ally. This, Krieger thinks, is why such people have turned on Israel with vitriolic fury: "Those Americans who have denounced Israel's invasion of Lebanon eventually may forgive Israel for defending itself, but they may never forgive Israel for illuminating our own confusion and cowardice."

Again Anthony Lewis offers himself as a good illustration. Indeed, the terms in which he has denounced Israel's invasion of Lebanon are strongly reminiscent of the hysterical abuse he used to heap on the United States in Vietnam. This being so, it is worth remembering that Lewis called the Christmas 1972 bombing of Hanoi—in which by the estimate of the North Vietnamese themselves no more than 1,600 were killed—"The most terrible destruction in the history of man" and a "crime against humanity." It is worth recalling too that only days before the Khmer Rouge Communists would stake a claim to precisely that description by turning their own country into the Auschwitz of Asia, Lewis greeted their imminent seizure of power with the question: "What future possibility could be more terrible than the reality of what is happening to Cambodia now?" Yet with that record of political sagacity and moral sensitivity behind him, Lewis has the effrontery to instruct

Israel on how to insure its security, and he has the shamelessness to pronounce moral judgment upon the things Israel does to protect itself from the kind of fate at the hands of the Arabs that has been visited by the Communists upon South Vietnam and Cambodia.

The Bible tells us that God commanded the ancient Israelites to "choose life," and it also suggests to us that for a nation, the choice of life often involves choosing the sacrifices and horrors of war. The people of contemporary Israel are still guided by that commandment and its accompanying demands. This is why Israel is a light unto other peoples who have come to believe that nothing is worth fighting or dying for.

But there is more. In the past, anti-Semitism has been a barometer of the health of democratic societies, rising in times of social or national despair, falling in periods of self-confidence. It is the same today with attitudes toward Israel. Hostility toward Israel is a sure sign of failing faith in and support for the virtues and values of Western civilization in general and of America in particular. How else are we to interpret a political position that, in a conflict between a democracy and its anti-democratic enemies, is so dead set against the democratic side?

Even on the narrower issue of American interests, George Ball, Anthony Lewis, and those who share their perspective are so driven by their animus against Israel as to think that (in Lewis's astonishing words) "Looking at the wreckage in Lebanon, the only people who can smile are the radicals and the Russians." Yet consider: Israel, an American ally, and armed with American weapons, has defeated the Syrians and the PLO, both of them tied to and armed by America's enemy, the Soviet Union. Are the Russians insane that this should cause them to smile? The military power of the PLO, representing the forces of radicalism and anti-Americanism in the Middle East, has been crushed; and (unless Ball and the others, who are so desperate to save it, should work their will) its power to terrorize and intimidate may also be destroyed, leaving the way open for such forces of moderation as may exist in the Arab world to come forward. How should this make the radicals smile and the United States weep? Egypt, America's best friend in the Arab world, has been strengthened and the policy of accommodation it has pursued toward Israel has been vindicated in comparison with the rejectionist policies of Syria and the PLO. Can this be good for the Russians and damaging to American interests?

George Ball says that it can be and that it is. But this is so palpably absurd that it cannot be taken as the considered judgment of an informed and objective mind. Therefore if it is proper to indict anyone in this debate for bias and insufficient concern for American interests, it is Ball who should be put in the dock and not the Jewish defenders of Israel against whom he himself has been pleased to file this very indictment.

In the broadside from which I have borrowed the title of this essay, Emile Zola charged that the persecutors of Dreyfus were using anti-Semitism as a screen for their reactionary political designs. I charge here that the anti-Semitic attacks on Israel which have erupted in recent weeks are also a cover. They are a cover for a loss of American nerve. They are a cover for acquiescence in terrorism. They are a cover for the appeasement of totalitarianism. And I accuse all those who have joined in these attacks not merely of anti-Semitism but of the broader sin of faithlessness to the interests of the United States and indeed to the values of Western civilization as a whole.

BEIRUT & THE GREAT MEDIA COVER-UP

by Ze'ev Chafets

I

On April 23, 1981 hundreds of Syria's elite special forces gathered in designated meeting places near the northern city of Hama. They were led by Syrian President Hafez Assad's brother, Rifaat Assad, and they had come for a simple purpose—to teach the citizens of Hama a lesson. For more than two years, the Assad government had been plagued with civil unrest and political dissent. Syrian military installations had been sabotaged, government buildings attacked, and even the president himself was no longer safe. The source of this turmoil was the mysterious Muslim Brotherhood, an organization of fanatical Sunni Muslims dedicated to the overthrow of the government. No one knew precisely where the Brotherhood was headquartered, but the city of

Ze'ev Chafets, who was born in Michigan and moved to Israel in 1967, served as director of Israel's Government Press Office from 1977 to 1982. The present essay will appear in different form in his book, *Double Vision: How America's Press Distorts Our View of the Middle East*, which Morrow is bringing out in October. Copyright (c) 1984 by Ze'ev Chafets.

Beirut & the Great Media Cover-Up **as it appeared in** *COMMENTARY*, **Sept. 1984 from** *Double Vision: How the Press Distorts America's View of the Middle East*. *(c) 1985 by Ze'ev Chafets by permission of William Morrow and Co.*

Hama was widely considered one of its strongholds. The Assad brothers decided that the time had come to give its people a demonstration of good citizenship, Syrian-style.

Just before midnight, the troops were given the order to move. They streamed into the town and cut off several neighborhoods where Brotherhood sympathizers were believed to live. Then they systematically dragged hundreds of civilians, many of them teenagers, from their beds, lined them up against the walls of their own houses, and machine-gunned them to death. At first they left the bodies bleeding in the streets, for the edification of the townspeople; later, municipal garbage trucks scooped up the corpses and dumped them into open ditches. No official death toll was published, of course, but later estimates put the number as high as 350.

Readers who have never heard of this massacre (or who may have confused it with another, much greater massacre that took place in Hama in February 1982 and that claimed as many as 20,000 victims) are in good company. The foreign editors of most of America's newspapers have never heard of it, either. In fact, just about the only Americans who are aware of the slaughter are those who happened to read about it in an article on an inside page of the *Washington Post* two months later. There, under the headline "Syrian Troops Massacre Scores of Assad's Foes," the *Post*'s Editor Cody, writing from

Washington, told the story. Cody, one of America's most experienced Middle East reporters, noted that the first report on the massacre had been published in the French daily *Le Monde* on May 13, 1981 and that the *Post* had delayed its own article until it had been able to gain independent confirmation.

The *Washington Post*'s report was a considerable achievement—an American exclusive on a major political event in an important Middle East country. But why, with so many foreign correspondents in Beirut, all of them assigned to the Syrian beat, did it take two months for the story to emerge? And why did other news organizations—the *New York Times, Time, Newsweek* and the three networks, to name only some—never report it at all? In the seventh paragraph of his story, Cody gave a diplomatic answer:

> The massacre reports, in trustworthy and untrustworthy variations, have been discussed in Damascus and Beirut in the last two months. In an atmosphere created by the wounding of Reuters correspondent Berndt Debusmann, shot in the back by a gunman firing a silencer-equipped pistol, and threats against British Broadcasting Corp. correspondent Tim Llewellyn—both after stories considered by Damascus as unfriendly to Syria—the Hama reports have not been widely published from the area.

Cody's meaning was unmistakable—the reporters stationed in Beirut must have heard the story circulating there and had chosen to ignore it. They had remained silent in response to recent Syrian violence against journalists. They had, in short, decided to censor themselves.

II

It is hard to blame the correspondents in Beirut for being cautious. Muslim West Beirut, where most of them lived and worked, had been a battlefield since the onset of the Lebanese civil war in 1975-76. Following the intervention of Syria in the summer of 1976, the city and much of Lebanon came under military occupation and Beirut became an urban nightmare of random violence, terrorism and repression.

It had not always been that way. In the 1960's and early 70's, before the PLO arrived in Lebanon, destroyed the country's political and social equilibrium and plunged it into chaos, Beirut had been one of the most sophisticated cities in the Middle East, a city where the old colonial French influence was still strong and which, in contrast to the closed societies of the Arab world, was an oasis of tolerance and of what one American correspondent, John Cooley of the *Christian Science Monitor,* described as a "free and easy" press.

166

Then, in 1970, the PLO, whose armed presence in the kingdom of Jordan had already become an acute threat to the government there, lost a bloody war against King Hussein's troops. In the months following, almost the entire leadership structure of the PLO fled Jordan and relocated in Beirut, where it brought its armed militant presence to bear on the side of the Lebanese Muslims, much to the displeasure of the dominant middle-class Christians. It also brought a method for dealing with Western journalists that was both direct and brutal.

In those early days foreign reporters were considered enemies of the PLO unless proved otherwise; and certain subjects were off-limits to all journalists, friends and enemies alike. This approach actually began during the period that the PLO was still headquartered in Amman. In the late 60's, Milan Kubic, who covered the Middle East for *Newsweek,* filed a report about the PLO's contacts with European terrorist organizations. When it appeared, he was informed that an official of the PLO wanted to meet with him. He was taken to the office of the PLO's chief spokesman in Amman, where his life was threatened. On leaving Jordan, Kubic hired two part-time correspondents to "report" on the PLO, one the son of the legendary British leader of the Jordanian army, Glubb Pasha, the other Mark (Abdullah) Schleifer, a Jewish convert to Islam and an anti-Israel propagandist. Both were, presumably, closer to what the PLO had in mind.

After its exodus from Jordan, the PLO began expanding its power in Lebanon. Its base was the hundreds of thousands of Palestinian Arab refugees in the country, and it joined forces with radical Muslim groups in a rough alliance against the Christians. By 1973, there was sporadic violence throughout the country, and in the spring of 1975, full-scale civil war erupted. The small community of foreign journalists in Lebanon was reinforced to cover the fighting. The PLO was particularly sensitive to the fact that its policies and methods were now under the scrutiny of a comparatively large group of Western reporters, and it undertook some of the same tactics that it had employed in Jordan in order to insure that its "enemies" in the Western press remained at arm's length.

One such, ironically, was William Marmon of *Time,* whose Middle East tour had begun in 1973 when he became *Time'*s bureau chief in Israel. He soon established himself as one of the journalists most critical of Israel and sympathetic to the Palestinian Arab cause. His wife had a job teaching at Beir Zeit, the Palestinian-Arab college on the West Bank that was a hotbed of anti-Israel sentiment. All this, he assumed, would stand him in good stead when, in 1975, *Time*—which was itself in the process of adopting a position more sympathetic to the Arabs—transferred him from Jerusalem to Beirut.

He was wrong. During the summer of 1975 Lebanese security officers came to Marmon's office and told his local assistant, Abu Said, that Palestinian intelligence had learned about Marmon's Jerusalem years and was planning to kill him. Abu Said, himself a Palestinian Arab, learned that the threat had come from the PFLP faction of the PLO. Marmon contacted the American embassy in Beirut; he was told that although there was no information regarding this particular threat, the embassy's policy was to take these matters very seriously.

Marmon decided to stay on in Beirut. He sent Abu Said to mediate, and his assistant was apparently able to convince the Palestinian terrorists to drop the threat. The correspondent remained in Beirut throughout the fall of 1975, a period in which *Time's* office was shelled and the civilian slaughter in the city was, in Marmon's words, "the worst I have ever seen." On New Year's Eve, Abu Said came to see him. He had word that PLO gunmen had been looking for Marmon the night before but had gone to the wrong apartment. This time the message got through. Marmon took the first flight out, and never again returned to an area under the control of the PLO. Even today he does not know how his name got on the enemies' list.

Another member of the American press who ran afoul of the PLO in 1975 was Philip Caputo, a former Marine officer in Vietnam and future novel-

169

ist, then the Beirut correspondent of the *Chicago Tribune*. He had already had a run-in with the PLO two years earlier, when he had been detained in Beirut on charges of "spying" and held for five days. Upon his release, he had written an emotional account of his ordeal for the *Tribune*. As often happens with the PLO, Caputo had received profuse apologies from the organization when, after scaring him out of his wits, it finally released him.

But Caputo's problems with Beirut's armed thugs were not over. On October 26, 1975 he filed a report to the *Tribune,* and left his office. He had not gone far when he was stopped at a checkpoint by "leftist militiamen." As Caputo later described the incident:

> They checked my credentials and told me to walk down to Hamra Street, a distance of about one hundred yards. I had gone about thirty yards when one of them fired a shot at me. I shouted at them to stop, but then another joined in and fired a burst of bullets, one of which literally went through my hair. I ran zigzagging and rolling low, and was grazed across the back and arms by flying bullets. Then one hit me in the right ankle and just as I reached the corner another one got me in the left ankle. I crawled down Hamra Street toward the Central Bank and a householder took me in.

Caputo was taken in an armored car to a nearby hospital; later, he was evacuated to the United States. When the *Chicago Tribune* reopened its Middle East office, it was in Tel Aviv.

By the summer of 1976 Beirut had become, in the words of James Markham of the *New York Times,* "the most savage and uncivilized place on earth." Tens of thousands of civilians had already died in the fighting and the Muslim-PLO alliance seemed to be winning. It was then, at the ostensible invitation of the hapless and almost fictional Lebanese government, that Syrian forces entered the country and began to intervene on the side of the Christians. The press corps now had a new threat to contend with.

III

Syria's first move against the press in Beirut was directed at the local Lebanese media, and it was carried out with the cooperation of the Lebanese government. On January 4, 1977 the government imposed a state of national emergency, and with it, new and, for Lebanon, unprecedented curbs on freedom of expression, including a ban on the right of assembly and the institution of press censorship. Syrian forces also shut down seven local newspapers, including the relatively independent *al-Nahar,* through the simple expedient of seizing printing presses and locking employees out of the buildings.

By 1978, the Syrian occupation was a fact of life, and Beirut was totally divided between Christian East and Muslim West. Syria abandoned its alliance with the Christian forces; Damascus was now cooperating with the PLO, and together they controlled West Beirut. Armed "fighters," some of them not more than fifteen or sixteen years old, roamed the streets, brandishing Russian-made assault rifles. Almost every journalist stationed in Beirut had had a close scrape or two.

During these years, Syrian pressure on the local press waxed and waned as circumstances dictated, but in 1980 it hit a high point with the murders of Salim Lawzi and Riad Taha. Lawzi, a Sunni Muslim who during the 1970's had built a reputation as a moderate and thoughtful journalist, as well as fierce antagonist of the Assad regime, had moved his journal *al-Hawadess (Events)* to London in 1977. In Lebanon for his mother's funeral in February 1980, Lawzi was kidnapped. On March 6, 1980, the *New York Times* reported:

> The tortured body of one of the Arab world's most influential editors, who had been kidnapped by unidentified gunmen ten days ago, was discovered by a shepherd in a wooded area near here last night...
>
> Mr. Lawzi had been critical of the leadership of a number of Arab countries, notably Syria and Libya...

172

The *Times* article cautiously refrained from speculating on the identity of the "gunmen" who had abducted and mutilated Lawzi, but at the bar of the Commodore Hotel, the foreign-correspondents' gathering place in Beirut, various theories, most of them related to the dread hit teams of Rifaat Assad, were propounded. Needless to say, the murderers were never caught.

On July 23, 1980 Beirut was shocked once again to learn of the assassination of Riad Taha, a long-time president of the Lebanese publishers association. Despite the fact that the assassination had taken place in broad daylight, the police were, as usual, unable to find any clue regarding the identity of the murderers, who were rumored to be terrorists working for the Iraqis or the Syrians. That same day Charles Rizk, the Christian head of Lebanese television, resigned his post after having been kidnapped and held for four hours by "unidentified gunmen," and the publisher and editor of *al-Nahar* fled Beirut. The terror had become an epidemic.

With the Lebanese press largely frightened into silence, the Syrians turned their attention to the remaining independent journalists in West Beirut—the foreign press corps. Syria itself was in the throes of a brutal crackdown on dissent; thousands of Syrian civilians were being arrested and hundreds murdered. The regime in Damascus totally controlled the news within the country, and by carefully monitoring the

173

entry of foreign correspondents, it tried to keep word of its bloody reprisals from reaching the outside world. But Beirut, as a listening post next to Syria, was a threat. Enemies of the Assad regime smuggled out information to foreign reporters, who in turn published it and even beamed it back to Syria via the BBC or Voice of America.

In the spring of 1980, the unrest in Syria was reaching a peak. Most correspondents, unable to get an eyewitness view of the fighting, were forced to rely on secondhand accounts and diplomatic leaks. Somehow Berndt Debusmann, Beirut bureau chief for Reuters, got hold of information about a near-insurrection against the Assad regime in the northern port city of Latakia, and got it published. On June 5, Debusmann and his wife were leaving a dinner party at the home of a fellow correspondent in West Beirut shortly after midnight. As they were getting into their car, another automobile with several men in it pulled up; they fired five shots with silenced pistols and then sped away. Debusmann, shot in the back, was rushed to the American University hospital. Later, he was transferred to a hospital in Cyprus and subsequently relocated by Reuters.

The attempted murder of Debusmann did not come as a complete surprise. After his reports on Assad's difficulties had begun to appear, Debusmann was visited by an officer of the Lebanese security police, which under the Syrian occupation was a toothless but sometimes well-informed organization. According to the British *Observer,* Debusmann was warned that two armed Syrians were looking for him. This incident was followed by repeated telephone calls to the Reuters office in Beirut attempting to ascertain Debusmann's whereabouts and on one occasion a visit to the office by a Syrian "journalist" who asked for a recent photo. Friends advised Debusmann to leave Beirut, but he refused.

Following the incident, Reuters sent out a story that stated, "There was no known reason for the shooting." Reuters, which must have known about the repeated Syrian threats to Debusmann, chose to cover them up. But Debusmann's colleagues in Beirut and throughout the Middle East were perfectly aware of the facts.

The party Debusmann had been attending on the night he was shot was held at the home of BBC correspondent Tim Llewelyn. It was the last one that Llewelyn ever gave there. For the BBC correspondent, who had watched the shooting of Berndt Debusmann from his upstairs balcony, would within weeks himself be forced to flee from Beirut ahead of the Syrian assassins.

The threats against Llewelyn and his backup correspondent, Jim Muir, came after they had persistently reported on internal unrest in Syria. In July 1980 a Syrian go-between informed several diplomats in Damascus that Llewelyn and Muir were going to be killed, and they passed the message along. The British embassy protested to the Syrian authorities but was told, with what the British *Economist* described as "laughable cynicism," that security in Beirut was the responsibility of the Lebanese government. That was enough. Llewelyn and Muir sought refuge in Cyprus, where they waited for several weeks while the BBC reportedly tried to negotiate the terms of their return to Lebanon. It was a lost cause. Llewelyn, like Debusmann, was reassigned to East Africa. Muir remained in Nicosia. And the BBC's new Middle East correspondent, Gordon Leach, took up residence in Cyprus. The BBC's Beirut operation had been closed down.

The reign of terror did not end there. Later that month, *Figaro* correspondent Jorg M. Stocklin was, in the words of *New York Times* Beirut correspondent John Kifner, "suddenly pulled out [of Lebanon], and word about town was that he, too, had received a warning from the Syrians."

Reporters in Beirut clearly recognized the organized, explicit threat posed by the Syrian government, but they found it difficult to respond directly. In the summer of 1980, a group of them held a secret meeting to discuss what might be done. They agreed, as one later wrote, that their "only protection lies in achieving maximum publicity" in order to show the Syrians that attacks on journalists would be counterproductive. They feared, however, that articles on the situation written from Beirut might lead to further harassment and violence. They decided instead to ask their home offices to print editorials and columns on the subject. Very few did so.

IV

Ironically, Syrian violence against the press, intended to silence criticism, had another, perhaps unanticipated, effect—it made the PLO look good by comparison. From the time the Syrians arrived in the mid-70's, most of the Commodore Hotel correspondents believed that, at least in terms of its dealings with the press, the PLO could be counted among the "good guys"—helpful, and somehow even protective. As Edward Cody of the *Washington Post* put it, "You do not have to fear the PLO when you write about Palestinian affairs." Many of the Beirut veterans took as a proof of the organization's benevolence the fact that it accepted occasional unfavorable press stories, and they contrasted this apparent sophistication with the rigid intolerance and bloody-mindedness of the Syrians.

What many of the correspondents failed to see was that the PLO's liberality was hardly more than the willingness of a violent, powerful group to establish ground rules and then to allow the reporters to play by them. Journalists were free to write—as long as they avoided certain "sensitive" subjects. Western reporters were welcome in Beirut—provided that they were not considered "hostile" to the Palestinian revolution.

Most of the Beirut press corps never saw the PLO's stick—they were too busy chewing on its carrot. That carrot was the permission the PLO gave them to work in the Lebanese capital and its assistance in covering its own secret, semi-underground activities. Still, in the backs of their minds, even the most obtuse journalists knew that the stick existed.

In May 1979 Robert Pfeffer of *Stern* magazine was murdered in Beirut. The thirty-eight-year-old German was working on a book about contacts between the PLO and the Baader-Meinhof gang and other European terrorist groups. As usual in Beirut, the murderers escaped, and there was no serious investigation. But most of Pfeffer's colleagues guessed the identity of the murderers. As Doyle McManus, now of the *Los Angeles Times,* was later to observe, "Obviously, Bob Pfeffer got killed, or at least most of us believe he got killed, for looking into the connection with Baader-Meinhof and the PFLP."

Following Pfeffer's murder, the Beirut press corps stayed away from the subject of the PLO's contacts with European terrorist organizations. As for the PLO itself, having established the limits of its tolerance, it turned back to the job of cultivating and befriending individual journalists. In the lawless atmosphere of Beirut, the organization could portray itself as the guardian of the press—presumably from the same Syrians with whom, despite periodic tensions, it was allied.

In conformity with the PLO-dependent security system, Western reporters became, in effect, accomplices to their own isolation and supervision. They clustered around the Palestinian-run Commodore, where they knew that their movements, contacts, and outgoing communications would be monitored. Some of those with separate offices in the city found that they needed local Palestinian employees in order to establish contacts and guide them through the complexities of life in Beirut. These assistants were, in many cases, subject to the discipline of the PLO; if the organization was circumspect in its dealings with most foreign reporters, it could afford to be far less so in its demands on its fellow Palestinians or Lebanese Muslims.

Even in their own homes, some journalists were "protected" by the PLO. Peter Ranke, Middle East correspondent for Springer publications, was once told by a colleague he visited in West Beirut that he was regularly watched by a PLO guard who lived in the basement of his building, ostensibly to protect stores of beer and coffee but actually to spy on the foreign residents of the apartment house. Ranke was skeptical until, as if on cue, the Palestinian guard appeared at the German journalist's door. As Ranke watched, astonished, the PLO man looked around the apartment, asked for a cold beer, and then left.

179

Sometimes PLO "protection" was totally shameless. After the murder of Robert Pfeffer, the PLO put out the word that *it* was conducting an investigation, and it did the same after the murder in 1981 of ABC's Sean Toolan. These investigative efforts by the suspects themselves were, apparently, taken at face value by a number of journalists in Beirut, who by that time had adopted an unquestioning belief in the PLO's role as their benefactor.

Many in the Beirut press corps also came to feel that they had a special obligation to help the PLO make its case in the West. Vincent Schodolski, former bureau chief of the UPI in Beirut, once told an interviewer, "I think people here try to keep balance, but you're here and have daily access to the Palestinians. You see the people, you see the refugee camps, you're bound to tell the story as you see it." Others were deeply committed to the Third World view of national liberation and wished the Palestinian revolution well. (This group included both serious ideologues and thrill-seeking groupies.) The sympathetic view of the PLO also colored the press corps' relations with Lebanon's Christians. Despite the fact that half the Lebanese story was on the Christian side, few foreign reporters visited that sector with any frequency, and virtually none lived there.

Some even encouraged their visiting colleagues to keep away from the Christian part of town. Former ABC *20/20* producer Barbara Newman, who came to Lebanon in 1980 to film part of a documentary, surprised and dismayed the ABC bureau in Beirut by planning to stay at the Christian-run Alexandre Hotel and not at the Commodore. The reaction caused the documentary's correspondent, Geraldo Rivera, to book rooms in both places and to ferry from one side to the other. Rivera was told by the late Lebanese leader Bashir Gemayel in 1980 that he was the first American television reporter to stay overnight in East Beirut.

Few professions are as vulnerable to the herd instinct as journalism, and once attitudes in the Beirut press corps were struck, they stuck: the PLO did not have much need to practice intimidation on the regulars in the Commodore Hotel. When it came to visiting journalists, however, the PLO had less reason to pull its punches. Correspondents who worked outside of Lebanon, and who had not been exposed to the influences that shaped the perceptions of their Beirut-based colleagues, could not be relied upon to respect, or even be aware of, PLO sensibilities. Many of these journalists were subjected to PLO threats or were simply not allowed to come to West Beirut at all.

Hans Benedict, one of the most widely respected European journalists, found himself a victim of "preventive intimidation" when he became diplomatic correspondent in the Middle East for Austrian national television in 1979. He applied to the Lebanese embassy in Vienna for a visa, and was astounded to learn that the answer was no. Even more amazing, a senior Lebanese diplomat told him that the decision had been made not by the Lebanese government but by the PLO.

Benedict had become unpopular with the PLO when he interviewed its Austrian representative, Gazi Hussein, in the fall of 1978 and asked about the Coastal Road massacre of Israeli civilians near Tel Aviv the previous spring. Hussein answered forthrightly that terrorism against Israelis, including women and children, was a legitimate tool of the Palestinian revolution and that the PLO would continue to use it as it saw fit. When the interview was aired, it caused a stir in Austria and was a major public relations setback for the Palestinians.

The Lebanese diplomat who returned Benedict's visa application was apologetic. He told Benedict that applications for Lebanese press visas had to be authorized by PLO headquarters and "if we ask them for a visa for you, they'll be on the lookout for you at the airport." Benedict, who first started covering the Arab world in 1946 and served as a correspondent for AP behind the Iron Curtain for more than fifteen years, knew a death threat when he heard one. He did not get to the Lebanese capital until the PLO departed in August 1982.

Perhaps the most blatant threat was directed against Geraldo Rivera. In early 1981, after meeting with Israeli experts on the PLO and interviewing

PLO prisoners in an Israeli prison in the course of preparing a documentary on terrorism, Rivera flew to Beirut via Rome. The next day, he and Barbara Newman were taken by ABC's Beirut correspondent, Jerry King, to a meeting with PLO spokesman Mahmud Labadi. Several armed men were in the room when the three arrived, and they remained there throughout the meeting. "I've been in very tight scrapes in my professional life," Rivera later recalled, "and those red flags don't get hoisted very often, but I definitely had a feeling that there were warnings implicit in almost everything Labadi said, in his entire attitude."

During the time Rivera worked on the documentary in Beirut, the warnings remained implicit. But when it was broadcast, the PLO's reaction crystallized. Rivera's colleagues in Beirut passed along the message: "Don't come back to West Beirut, or else. . . " He also received telephoned death threats at his home in California. During the 1982 war, Rivera, like hundreds of other Western newsmen, found himself again in the Lebanese capital, in this case to do an exclusive interview with Lebanon's president-elect Bashir Gemayel. He checked with contacts and colleagues on the west side of the city to make sure that he could cross the border and do some reporting there. "I was told point-blank, and by more than one source, never to come back to West Beirut, to Palestinian territory. I was told that I had a death warrant out for me."

The spring of 1981 was a time of considerable tension in Lebanon. Israel and Syria were facing off over the introduction of Syria's Soviet-made SAM missile system in Lebanon's eastern Bekaa region, and Israel was pursuing a policy of preemptive strikes against PLO concentrations in the southwestern coastal area. The Beirut press corps was overworked and tense, expecting a major Israeli assault. One day late in May, three American correspondents, Jonathan Randal of the *Washington Post* and William Farrell and John Kifner of the *New York Times,* decided to take some time off and have what Farrell later described as "a civilized dinner party, a dinner-jackets-in-the-jungle kind of evening" at Kifner's home in West Beirut. At about 11:30 their dinner party was interrupted by a telephone call. Someone informed Kifner that the long-anticipated Israeli raid on PLO bases in the Damur area was taking place.

Despite the late hour, the three decided to investigate. Their first stop was the Commodore Hotel. The consensus at the bar was that if there was a raid, it was probably a limited one; but Randal, Kifner and Farrell decided that the tip was worth checking. Julian Nundy of *Newsweek* and William Foley, an Associated Press photographer, asked to come along and the five piled into Kifner's car and headed toward Damur, about fifteen miles south of Beirut. They never got there. At the outskirts of the city they

184

were cut off and pulled over by a Red Crescent ambulance belonging to the PLO's first-aid and medical organization. Gunmen armed with assault rifles pulled them out of the car and demanded to see their identification papers, which they produced.

The armed men, members of the PFLP-GC faction of the PLO, examined the reporters' credentials, and decided to haul them in. Farrell later recalled:

> They booked us, police style, put our belongings in envelopes and took us to an area with narrow, high-ceilinged, almost coffin-like cells, about six-and-a-half feet long by three-and-a-half wide. They had steel doors with a little hatch you couldn't see out of at all. There were no toilets, just a foam rubber pallet on the floor. It was hot as hell inside.

After about two hours, the reporters were stripped and searched. Later they were taken, one at a time, into an interrogation room, where they were questioned by two men. Not everyone got the same treatment. At least two feared that their lives were in danger. So, apparently, did their colleagues in town, who engaged in a frantic search throughout Beirut for the five journalists, contacting, in the process, senior officials of the PLO (a fact which lends weight to the supposition that the PFLP men were aware of the journalists' identities early on).

At about five p.m., the five were reunited for the

185

first time in fifteen hours. They were taken to another building, where they received profuse apologies, and were then released. When they were freed, Kifner raised the question of whether the story should be reported. *Time* later quoted one of the journalists as saying: "We made an informal agreement that we would not write about the incident. The stories would have just embarrassed everyone involved." Especially the PLO.

V

The story of Palestinian-Syrian-controlled West Beirut between 1975 and 1982 is thus one of terror against journalists—Syrian terror wielded like a baseball bat, with crude, broad strokes; PLO terror, a scalpel used with discrimination and subtlety. Some resisted and paid with their lives, their careers, or their access to Beirut; others succumbed, wholly or partially, to the threats, the pressure, and the inducements to "get on the team." And in the case of the PLO, many journalists did not need much encouragement.

Much of what went on in Lebanon and neighboring Syria was only partially reported or rarely mentioned—the excesses of the Assad regime, the PLO mini-state in South Lebanon, Palestinian links with international terrorists, and so forth. As in all cases of self-censorship, it is impossible to know *what* was being covered up; and in the case of Beirut, the problem was compounded by an even greater omission—the failure or outright refusal of Western news organizations to tell the truth about pressures and threats directed against their journalists in the Arab world.

This refusal was at variance with normal journalistic practice; more importantly, it meant the public could not properly evaluate the credibility of news reports from much of the Middle East. Readers and viewers who were unaware of the atmosphere of intimidation and violence that existed in Beirut, for example, could not know that much of the news from there between 1975 and 1982 was filtered through a veil of fear, caution, and self-censorship; nor did they have any idea that there was news they were not getting at all, because some reporters had been driven out of the Lebanese capital. Censorship in Lebanon was accomplished by terror, exclusion, and expulsion —yet, remarkably, most news organizations acted as if the public had no right to know that it was going on.

There were, of course, exceptions. The PLO's abduction of Philip Caputo in 1975 was given considerable publicity by his paper, the *Chicago Tribune. Newsweek,* in the summer of 1976, printed a page-long story on the violence against foreign correspondents, including two of its own reporters, in Beirut. The imposition of Syrian-inspired censorship in early 1977 elicited a few critical articles in the Western

187

press. But as the civil war dragged on and the Beirut-based correspondents got used to the situation and made their accommodations with it, less and less was mentioned about the pressure they faced. From mid-1976 until the summer of 1980, a four-year period in which a number of journalists were killed or harassed and the Lebanese press was effectively muted, almost nothing was reported by the American media about the situation in Lebanon. The murder of Robert Pfeffer, a politically motivated assassination, was barely noticed; the abduction and killing of Salim Lawzi, which shocked and frightened the Beirut press corps, was briefly noted in a few major newspapers and ignored by almost everyone else.

News organizations whose own personnel were under attack often tried to play down the incidents. *Time,* for example, sought to keep the plight of William Marmon a secret. When the two BBC correspondents Tim Llewelyn and Jim Muir were driven out of Beirut in 1980, the BBC at first said nothing, in the apparent hope that it could negotiate their return. When that failed, it made a belated and terse announcement about the situation and continued to "report" on Lebanon from Nicosia, Cyprus. The BBC's public, which included not only Great Britain but millions around the world who depend on the World Service for independent and comprehensive news was effectively shut out of the Lebanese capital. Most had no idea that this was so.

Reuters, the world's largest news agency, was no more forthright when Berndt Debusmann was shot. It reported the incident but made no mention of the previous Syrian threats to the correspondent, and compounded omission with distortion by saying that "there was no known reason for the shooting."

Only a handful of newspapers addressed the issue editorially, among them the British *Economist* and the *Guardian*. The *Guardian* noted: "Although the BBC and Reuters were well aware that Syria was responsible for the intimidation of their reporters, neither organization felt able to publicize the fact." The *Economist* was blunter:

> The Syrians have thus forced the represent-
> atives of the BBC and Reuters out of Leb-
> anon by terrorism and have got away with
> it without even being named. Foreign and
> local pressmen in Beirut were all in favor
> of a concerted exposure of the Syrian role,
> but when the two leading British news or-
> ganizations declined to name any names,
> the protest collapsed.

Throughout the next two years, this pattern continued. The 1981 murder of ABC correspondent Sean Toolan was given a single 30-second mention on his own network, while the other two networks ignored it completely. The *New York Times* and the *Washington Post* reported it briefly, and only the *Los Angeles Times* gave the murder serious attention.

Other outrages against newsmen in Beirut, including the death threats that resulted in the December 1980 flight from the city of CBS's Larry Pintak, threats against Neal Temko of the *Christian Science Monitor,* and, preeminently, the seizure of the five American correspondents in the summer of 1981, went mostly unreported.

Although the primary victim of this silence was the public, whose right to know was being subverted by a combination of Arab terror and journalistic acquiescence or indifference, there were serious consequences for Israel as well, which was engaged in a struggle with both the PLO and Syria. If the press in Beirut was not reporting fully out of a fear of Arab reprisal, then Israel was being forced to fight the war for Western public opinion with one hand tied behind its back. People who knew little about the PLO's operations in southern Lebanon or its connections with international terrorist groups or about the internal situation in Syria often found Israel's concern about these matters "paranoid" and its attempts to deal with them overreactive. Moreover, when Israel tried to point out what was happening in Lebanon or Syria, its arguments had little credibility—after all, there were plenty of American and European reporters in Beirut who would surely be aware of a Palestinian "mini-state" in south Lebanon if one existed, or of large-scale massacres in Syria.

The notion that the intimidation of Western

journalists in Beirut was working—to Israel's detriment—began to sink in after the murder of Salim Lawzi in early 1980. As the director of Israel's government press office, I was then in close contact with many of the foreign correspondents in the Middle East. Some of them who visited Jerusalem told hair-raising stories about personal experiences they had had; many admitted that there were now subjects that they would not report. For almost two years I waited for an article on how the press was being abused in Lebanon. Finally, in February 1982, I decided to raise the issue myself.

The immediate stimulus was an ABC documentary about the West Bank entitled "Under the Israeli Thumb." The program was exceptional in the harsh accusations it made about the occupation of the West Bank and in its refusal to present any Israeli point of view. I knew that ABC had recently had difficulties with the PLO in Beirut, and I thought there might be some connection. I called David K. Shipler of the *New York Times,* who was widely admired for his ability to understand and convey the feelings of all sides in the complex Arab-Israeli equation, and suggested an on-the-record discussion of the issue.

My interview with Shipler, which lasted about an hour, was printed two days later in the *International Herald Tribune.* The Paris-based *Tribune,* widely distributed in Israel, is published as a cooperative venture of the *New York Times* and the *Washington*

191

Post. Shipler had done his usual accurate job. He began by setting forth my central contention—that terrorism was being used against correspondents in Beirut—along with my qualification that it was very often the news organizations, concerned for the safety of their personnel, who decided on self-censorship. The interview then went on to my suspicion that ABC had been trying to ingratiate itself with the PLO by doing puff pieces on the organization. I also mentioned the shooting of Berndt Debusmann of Reuters and the warning to BBC reporter Tim Llewelyn, and noted that the BBC had tried to cover up the latter incident and that it still had no regular correspondent in the Lebanese capital. I also raised, without mentioning any names, the hitherto unreported 1981 abduction of the five American reporters, including those from the *New York Times* and the *Washington Post,* who were seized and held by the PFLP-GC.

Although the interview appeared promptly in the *International Herald Tribune,* it was not published in the *Times* until February 14, and then only after the two paragraphs about the *Times* correspondents and the apparent decision to keep their detention a secret had been cut.

The *Times* had thus confirmed my original charge—that news organizations in the U.S. and elsewhere were committing acts of self-censorship to protect their own interests. I asked William Claiborne, the Jerusalem-based correspondent of the *Washing-*

ton Post, if the *Post* might be interested in *this* story, but after checking with his home office he said no. Norman Kempster of the *Los Angeles Times* thought it was a good story, but his foreign editor evidently did not. I had better luck with Tim McNulty of the *Chicago Tribune.* Three days later, that newspaper became one of the first to report on the *Times'*s censorship of my charges that it had committed self-censorship.

The Israeli media also seized on the story. The *Jerusalem Post* carried a front-page article, several Hebrew papers gave it headline treatment, and the national radio led its morning news bulletins with the incident. Now, I was certain, the wire services, AP and UPI, would pick it up and send it out to their thousands of clients. But neither would touch it. They first mentioned the affair ten days later, after both *Time* and *Newsweek* had devoted full pages to it in their "Media" sections—one of the rare occasions when the wire services have been scooped by weekly magazines.

On February 18, four days after the sanitized interview appeared, the *Times* published a follow-up entitled "Official in Israel Assails the Times." It now reported my criticism of the paper for deleting the story of the detention of the two *Times* correspondents, and then went on:

Craig H. Whitney, deputy foreign editor of the *New York Times,* said... "It is the pol-

193

icy of the *Times* to report difficulties encountered by its correspondents in the
course of reporting only if the difficulties
themselves become news and we did not
consider this such a case, then or now."

This was apparently a new policy. A recent,
prominently displayed, article by Youssef M. Ibrahim, an Egyptian-American who then worked for the
Times, had described his crossing from Jordan into
Israel by way of the Allenby Bridge. He had arrived
at the bridge unannounced, carrying tapes of conver-
sations with leaders in the PLO and correspondence
among various PLO officials. These aroused the interest of Israeli security officials. Ibrahim was questioned for about five hours and then allowed to drive
to Jerusalem. Some of his notebooks were examined
and returned a day later. In the shuffle, a pair of
pants got lost. Ibrahim was understandably agitated,
especially about the five-hour delay, and proved it by
writing a tough piece which the *Times* published. But
he had never been locked up in a cell or threatened by
gunmen, nor was he held overnight. Was his experience more newsworthy than that of his colleagues
in Beirut?

Then there was the article by Martin Tolchin, the
Times White House correspondent, about his experience trying to get permission to cross from Jordan
into Israel via the Allenby Bridge. In this article, Tolchin described his feeling that he and his family had

194

been treated rudely by the Jordanian bureaucracy because they were Jewish. Certainly Tolchin's experience was unpleasant and aggravating, but it was a far cry from twenty hours in a PLO slammer. If the *Times* had a policy of not printing stories about difficulties encountered by its journalists "unless the difficulties themselves became news," it was a rather selective one.

On February 22, twelve days after the interview had first run in the *Herald Tribune,* the *Times* made an effort to rectify matters with a piece entitled "Reporter's Notebook: Fear Is Part of the Job in Beirut." In it, John Kifner described the conditions under which he and his colleagues were forced to work and the possible implications for the reader who expected full and comprehensive information. In Beirut, Kifner admitted, "a journalist must often weigh when, how, and even whether to record a story." The piece was somewhat bland and defensive in tone, but at least it confirmed the existence of serious harassment of journalists in Beirut.

Although Kifner did not say so in his article, he was very nervous about having had to write it. He made an unusual request—that the *Times* run the article in New York but keep it out of the *International Herald Tribune,* the reverse of what had happened with my interview with Shipler. The *Times,* once again bowing to the fear of Arab violence, agreed. But by mistake the *Tribune* did publish the

195

article. At this point, Kifner decided it would be a good time to go elsewhere for a few days. His hurried departure from Beirut might have gone unnoticed but for an article by the London *Observer*'s news service which stated that Kifner had left because of threats he received after his February 22 story was published in the *Tribune.* The *Observer* article was written by its Beirut correspondent, Colin Smith, who did not ask to be anonymous. In an effort to protect him, however, the *Observer* left his name off the story and by-lined it only "A Special Correspondent," a designation that greatly concerned Smith's stringer in Beirut who feared that he, and not Smith, might be held accountable by local gunmen.

If the *New York Times* finally dealt with the story, other American news organizations were less forthcoming. *Newsweek,* for example, carried an article, "Who's Afraid of the PLO?," that was written in part by Julian Nundy, who had been one of the five detainees. The article, which did not explain why Nundy had failed at the time to report on his detention, sought to minimize the whole event by noting that the correspondents had been held and then released "with profuse apologies." Missing from the *Newsweek* account (but included in *Time*'s article on the incident that same week) was the fact that the reporters had been abducted at gunpoint, and that at least two of them had felt their lives were in danger.

Throughout the controversy, only one of the

American news organizations whose reporters had been involved in the PLO abduction—the *Washington Post*—managed to keep the whole matter blacked out of its news pages. Finally, several weeks after the incident, Martin Peretz of the *New Republic* exposed the *Post*'s stonewalling. In "A Journalistic Cover-Up," Peretz noted that "the *Washington Post* hasn't given the story an inch" and revealed, for the first time, the names of the abducted reporters.

The *Post*'s vehicle for finally addressing the controversy was an op-ed article by the foreign editor, Jim Hoagland. Writing on March 4, Hoagland conceded that there was "something" in my charges—at least with regard to the Syrians. As for the PLO, however, he described it as a benevolent force which "tacitly provides protection for the American embassy and [has] as often pulled correspondents out of scrapes as imperiled them." Regarding the failure of Jonathan Randal to report on his detention by the PLO, Hoagland admitted that "in retrospect Randal was probably a bit too phlegmatic in dismissing [it] so lightly," but he also cited *Post* correspondent Edward Cody on the exquisite symmetry of the threat to journalists. "You know that you can get picked up by Palestinian kids with guns anytime you do your job. Or you know you may be bombed by Israeli jets. That does not mean you write any differently." No doubt even Cody had not intended to say that Israel was carrying out air raids on journalists in order to

197

intimidate them. Yet Hoagland made it seem that Israeli jets posed the same threat to press freedoms as the "Palestinian kids" who had murdered Robert Pfeffer, threatened Geraldo Rivera and Hans Benedict, and driven Milan Kubic and William Marmon out at gunpoint.

Worst by far, however, was Hoagland's version of how the entire incident of the five reporters' abduction had first come to light. He wrote:

> Chafets said that one of the reporters, William Farrell, formerly Jerusalem correspondent for the *Times* and now based in Cairo, had subsequently told him the five were "held for a number of hours and threatened and frightened."

I had, in fact, never mentioned Farrell's name at all, never mentioned *any* names, and certainly had not said what my source for the story was. Hoagland, by publicly naming Farrell, who was still stationed in the Middle East, as a source of information for an Israeli official, was making a charge that could get the *Times* reporter into serious trouble in the Arab world. Hoagland had never contacted me to check this point. I later learned he had never bothered to contact Farrell, either, who was badly frightened and upset by Hoagland's article.

I immediately wrote a letter to the *Post* setting the record straight and challenging Hoagland to produce evidence that Farrell had told me of the incident. It took six weeks and three transoceanic telephone calls for the letter to be published, along with the following note:

> Mr. Hoagland replies: "In July 1981, Mr. Chafets told William Claiborne, the *Washington Post*'s Jerusalem correspondent, that Mr. Farrell had recounted the Damur incident to him that month, and Mr. Chafets confirmed that fact in an on-the-record interview with Mr. Claiborne on February 15, 1982."

This was a plain lie. There had been no interview, just a private conversation in which I had tried to interest the *Post* in the self-censorship issue and in which Farrell's name had not figured at all. When I asked Claiborne about this, he readily agreed the facts were as I had stated them, and confessed he did not know what the *Post* was up to.

On April 28, the *Post* ran a "correction," signed by William Claiborne:

> On April 17, the *Post* published a letter from Ze'ev Chafets denying that he had publicly said that William Farrell of the *New York Times* had told him of the detention of five Western reporters in Beirut in 1981 by Palestinian guerrillas. Through an error it was stated in a response that my conversation with Mr. Chafets on this point of February 15 was on the record.

Mr. Chafets did not address that point on
the record during the February 15 conversation, and continues to refuse to say for
the record if he had discussed the incident
with Mr. Farrell.

The *Post*'s behavior in this matter sheds some
light, I think, on its recurrent problems with accuracy. The formula is one part carelessness, one part
arrogance, with a big touch of bias thrown in. The
bias in this case may have to do with the fact that the
good name of the PLO, whose cause the *Post,* under
Hoagland's guidance, had adopted, was being called
into question.

For as a cursory look through the *Post*'s back
issues reveals, the paper often publicizes the difficulties its reporters encounter in the line of duty, even
when these difficulties are considerably less serious
than abduction at gunpoint. There was, for example,
"Rumanian Agents Blunder After Visiting Newsman," by correspondent Michael Dobbs, a seven-
teen-paragraph article about being followed on a visit
to Rumania; or "Interrogation—Post Reporter Runs
Afoul of Bolivian Army," twenty-two paragraphs devoted to Charles A. Krause's arrest and interrogation
by "five army intelligence agents, one of them armed
with a submachine gun." The whole episode lasted,
according to Krause, nearly three hours, and he was
never threatened physically. Other stories in recent
years included a report that Indonesian authorities

had refused to renew the visa of a *Post* stringer; a long article on reporters' working conditions in Poland; and a piece stating that the *Post* correspondent in Moscow had been called in by Soviet authorities for a fifteen-minute meeting in which he was "rebuked" for some allegedly "slanderous assertions" about the USSR. Only when the "authorities" in question were ones the *Post* had been touting as moderate and responsible did the incident cease to be newsworthy.

Nor has the *Post* correspondent Jonathan Randal always been so "phlegmatic" when he has come under attack—even in Beirut. In 1975 he published a stirring first-person article entitled "Morning in Rebel Hands," recounting how, just after dawn, armed men had burst into his room, arrested him, and taken him and some of his belongings into headquarters. His detention that time lasted not twenty hours but only a couple. Randal was not locked up, merely questioned and then taken to the home of his old friend, the Algerian ambassador. Yet the grippingly written article—in which the reader learned, among other things, that Randal had worked in Vietnam, that Randal had worked in Algeria, that Randal spoke French, that Randal was cool in tight situations, and that Randal slept in boxer shorts and a black T-shirt—was presumably intended to convey a sense of the perilous situation in Beirut. If so, it is hard to see why what happened to Randal in May

1981 should have been any less revealing of the climate or less interesting to *Post* readers. But that, perhaps, is the point. In October 1975 Randal's abductors were "members of two Lebanese Communist outfits," not members of the PLO.

VI

Taken together, the incidents recounted here add up to a depressing chapter in Western journalism. The essence of journalistic credibility is candor, both in what is reported and about what restrictions and constraints limit or influence that reporting. But at one time or another over a period of some seven years, Reuters, *Time, Newsweek,* the *New York Times,* the *Washington Post,* CBS, ABC, the Associated Press—to name only some—played an active part in hiding from the public many of the facts about what was happening in Lebanon in general and, in particular, the way in which their newsmen were being subjected to intimidation and violence there. By acquiescing in this state of affairs through silence, cover-up, and other accommodations, some of which are known, others of which we can only speculate about, the Western news organizations betrayed their readers, their traditions, and their own standards.

'TIME' AGAINST ISRAEL

by Rael Jean Isaac

For the last seven years, and with accelerating tempo after 1977, *Time* has engaged in vigorous adversary journalism against Israel. In doing so *Time* has practiced subversion — literally, "the turning of a thing upside down or uprooting it from its position." *Time* is not simply inaccurate: it stands facts, words, and moral principles on their heads to achieve its portrait of the Arab-Israel conflict.

Time's coverage of Israel up until 1970 was reasonably balanced. After Nasser's death, *Time* began to shift blame for the stalemate in the Middle East. The 1973 war brought a substantial tilt against Israel, leavened for a while with a certain disarming frankness. Thus on March 10, 1975, *Time* reported that Israel's enemies, in taxing the economies of Israel's friends, were taxing their loyalties, and noted "Western Europe appears willing to bargain away Israel's security for access to oil." Only gradually did *Time* internalize constraints into principles. The process was complete by 1980. On April 14 *Time* raised the possibility that the

Rael Jean Isaac is the author of Israel Divided *(Johns Hopkins) and* Parties and Politics of Israel *(Longmans).*

Rael Jean Isaac is a member of the Executive Committee of Americans For A Safe Israel.

Reprinted by permission of THE NEW REPUBLIC, (c) 1980 The New Republic, Inc.

growing number of supporters for the Palestinian cause was, in Israeli ambassador Yehuda Blum's words, "a sorry parade of nations supplicating the Arab oil gods"—only to dismiss this view in the same article as "a dangerous misapprehension of the Begin government." By 1980 it was hard to talk of a dual standard in *Time:* it now has no standards whatsoever in its coverage of the Arab-Israeli conflict.

Since 1977, except for a two week honeymoon in which Begin basked in Sadat's reflected glory after the signing of the peace treaty, Israel has been able to do no right. *Time* reacted to the Israeli elections of May 1977 with a stream of calumny. The new prime minister, Menachem Begin, who had led a parliamentary opposition party for 29 years, was repeatedly described as a "terrorist." In its first major story following the election, *Time* introduced Begin to its readers with the words "rhymes with Fagin." (Why not "Reagan" rather than the anti-Semitic Dickens caricature?) Apparently sending its fact-checkers home so they could not interfere with the rush of editorial inspiration, *Time* went on to report falsely that Begin's men "tortured two British soldiers to death," "massacred," "mutilated," and "raped" innocent villagers, and that Begin himself, after the sinking of the Irgun Ship, the *Altalena,* vowed to "see to it that the state of Israel sinks with us."

On the first anniversary of Begin's election, *Time*'s former Jerusalem bureau chief Donald Neff offered a lengthy evaluation of Israel's prime minister. Neff announced that "all the worst fears, and more, of his critics" had come to pass and that Begin, "more than any other man, has set back the chances for peace in the Middle East." Neff went on to accuse Begin of being inflexible, myopic, hard-lining, deceptive, tiresomely preachy, self-righteously arrogant, and "totally insensitive to any problems beyond those of Jewish Israel." Neff sums up with the title of the *Time* essay, which he attributes to an unnamed diplomat— Begin is "Beyond the Pale."

In the slow negotiations following Sadat's visit to Jerusalem, Begin was repeatedly singled out for blame. On March 6, 1978, *Time* announced that "dispassionate observers" put the blame on Israel; on March 20 that Begin showed "scant willingness to make the kind of concessions that a peace agreement will require"; on September 11 that "Begin does seem to bear by far the greatest responsibility for the current impasse"; on September 18 that "most U.S. officials and experts agree that Begin has been considerably less willing to compromise than Sadat"; and on December 25 that "on balance Israel has been the less compromising and more frustrating negotiating partner." *Time,* unlike other Begin detractors, managed to transform its contempt for Begin into a contempt for Israel itself.

Time judged Sadat in terms of a different set of assumptions and expectations. On January 20, 1978, *Time* reported flatly that Sadat could not be expected to make any concessions: after coming to Jerusalem "he could not give up any more on Sinai, the Palestinian issue or Jerusalem." Sadat's periodic suspensions of the talks did nothing to cloud his image for *Time;* after one such suspension, the magazine editorialized that Sadat had "an almost mystical commitment to the peace process" (March 27, 1978). *Time*'s editors were so carried away by their view of Sadat as visionary peacemaker that they interpreted his assault on Israel on Yom Kippur of 1973 as an expression of his yearning for peace.

> Ironically Sadat started his peace campaign by going to war. The road to peace in the autumn of 1973 seemed totally blocked . . .. To coax some movement toward peace, Sadat made one of his swift, dramatic decisions. He chose to attack Israel.

Even more extraordinary, after the Camp David agreement was signed, *Time* concluded that "it was Begin who conceded the least" (October 2, 1978). Since Begin had given up the Sinai oil fields, air bases, and settlements, and agreed to a companion "framework" for the West Bank and Gaza, while Sadat had compromised on none of his demands (some were temporarily not pressed, such as Jerusalem, on which separate "letters of intent" were filed by the parties to the negotiations), *Time*'s judgment clearly reflected its skewed vision.

What is *Time*'s problem? In part, it is that *Time* does not take Arab statements "for internal consumption" as seriously as it takes those made to Western media and statesmen. That the Arabs want to drive Israel into the sea is old hat. That the PLO, even the fire-eating George Habash, is prepared to accept Israel is "news." But most importantly, *Time* gives weight and credibility to sources who tell the magazine's editors what they want to hear.

Malcolm Toon, formerly US ambassador to Israel and

more recently to the Soviet Union, has pointed out that in closed societies (he was speaking of the Soviet Union, but the point applies equally well to the dictatorships of the Middle East) the way to understand the country's strategy is to read

> statements in their own language and to their own people—rather than listening to gossip in the corridors of the United Nations or, worse, to misleading and ambivalent observations by... envoys sensitive and responding to the naiveté and wishful thinking of their American interlocutors....

But it is precisely these envoys who too frequently constitute *Time*'s source of information. *Time* habitually quotes Faruq Kaddoumi, for example, the PLO's envoy to the United Nations and Western capitals, whose job it is to present the PLO in an attractive light to foreigners. On October 3, 1977, *Time* asserted that "there was no progress on the basic issues of Israel's refusal to withdraw to its 1967 borders or to accept an independent Palestinian state on the West Bank." If, in the weeks between August 29 and October 3, *Time* had reported the public statements of Arab leaders, it would have been difficult to avoid recognition that the basic question was not Israeli withdrawal but Arab refusal to accept the existence of the state (see sidebar at end of article).

Moreover, without the glowing reports of previous weeks on the moderation of Arafat and Habash, *Time* would have found it difficult to treat Israel as a legitimate subject for American pressure. As it is, on October 3 *Time* included a feature "How to Lean on Israel"– remove the exemption of the United Jewish Appeal, cut back on military assistance, deny loans on favorable terms, refuse to deliver a promised nuclear power plant, end joint ventures, reduce support in international forums, abstain on anti-Israel votes in the UN, further publicize US disagreements with Israel, and publicly inquire about the treatment of what *Time* calls "political prisoners." *(Time* repeatedly talks of thousands of "political prisoners," the term suggesting that these are individuals imprisoned for their opinions. These are individuals sentenced for crimes, including formation of PLO cells and attacks on Israeli civilians. The term "political prisoner" is no more appropriate in this case than it is to the convicted criminals in the United States dubbed "political prisoners" by Andrew Young.)

In seizing almost exclusively upon Arab "private" statements, *Time* in these five weeks was not simply providing partial information, but "disinformation," information deliberately provided to mislead Western media about Arab, and especially PLO, intentions. Nothing that *Time* claimed had happened or was about to happen actually transpired then or later. The October 10 edition of *Time* did not admit that it had been misinforming its readers for weeks; instead it announced that a PLO resolution, reaffirming an earlier 1974 resolution, was "more moderate in tone" because in calling for a state to be created on any soil given up by Israel, it dropped the 1974 clause that designated such a state a base for further struggle against Israel. This was wrong: the PLO had explicitly renewed the 1974 resolution in its entirety. But what is more interesting is that *Time* finally allowed its readers to know that a state in the West Bank and Gaza had been specifically designated by the PLO as a base against Israel only when it erroneously reported that the clause had been dropped. Up to this point *Time* had repeatedly described the readiness to establish a state in land relinquished by Israel as proof of PLO "moderation."

Time eventually grew tired of falsely predicting that the PLO "will drop the most offensive passages from its Covenant" immediately prior to PLO or Palestine National Council meetings. There is no reference in *Time* to the meeting on May 31, 1980, of Al Fatah, repeatedly described by *Time* as the most "moderate" of the PLO's constituent organizations, at which it rededicated itself to the liquidation of the Zionist entity, "politically, economically, militarily, culturally and ideologically," Nor does *Time* ever explain why the PLO is so reluctant to change the Covenant, despite repeated predictions that it will be altered. Nor will readers learn from *Time* that on February 21, 1980, Nabil Ramlawi, the PLO's London representative, stated that the Covenant "is no less vital to the PLO than is the Proclamation of Independence and the Law of Return to the Zionists," nor that on March 4, 1980, the PLO's Abu Ayyad asserted "it is impossible to alter the Covenant"; nor that on March 26, 1980, PLO spokesman Abu Sharar asserted that the Palestinian Covenant "defines the PLO's struggle." In other words the destruction of Israel is the central demand Palestinian Arabs make on themselves, other Arabs, and the world. The obligation to "liquidate the Zionist entity" is as "sacred" to the PLO as national independence is to Israel.

Time replaced its predictions about changes in the PLO covenant with reports that the PLO has "de facto" recognized, is recognizing, or will recognize Israel. As recently as October 6, 1980, under a headline "Arafat's Nudge: Inching Towards Recognition?" *Time* reported that Arafat, at a communist-sponsored peace conference in Bulgaria, spoke to four Israelis. *Time* finds this a highly significant event and asserts that the "decision of the PLO leader to make so conciliatory a gesture" lends credence "even to some Israelis" to a remark made by Morocco's King Hassan the previous week that the PLO was ready to accept Israel. While *Time* points out that the Israelis were members of the Communist party, it fails to mention that the Israeli Communist party is the channel through which Israeli Arab Nationalists express their rejection of the Jewish state. No wonder Arafat said he was happy to meet "the peace forces of Israel."

But *Time* is not content with subverting the facts. *Time's* use of words like "peace," "moderation," and "democracy" verges on Orwellian doublethink. Prior to president Sadat's 1977 visit to Israel, a time when there was no indication that any Arab state was willing to make peace with Israel, *Time* informed its readers week after week that the Arabs sought "peace." On May 9, 1977, *Time* reported that Jordan's King Hussein was "pessimistic about Israel's willingness to make peace"; on May 23 that Assad of Syria said a

Palestinian state was necessary for "peace"; and on July 25 that Arab nations "sincerely believe that the only road to peace leads through the White House." After Sadat's visit, when the Arab states mounted a virtually solid rejectionist front, *Time* continued to assert that "peace" was their target. On December 5, 1977, *Time* wrote that although the rhetoric from Damascus was "pure vitriol," Assad "basically is as committed to peace talks as Sadat." Although by mid-1978 Hussein had made clear his unwillingness to negotiate with Israel, *Time*'s conclusion on May 29, 1978, was that Hussein felt Carter was incapable of obtaining the concessions needed "to permit a peace settlement."

Time never explores what it is that Arab leaders mean when they say they seek "peace." But Iraqi president Ahmad al Bakr had already performed this service quite succinctly. "We hope the forces of peace will strengthen their struggle of solidarity with the Arab liberation movement," said al Bakr, "and will work toward the liquidation of the imperialist Zionist aggression." Syria's Assad also defined peace in an interview with an Arabic paper: "The October War expressed our will to regain occupied Arab land and the Palestinian Arab people's usurped rights. Anyone who fights for the homeland is a fighter for peace." When in September 1977, 21 Arab foreign ministers called for peace based on the right of return, of self-determination, and of an independent state, *Time* described it as "the last hurrah of the moderates." But the foreign ministers were merely reiterating the PLO formulas which had been devised in 1964, three years before Israel captured the West Bank and

Gaza. *Time*'s "last hurrah of the moderates" was well understood in the Arab world as a call for peace to follow the destruction of Israel. The PLO also clarified its understanding of peace. The Palestine National Council has asserted that it refuses to accept UN Resolution 242 because it recognizes "a partial peace" instead of "a permanent peace." A partial peace, as the PLO defines it, exists while Palestinian rights have not been realized in full. Permanent peace is the liquidation of Israel.

Democracy is another term which *Time* applies in extraordinary fashion to the Arab world. *Time* entitles its October 24, 1977, article on the PLO, "Democracy Gone Wild." *Time*'s headline certainly suggests that something is amiss, but the average *Time* reader is not likely to feel that too much democracy warrants excessive censure. According to *Time,* Arafat was only the first among three million Palestinian equals and maintained his leadership by "force of personality." *Time* did take note of conflicts among rival groupings and asserted that in moments of "extreme crisis for the PLO debate is suspended and democracy begins (or ends) at the barrel of a gun." But surely the point of democracy is that even in moments of crisis, decisions are made by votes, not guns.

Time's depiction of the PLO as a democracy cannot be discounted as a one-time aberration. On May 14, 1980, *Time* called the 100-member Palestine National Council "probably the most democratic institution in the Arab world." But there are no elections in Palestinian camps; ironically, the most democratic institutions in the Arab

212

world are the elected city councils on the Israeli-occupied West bank, made up primarily of Palestinian hard-liners. The only Arab press operating in conditions of relative freedom is also in the West Bank or in Israel proper. (Scarcely less remarkable is *Time*'s use of the term "desert democracy" for Saudi Arabia (May 22, 1978). Though *Time* admits that Saudi Arabia has no parliament, no parties, not a single elected official, and that absolute power resides in the hands of the royal family, Saudi Arabia is "democratic" because even humble subjects have access to the ruler, to whom they can present complaints.)

Time takes up another treasured term of Western democracy, "self-determination," only to subvert its meaning. According to *Time,* the chief obstacle to a comprehensive peace is Israel's reluctance to grant the Palestinians what *Time* calls "true self-determination." But to Americans self-determination assumes freedom of speech, a free press, and a multi-party system which gives the people the ability to change the men responsible for creating public policy. As political scientist Paul Eidelberg has observed, the "self-determination" exercised in Arab countries is that of ruling cliques — not at all what Americans have in mind by the term. Were the Palestinian Arabs to exercise self-determination, not only would their form of government deny the freedoms that give self-determination meaning, but that government would be committed to the destruction of Israel — the only country in the Middle East where those freedoms are enjoyed. (If *Time* means "national self-determination," Flemings and Walloons in Belgium, Welsh

213

and Scots in England, Basques in Spain, Bretons and Cor-
sicans in France, Kurds in Iraq, and Pushtus in Pakistan
all would qualify better for sovereignty than the Arabs of
Palestine.)

Even the simple word "moderate" is shorn of traditional
meaning. As early as January 27, 1975, *Time* reported that
the moderates "dominate the PLO." For several years
thereafter *Time* variously described Arafat as "relatively
moderate," "somewhat moderate" and "just plain moderate."
When, following Sadat's trip to Jerusalem, the PLO murdered an Egyptian representative, *Time* had doubts. The
solution: on March 27, 1978, *Time* reported that Arafat and
the PLO have returned to a "policy of militancy" after "3½
years of relative moderation." Arafat was a "moderate" suffering from radical pressures. Arafat was restored to full-
fledged moderation on May 15, lost the title temporarily
after the Camp David agreements (on September 18, 1978,
the PLO is actually described as "radical"), and regained
it on January 29, 1979, when he was described as "relatively
moderate."

Since Arafat is the leader of the world's major terrorist
organization, it is reasonable to ask by what criteria *Time*
judges him to be moderate. The answer, presumably, is "in
relation to George Habash." By this token Stalin and Hitler
could be called moderates, for both were pikers in mass
murder compared to Mao Zedong who, according to the
Guinness Book of World Records, may have been responsible for the death of twice as many people as these two
European dictators combined. In any case there is no

evidence that Habash is responsible for more murders than Arafat or would, if he could, inflict a harsher fate on the Jews of Israel. The differences between the two men seem to be simply on the level of short-range tactics.

Time similarly divides the Arab states into moderates and radicals without discernible reason for doing so. Since moderates and radicals do not differ in their attitude to Israel, one might suppose that *Time* was dividing these countries on the basis of their attitude to the United States—except that Syria, a Soviet client, is a perennial *Time* "moderate." When, following Sadat's trip to Jerusalem, *Time*'s moderates joined the rejectionists, *Time* solved the dilemma by simply continuing to call some of the rejectionists moderate. Thus on July 24, 1978, *Time* talks of Egypt's "moderate Arab allies" when they were nowhere in sight. *Time* supplies a running series of apologies for the moderates; the Saudis "could not" publicly support Sadat because of their concern that this would help the Soviet Union (December 12, 1977), Hussein wants to remain "an uncommitted moderating force" (December 26, 1977), Camp David "caught the moderate Arabs by surprise" (October 2, 1978). Why joining the rejectionists to attack Israel, Egypt, and the United States would hurt the Soviet Union or contribute to the cause of moderation, *Time* does not explain. Saudi Arabia's call for a *jihad* against Israel in August 1980 did not impair its moderate credentials for *Time*.

Although there is no state about which *Time* writes more respectfully, it is hard to see why Saudi Arabia should ever have been given the title of "moderate" in relation to the Arab-Israel conflict. Second to none in anti-Israel sentiment, chief bankroller of the PLO, it is of all Arab states the most viciously anti-Semitic. Before reaching its present state of obsequiousness, even *Time* noted (April 7, 1975) that King Faisal handed out the notorious Protocols of the Elders of Zion to visitors and that Saudi Arabia routinely refuses Jews entry to the country.

Time's use of "moderate" is even more bizarre when contrasted with its use of "intransigent." *Time* applies that word very sparingly to the Arab world: after 1977 it is used only to describe George Habash and the Iraqi leadership. But Israel is called "intransigent" so frequently that the word takes on the character of a Homeric epithet. When *Time* wanted to castigate South Africa's then prime minister Vorster, the Israeli prime minister was the only figure of sufficient turpitude to offer a worthy parallel: Vorster was "as intransigent as Golda Meir" (June 27, 1977).

Semantic subversion of a more subtle sort is apparent in *Time*'s treatment of "terrorism." As early as March 17, 1975, in an article describing a PLO attack on the Savoy Hotel in Tel Aviv, *Time* variously calls those who staged the assault "commandoes," *"fedayeen,"* and "guerrillas"– and uses the word "terrorists" only when quoting an Israeli statement. (In the same issue there is an article on the Baader-Meinhof: here *Time* has no hesitation in speaking of a "terrorist gang" engaged in "terrorist acts.") Sometimes *Time* does not even seem too sure if attacks on Israeli civilians should be termed terror at all. In an October 31, 1977, ar-

216

ticle on the problem of world terror *Time* declares that the Popular Front for the Liberation of Palestine is the most likely of the six major groups in the PLO "to spearhead a resurgence of terror." Since terrorist operations against Israel by all these groups had continued unabated, this suggested that assaults on Israel did not count.

Another way *Time* removes the PLO's sting is by describing it as a social welfare organization. On July 18, 1977, *Time* reports on the PLO's factories that provide jobs for disabled *fedayeen* and Palestinian women in "handicrafts, ready-to-wear clothing, furniture building and filmmaking." On April 14, 1980, *Time* reports that the PLO "runs hospitals and clinics, dispenses social security benefits, sponsors trade unions and even associations for writers, poets and painters." *Time* lets us know (nice touch) that the PLO makes toys.

More important, by using "Palestinians" and "PLO" as interchangeably as "United States" and "Uncle Sam," *Time* gives the reader the impression that all Palestinians are PLO terrorists—or that the PLO is a nation seeking "self-determination." In the 1977 article on world terror, *Time* includes "the Palestinians" as one of five major terror organizations outside West Germany. Terrorism by the Palestinians can be expected to continue, says *Time,* if they "are not suitably represented at a Geneva peace conference." But for the most part *Time*'s accent is on showing that the PLO are the Palestinians. Can four million people be terrorists? *(Time* rapidly escalates its estimate of the number of Palestinians: on October 24, 1977, there are three million

217

Palestinians; on December 5, 1977, less than two months later, there are 3.4 million; three months after that, on March 27, 1978, there are 3.8 million, and on April 14, 1980, there are "nearly four million.") If, as *Time* repeatedly tells its readers, the Palestinians are a people seeking self-determination, and the PLO are the Palestinians, it follows that the PLO is a nation, not a terrorist organization.

The cumulative effect of *Time*'s misuse of words is perhaps more serious than its inversion of facts. While the reader of *Time* may not learn the true facts elsewhere, he certainly could absorb the information if presented with it. But when new meaning is given to words, the impact is below the level of consciousness. What *Time* has done to the reader's vision of the world through the corrupt use of language is probably irremediable.

THE WAR IN LEBANON
by Frank Gervasi

An old adage has it that truth is the first casualty of war. The maxim was abundantly confirmed by Western journalists last summer during Israel's war against the Palestine Liberation Organization in Lebanon. The opportunity for fair, balanced reporting was unique; correspondents of both the print and electronic media could cover the fighting from both sides simultaneously. Unfortunately, however, the overall results were more often misleading than illuminating and, on the whole, considerably less than objective.

There were notable exceptions, of course. Much of the coverage, however, especially when it originated from Beirut while that city remained the "capital" of the PLO's virtual state within a state in Lebanon, was remarkable mainly for its distortions of the truth. From the moment the Israeli incursion began on the morning of June 6 until the horrendous mid-September massacre of Moslem Palestinians by Lebanese Christian militiamen, egregiously distorted accounts flooded the public in print and over the air.

Reprinted by permission of CENTER FOR INTERNATIONAL SECURITY, (c)1984 Center for International Security.

219

Indeed, not since Hitler and Goebbels perfected the technique of The Big Lie back in the 1930s was truth more blatantly violated for evil ends than during the bloody summer of 1982. Historically, those who would destroy a people first destroy its good name. Throughout most of the fighting in Lebanon, particularly in the early stages, media seemed intent upon destroying Israel's credibility and its image as a stalwart democracy. Veracity often gave way to mendacity.

"Every man has a right to his opinion," the late Bernard Baruch once said, "but no man has a right to be wrong in his facts." And the facts about Israel's incursion, code-named Operation Peace for Galilee, were often twisted or ignored altogether by foreign correspondents under pressure to produce sensational stories to sell newspapers or to boost TV news ratings.

Media in general, but television in particular, tended to depict the Israelis as brutal invaders bent less upon victory over their longtime PLO tormentors than on the extermination of Palestinian Arabs as a people, naturally with resultant deadly consequences to whatever Lebanese civilians who happened to be in the way. In many correspondents' accounts, the Israelis emerged as the villainous conquerors of a foreign Arab land while Yassir Arafat's terrorists—almost invariably identified as "freedom fighters" or "guerrillas"—were characterized as heroic defenders of a righteous cause.

The world was made to see Israel's military action as a gratuitous onslaught on a small, defenseless Lebanon whose sole guilt lay in having given shelter to the "resistance movement" of Palestinian Arabs seeking fulfillment of "legitimate rights." In some dispatches obscene comparisons were made between the Israelis' campaign against the PLO and the Nazi Holocaust.

Television's Role

The chief offender, however, was television. Rarely did the electronic media bother to explain that the PLO's strongholds, for instance, were purposely located in or near civilian centers, thus rendering civilian casualties inevitable. *All* the major American networks, furthermore, showed Israeli tanks and artillery rolling past the ruins of Tyre, Sidon and Damour—cities which already had been heavily damaged by the PLO—creating the impression that what the viewers were seeing was the result of Israeli military action. Little attempt was made by anchormen or commentators to explain that the battered homes, churches and shattered public buildings so dramatically portrayed in full color on TV screens were at least as much the result of previous PLO depredations as they were the consequence of Israeli combat action.

Seldom, moreover, were TV viewers told that the

places shown had served as redoubts for PLO troops and were therefore logical targets for Israeli bombs or shells. Nor were TV watchers informed that before every assault on population centers the Israeli Air Force dropped leaflets urging the inhabitants to flee to safety. The drops were almost invariably followed by loudspeaker announcements from Israeli sound equipment warning civilians of impending danger and providing explicit information—in Arabic—about safe escape routes to nearby beaches or mountains.

The Israeli army actually sustained greater casualties because of its efforts to spare civilians, but this fact never emerged in TV broadcasts. Instead, TV audiences were told that Israel was "carpet bombing" the cities, town and villages of southern Lebanon, and "slaughtering" the civilian population as part of a systematic policy of "decimation" against Palestinian Arabs. Incredibly, one wire reporter (Helen Thomas, of UPI) went so far as to compare the Israeli action in Lebanon to the Soviet invasion of Afghanistan. By and large, however, when compared with TV coverage, the print media at least strove for fairness and even-handedness.

The Big Ad Lie

Meanwhile, pro-PLO elements in the USA were quick to seize the occasion for a propaganda holiday of flagrant misinformation and *dis*information. Full-

222

page advertisements appeared in such leading newspapers as *The New York Times* deploring the "wholesale killing and destruction" in Lebanon, using statistics manufactured by the PLO itself and released through the International Red Cross. The first full-page ad (June 20, 1982) claimed that the "Death and Devastation" wrought by the Israelis in Lebanon had caused "40,000 killed and wounded" and made "700,000 homeless."

The advertisement was signed by some 200 or more or less prominent intellectuals—Gentile and Jewish—professors, clergymen, politicians and writers. The signers were headed by Senator James Abourezk, whose anti-Israel bias is well and widely known, the Berrigan Brothers, Congressman Paul McCloskey, and Noam Chomsky, who, according to George F. Will (*Newsweek,* August 2) has collaborated with a French author in claiming the Holocaust of Hitler's time never happened. Few of the signers, if any, qualified as objective students of the Arab-Israeli struggle in the Middle East. But the damage they did to Israel's image as a free, progressive democracy—the only such society in the whole of North Africa and Southwest Asia—proved almost irreparable. Accompanying as it did the twisted accounts provided by TV—and by some newspapers and newsmagazines—the advertisement provided a distorted but enduring perception of Israel's war in Lebanon.

As a veteran correspondent who has known war—oftener than not at combat level—since the late 1930s, I strongly suspected that the figures cited in the pro-PLO ads, in some reporters' dispatches and in many TV broadcasts were either gross exaggerations or outright lies manufactured by the able propagandists of the PLO. Given the nature and speed of the Israeli advance, it was inconceivable that there had been "40,000 killed and wounded." By the third week in June, the Israeli military operation, although considerably more than "police action," was still substantially less than a full-scale war, and had moved so quickly that Israeli forces were already at the gates of Beirut.

At the time, the Israelis' own dead numbered fewer than 200. Clearly, there could not have been such serious fighting as to have caused 40,000 dead—or even 10,000, as was subsequently claimed by Beirut—on the other side. Otherwise, by the time the sensational ads appeared, the TV screens would have been filled with piles of corpses and with images of hospitals overflowing with wounded.

Moreover, since the entire population of southern Lebanon in the area of Israel's military operations—south of Beirut and west of the Bekaa Valley—was known to comprise only 510,000 inhabitants, it was hardly possible that 700,000 had been made homeless. But the figures were widely accepted even by Secretary of Defense Caspar Weinberger. Furthermore, much of the territory involved is made up of Christian and Shia Moslem towns and villages friendly to the oncoming Israeli forces, in which no fighting occurred. By no stretch of the imagination, therefore, could the population in the limited areas of actual combat have equaled the 700,000 figure of homeless refugees cited by the ad in question.

Lebanon at First Hand

As a longtime Middle East watcher, I was determined to see for myself what was really happening in the area, and made two trips to Israel and Lebanon. The first, on behalf of Network News, a Washington-based feature service, spanned five weeks from June 22 through July. The second, undertaken under the auspices of the Center for International Security, covered the period from mid-August to September 5.

Arriving in Lebanon during the third week of the hostilities, I visited the entire southern region from the border to East Beirut, which by then was securely in Israeli hands. Like Martin Peretz, of *The New Republic*, I found that much of what I had read in the newspapers and newsmagazines—and even more of what I had seen and heard on television— was "simply not true." Worse, it grievously damaged the reputation of America's only trustworthy ally in the region, indeed, in the whole of what is commonly called the Arab World, which is neither wholly "Arab" nor even an approximation of a "world."

I found no signs of "carpet bombing" by the Israeli Air Force (IAF), certainly nothing comparable to what I had seen as a correspondent in Sicily, northern Italy and southern France during the Allied advances in those areas in World War II. Nowhere did the IAF do to Lebanese population centers what the Allied air forces did to Anzio, Cassino, or Naples back in the 1940s. On the contrary, the visible evidence pointed to extreme care on the part of the IAF in its choice of targets, even along the coastal battlefields in and around Tyre and Sidon where the worst fighting occurred in the Israelis' drive toward Beirut.

Mosques, for instance, were meticulously spared, as were hospitals and schools unless antiaircraft guns were mounted on their rooftops by the PLO (as they often were), or the buildings were known to have become depositories for PLO munitions or to have been converted into training schools for PLO terrorists.

Meanwhile, Israeli ground forces took all possible precautions against needlessly tearing up tobacco fields, vineyards, banana plantations, orchards and olive groves. In fact, there were no indications anywhere of wanton Israeli destruction. This is not to say there was no damage to homes and public buildings. Wherever advancing Israeli tanks or troops were fired upon from schools, hospitals and other buildings in highly concentrated residential areas, the Israelis fired back, causing unavoidable civilian casualties. It may fairly be said, however, that the Israeli armed forces took extraordinary care to minimize civilian casualties and were largely successful.

By mid-July, I had canvassed hospitals in the coastal cities where there had been heavy fighting. In Tyre, local Lebanese officials said that their city had suffered 56 dead and 96 wounded, only 20 of whom were still hospitalized when I visited the place. In populous Sidon, there were, by official count, 265 dead and about 1,000 wounded, of whom some 300 did not require hospitalization. But what of Palestinian Arab "civilian" casualties in or near the southern fields of battle?

Before the start of the siege of Beirut (incidentally, it was never a "siege" in the strictest military sense of the word, for the besiegers periodically allowed the besieged to receive food, water and medical supplies, denying them only gasoline and munitions) the heaviest civilian casualties occurred in the so-called "camps" of the Palestinian Arab refugees. I visited two, one at Ein el-Hilwe, near Sidon, and the other at Rashediye, on the outskirts of Tyre. The "camps" were really typical Arab towns with squat one-story row houses solidly constructed of reinforced concrete around small patios or gardens. Both refugee communities were badly damaged, the IAF having hit at least one house in every three or four. Nearly every one of the demolished homes, however, was erected over, or adjacent to, deep underground bunkers which usually had served as storehouses for PLO weapons and ammunition. Casualties in the two camps, according to the local *muktahrs,* totalled between 1,000 and 1,200, far too many from a humanitarian point of view, but far fewer than PLO propagandists would have the world believe.

At predominantly Christian Nabatiyeh, inland from the potted and rutted north-south coastal highway which, by the way, was already heavy with the southbound traffic of refugees returning from Beirut and other points to the north and west of the battle zone, town authorities told me that they had sustained 10 dead and 15 wounded during the fighting between Israeli troops and retreating elements of the PLO. And in Nabatiyeh, in mid-July, life was already returning to normal. Cafes and hotels had reopened and were crowded with well-dressed young men taking their ease over elaborate meals, sucking on their water-pipes, playing the imported Bally-made slot machines in the lobbies, and ogling the comely, fashionably-attired young women who paraded the main street in twos and threes in the late afternoon sunshine.

Driving southward over winding, narrow mountain roads I saw town after town, village after village, untouched by war. Like Nabatiyeh, Jezzine, a lovely mountain resort town, was also crowded with Lebanese refugees from Beirut and the Syrian-occupied Bekaa Valley. Here, too, there were few signs that war had passed.

Indeed, what I saw in an intensive tour of the battlefields and rear areas was not an Israeli war of conquest but a war of liberation. The Lebanese, Moslems as well as Christians, showered the advancing Israelis with rice and flowers, the traditional gifts of welcome, and thanked them for having removed the oppressive presence of the PLO whose brutal occupation had made life miserable for the inhabitants.

On each of five one- and two-day visits to the war zone, I talked with Lebanese doctors, lawyers, merchants, municipal officials and individuals chosen at random in Tyre, Sidon, and the northern outskirts of Damour, East Beirut and, finally, West Beirut itself. Many spoke English or French, hence I did not require the services of my Arabic-speaking Israeli escort officers, and could converse freely with the persons I interviewed. Moslem and Christian Lebanese alike expressed themselves happy to be free at last of the PLO's interference in their daily lives. Some Christian Lebanese even rebuked the Israelis for not having come sooner. More significantly, perhaps, they could not understand why their plight was not known to the outside world. This complaint, after investigation, proved to be well-founded.

The Seven-Year Rape

Beginning in 1975, the PLO ruled over the Lebanese population through coercion, intimidation and force of arms. In the absence of any semblance of law and order, life and property were in constant danger. The people were in fact hostages of the PLO. This intolerable state of affairs was not unknown to the many foreign journalists, diplomats and business-men stationed in Beirut. Yet, there was no public out-cry abroad, not even after the situation was graphi-cally described by Suleiman Franjieh, Lebanon's president in the mid-1970s, in his farewell radio ad-dress to the nation on September 19, 1976. As reported by the Associated Press, the retiring presi-dent said, in part:

> "They (the Palestinian Arabs) came to us as guests. We awarded them every possible hospitality but eventually they turned into savage wolves. They sought to kill their hosts and become masters of Lebanon. In-deed, our guests have already sabotaged Lebanon's executive, legislative and judi-cial authorities, as well as the nation's regular army..."

The following month, Ambassador Edouard Ghorra, Lebanon's Permanent Representative to the United Nations, was even more explicit about what was happening to his country. In a speech to the U.N. General Assembly on October 14, 1976, Ambassador Ghorra protested that PLO groups had "increased the influx of arms into Lebanon, and transformed most—if not all—of the refugee camps into military bastions where common-law criminals fleeing from Lebanese justice found shelter and protection."

"Those camps," Ambassador Ghorra said, "became in fact centers for the training of mercenaries sent there and financed by other Arab states. Palestinian Arab elements belonging to various organizations resorted to kidnapping Lebanese—and sometimes foreigners—holding them prisoners, questioning them, torturing them, sometimes killing them. They committed all sorts of crimes in Lebanon. They smuggled goods and went so far as to demand 'protection money.' It is difficult to enumerate all the illegal activities committed by those Palestinian elements..."

But the world at large remained unmoved, although Dr. Wilson Salim, a distinguished Lebanese Christian physician, observed—in a pamphlet published in London in the early spring of 1982—that the PLO was shelling the homes of Lebanese day and night, mining their roads and causing much loss of life. "Many women and children have been killed," Dr. Salim wrote, adding that since the entry of the PLO in Lebanon, "we Lebanese have had little respite. Many of our people, for whom the constant tension became unendurable, have fled the country in fear of their lives..."

For the most part, however, the Lebanese people remained silent during the years of the PLO occupation out of fear of reprisals. Freed from restraint after the Israeli incursion, Father John Nasser, a Maronite priest from Aishiya, told reporter Aaron Dolev, of *Ma'ariv,* what the PLO did to his village.

"A thousand armed terrorists attacked Aishiya in force. They burst into the houses and dragged out the villagers, the members in all of about 100 families. They crowded most of them into my church, and locked us in. About 65 villagers remained outside. After about an hour had passed, those of us in the church heard shooting, burst after burst of machine gun fire. We were kept in the church for two days while the attackers ransacked and pillaged the town. When the raiders left, we found the bodies of the 65—all friends and relatives—lying dead in pools of dried blood. And Aishiya was no exception. Our beloved, unhappy Lebanon is full of Aishiyas..."

But the slaughter of innocents by the PLO was seldom publicized abroad. The PLO was understandably reluctant to allow Beirut-based reporters to witness what it was doing in the countryside. There were no TV cameras at Aishiya, nor were TV crews invited to record the PLO's massacre of civilians at Christian Damour in 1975-1976, or the Syrian shelling of Tel El Zatar where the victims were not Lebanese but Palestinian Arabs.

From time to time word of the horrendous events taking place in Lebanon did filter through to the West. There was heavy fighting between the PLO and its Christian and Shi'ite Moslem opponents in 1978. Radio Beirut claimed that during that year alone some 60,000 Lebanese were killed. In a rare glimpse into what was happening, *Time* reported that 400,000 Christians had fled from PLO terror in the Lebanese capital and that some 35,000 homes had been destroyed.

In 1979, Nicholas Tatro, of the Associated Press—one of the more fearless correspondents based in Beirut—wrote that 990 persons had been killed in the city. The following year Tatro, quoting police figures, wrote that 2,183 Lebanese were killed and 6,815 wounded in fighting between PLO "troops" and Lebanese forces. The Lebanese newspaper *A'Liwa'a* reported in April 1981, that in that month alone some 200 civilians were killed and 1,500 wounded by PLO and Syrian terrorists.

However, there was still no audible public outcry in the West. No full-page newspaper ads appeared in New York, Chicago and Los Angeles denouncing the activities of Yassir Arafat's organization and calling for a halt to the slaughter. The United Nations sat on its hands and while the PLO and its Syrian allies remained above criticism, the story of what was happening to once free, independent and prosperous

Lebanon remained untold. With the country's liberation from PLO domination, a brief reconstruction is now possible, and is essential to an understanding of the objectives and accomplishments, as well as the shortcomings, of Israel's Operation Peace for Galilee.

Background to Chaos

The PLO's first major base was Jordan, from whose territory it launched attacks against Israel. In 1970, when King Hussein realized that the terrorist organization seriously threatened his own regime, he sent his well-armed Arab Legion to crush the PLO, killing thousands of Arafat's followers and expelling the rest in an episode that entered Palestinian Arab history as "Black September."

Then as now, however, the Arab states were reluctant to grant the PLO sanctuary, and Arafat sought and found refuge for his forces in Lebanon. They brought with them the involvement in Lebanese affairs of those countries—Saudi Arabia and Syria, among others—which sponsor several of the PLO's eight main groupings.

Actually, the PLO had started creating bases in Lebanon in 1968, and by the Cairo agreement of the following year the country was pressured by the late Gamal Abdul Nasser, then Egypt's president, to allow the PLO what was tantamount to extra-territorial rights to run the Palestinian Arab refugee camps. Along with extra-territoriality went freedom to conduct terrorist activities against Israel.

The armed presence of the PLO in Lebanon grew through the 1970s, as did the PLO's harassment of the Christian population and attacks on Israeli civilians in Galilee and everywhere else. The PLO brought under its control certain areas, including such ancient Christian towns as Damour, from which thousands of inhabitants were driven out and slaughtered.

Lebanese efforts to curb the PLO were prevented by Syrian intervention, leading to a 1973 arrangement whereby the PLO was given even greater freedom of action. By 1975, the PLO was in effect a state-within-a-state with its headquarters in West Beirut. It interfered with the internal affairs of the country, defied the weak central government, made alliances with some of Lebanon's leftist internal forces, and exacerbated the ongoing feuds between the Christians and those Sunni Moslem groups which had allied themselves with the PLO. Lebanese Christians and foreigners were frequently stopped at gunpoint by PLO activists for body searches and examination of identity cards. In short, by 1975, Lebanon virtually belonged to Arafat and his terrorists.

In time, Israeli retaliation against attacks emanating from PLO bases in southern Lebanon led to the migration of some 300,000 Shi'ite Moslems from the south to Beirut, where tensions were further heightened between them and the PLO. Meanwhile, the PLO expanded its control over new areas of Lebanon including nearly the whole of the south and Beirut, the Bekaa Valley and the north. Internal disorders increased accordingly. Bank robberies, letter bombs, kidnappings, confiscations of private property and assassinations became almost daily occurrences. The Shi'ites added to the mounting chaos by creating their own paramilitary organization, the Free Fighters Front, to defend themselves against left-wing Sunni Moslem groups allied to the PLO.

The attempted assassination in 1975 of Pierre Gemayel—founder (in 1936) of the Maronite Christian Phalange and father of the recently murdered Bashir—precipitated major retaliatory action against the PLO. The fighting between Arafat's forces and the Phalange escalated into what came to be known in news dispatches out of Beirut and elsewhere as the Lebanese "civil war" but was really the PLO's war to subdue all of Lebanon. During the struggle the Lebanese civilian death toll rose to 100,000, some 50,000 children were orphaned and Lebanese in the tens of thousands were made homeless.

It may fairly be said, therefore, that the PLO was the main catalyst of the internal warfare that erupted in Lebanon in the spring of 1975. Meanwhile, the PLO entrenched itself among the population of southern Lebanon, cultivating ties with local leftist Moslems, training and arming their various private militias and gaining their support and trust. Gradually, segments of the Moslem community began looking upon the PLO as an ally whose aim was the concentration of all authority in Lebanon in PLO-Moslem hands. This eventually disrupted the delicate balance among the country's many ethnic and religious groups—Maronites, Greek Orthodox, Greek Catholics, Druze, and Shi'ite and Sunni Moslems—upon which the existence of the Lebanese government depended. The violent clashes of April 1975 between Christian and Moslem elements resulted in 18 months of bloody confrontations during which the central authority of the Lebanese government disintegrated.

The Extent of Syrian Aggression

Ever since Lebanon achieved independence in 1943, the various regimes which have ruled in Damascus have never concealed their desire to annex the country, always considering it really part of "Greater Syria." No Syrian government has ever accepted the reality of Lebanese sovereignty nor established diplomatic relations with Beirut. The Lebanese crisis of 1975-1976 gave Syria's Ba'athist leader, Hafez Assad, an opportunity to advance a long-standing Syrian ambition to extend its hegemony over its neighbor.

In June, 1976, Syria sent regular units of its army into Lebanon in the guise of a "peace-keeping mission" legitimized later, in October, when an Arab Summit Conference created an "Arab Deterrent Force" in Lebanon based on the several thousand Syrian troops already there. At first, Syria intervened on behalf of the besieged Christian community against leftist Moslem-PLO forces, and occupied much of Lebanon. When it became clear to Damascus, however, that the Christians opposed Syrian domination and were determined to resist it, Syria started coordinating its military efforts with those of the PLO and turned against the Christians.

In 1978, Syrian forces unleashed a violent offensive against the Christians in East Beirut, causing thousands of civilian casualties and destroying entire neighborhoods. The action was roundly condemned in London by *The Economist*, in its issue of October 7, 1978, as "sociological warfare...the application of military power against civilians to achieve non-military objectives...instead to cause as much disruption and suffering as possible by shattering the structure of organized social life..."

Between December 1980 and June 1981, the Syrians held the large Christian town of Zahle under siege, subjecting it to repeated shellings which killed thousands and wounded many more. Meanwhile, the Syrians stationed large numbers of troops in the Bekaa Valley where they also introduced powerful

Soviet-made, latest model SAM surface-to-air missile batteries giving Damascus virtual control of all of southern Lebanon and that part of northern Israel known as the Galilee.

The so-called "civil war" ended with Syria firmly entrenched in Lebanon, policing a substantial portion of the country in what was tantamount to a Syrian quasi-hegemony over its neighbor which Israel could not tolerate. During the years since 1973, the Syrians had moved from initial animosity toward the PLO, to rapprochement and, following the conclusion of the Egyptian-Israel Peace Treaty under the terms of the Camp David accords, to open alliance.

As of early June, 1982, Lebanon as a viable political structure had ceased to exist. In its place there existed only individual fiefdoms with about 100 different political groupings and at least 40 private armies. Beirut itself was divided into two zones, a predominantly Moslem West and a preponderantly Christian East. North of Beirut there emerged a Christian enclave based on Jouniyeh. The area further north was held by Sunni Moslems backed by the Syrians. In the south the area close to the Israeli border was controlled by Major Sa'ad Haddad, the Roman Catholic commander of a 2,000-man militia armed and supplied by the Israelis. Although Haddad's force was composed mainly of Christians, it also contained substantial numbers of anti-PLO Shi'ites. In 1979, Major Haddad, a former officer in

239

the Lebanese army, proclaimed an Independent Free Lebanon in a strip of land adjacent to the Israeli frontier about eight miles wide.

Following Israel's limited police action into southern Lebanon in March, 1978, planned to root out terrorist bases, the United Nations Interim Force in Lebanon was formed to assist in restoring peace in the area. But the UNIFIL territory soon was heavily infiltrated by PLO terrorists who established therein several bases from which attacks were launched on 23 Israeli towns and villages in Galilee.

It seems fair to state at this point that little of the background outlined above found its way into the dispatches of the correspondents of the print media covering Israel's Operation Peace for Galilee last summer, and even less in the segments aired by the TV networks.

Reporting from Lebanon before the Israeli incursion often took the form of black comedy rather than realistic appraisal of the confessional and personal factors involved. Throughout the "civil war" period that preceded the Israeli military action, the conflict was usually oversimplified as merely a struggle between a Christian Right and a Moslem Left. The Israeli military campaign against the PLO that began June 6 was similarly treated in simplistic terms as an outright "aggression" and was generally characterized as "expansionist," and even "imperialistic."

Meanwhile in that international community euphemistically known as the United Nations, hardly a voice was raised in condemnation of Syria's and the PLO's encroachment in Lebanon. From the beginning of Lebanon's nightmare in 1975 until June, 1982 neither the General Assembly nor the Security Council passed a single resolution dealing with the enormous tragedy that was being enacted under the eyes of numerous foreign observers. Both bodies, however, rarely missed an opportunity to condemn Israel for a multitude of mostly imaginary sins, going so far at one point as to equate Zionism with racism.

Yet, much of the responsibility for the Lebanese tragedy was attributable to the United Nations, which committed a historic blunder on November 13, 1974, when it illegally allowed Yassir Arafat to appear on the podium of the General Assembly to expound his widely publicized "real solution" to the "Palestinian problem"—a solution that would have merely "liberated" Israel from Israel. Overnight, the U.N. turned the arch-terrorist into an internationally recognized figure.

Crowned with a propaganda victory and clothed in his newly-won worldwide prestige, Arafat returned to Beirut as though to his own capital and unleashed his armed gangs. Four months later, in the early spring of 1975, Lebanon was swept into the bloody whirlwind erroneously called a "civil war." Thereafter, the world never again saw the true face of

241

the PLO. But in Lebanon, I met many Lebanese who recognized the PLO and its Syrian allies for what they really were and denounced them as murderers, rapists and thieves capable of almost unimaginable cruelties.

Atrocities Abounding

One of my many informants was Dr. Khalil Torbey, a distinguished Lebanese surgeon with degrees from Harvard Medical School and Boston's Massachusetts General Hospital. A portly gentleman in his early 50s, Dr. Torbey minced no words in describing his experiences during his country's torment under PLO-Syrian domination.

Torbey confirmed that since 1975 approximately 100,000 people were massacred by Arafat's minions and their Syrian partners. Many of the victims, he said, were not Christians but Moslems. Their deaths were callously used in a studied effort to make the world believe that what was happening in Lebanon was not a PLO takeover of the country but a "civil war" between its two main religious groups.

As a physician, Dr. Torbey was frequently called upon to attend to victims of PLO torture sessions which were usually conducted at the terrorists' "detention center" at Armoun, a village in the mountains east of Beirut.

"I know of cases," Dr. Torbey said, "of people being thrown into acid tanks and reduced to unrecognizable masses of porous bone. Many young girls came to me for abortions after being raped by PLO gangsters. Very often, mine was the only car circulating the perilous streets of West Beirut after dark to help some unfortunate victim or other of PLO or Syrian violence. I treated persons with arms severed by shelling, and men whose testicles had been crushed by torturers.

"I saw men—live men, mind you—dragged through the streets from fast-moving cars to which they were tied by their feet. All this, I am certain, was motivated in the early years by a desire to create the impression that a civil war was going on.

"In time, the Lebanese had nothing with which to defend themselves and no one to help them so that it was easy for the terrorists to take over homes, shops, garages, apartment houses—anything they wanted. Our children were growing up in terror and our people, robbed of their homes and belongings, were reduced to living like Bedouins, moving from place to place, seeking refuge from the terror. The lucky ones were received by friends or relatives in the hills and mountains to the north or south. The less fortunate lived like hunted animals."

243

Dr. Torbey himself was one of the victims of the technique employed by the PLO and its Syrian allies for the appropriation of property suitable to their purposes. Early in 1979, Dr. Torbey had nearly completed construction of what he described as "one of the largest medical facilities in the world, comparable to the Mayo Clinic" on ground close to the so-called Green Line that divided Beirut into a preponderantly Moslem western sector and a predominantly Christian eastern portion. Later that year, the Syrians attacked the Torbey Medical Center, drove out the defending forces of the enfeebled Lebanese Army, and took the place over as their main headquarters.

Another of my informants was Frederick El-Murr, a 54-year-old civil engineer and prominent Lebanese industrialist. Like Dr. Torbey, Mr. El-Murr was convinced that what had happened in Lebanon from 1975 onward, following Arafat's triumphal return from the United Nations, was not a "civil war, as the press hastened to characterize it, but a conquest of my country by the PLO and the Syrians."

"The terrorists," Mr. El-Murr added, "virtually destroyed with artillery and Katyusha rocket fire such Christian cities as Damour and Tyre, and badly damaged mostly Moslem Sidon. In West Beirut, hardly a building remains untouched. In 1978, the apartment building in which we lived in East Beirut was hit by PLO rockets 16 times.

"And we have seen mutilations and rape. I know

a worker in my factory whose mother was raped by PLO terrorists. A favorite method of ridding themselves of political opponents was to tie the feet of the male victims to separate cars speeding off in opposite directions. One such incident was witnessed by my 17-year-old daughter, Nada.''

Intimidating the Press

The outrages described by Dr. Torbey and Mr. El-Murr were comparable only to those perpetrated by the Nazis during World War II with refinements harking back to the Dark Ages. How did what both called "an organized gang of criminals" manage to impose a reign of terror and silence on a population of hundreds of thousands for more than seven years?

A partial answer was provided by Mr. El-Murr who said that the PLO had "plenty of money" with which to "persuade" Lebanese editors and journalists to write favorably about the PLO's so-called "revolution" or to remain silent. One editor whom the PLO could not "buy," Mr. El-Murr said, was his friend Salim El-Lawzi, owner of the independent Lebanese Arabic weekly, *El Hawadess*. Exactly how El-Lawzi was "silenced" I learned from other sources: Moslem newspapermen who preferred to remain anonymous.

El-Lawzi was a Lebanese patriot from one of the wealthiest Moslem families in West Beirut and, above all, a courageous journalist. He began warning his countrymen against the Palestinian terrorist organizations back in the early 1970s, when he saw that their ultimate goal was the creation in Lebanon of a state-within-a-state. Threats against his person started in the summer of 1975 by means of letters, telephone calls, and visits by PLO hooligans to his weekly's editorial offices located near the PLO-controlled neighborhood known as Burj al-Barajne.

El-Lawzi ignored the warnings until two explosive charges went off one night in the building that housed the weekly's presses, editorial rooms and administrative offices. The entire building collapsed. El-Lawzi moved to London where he revived his paper and continued his anti-PLO editorial policy. He stayed away from Beirut for three years but the desire to visit members of his family whom he had left behind got the better of him.

After obtaining a "safe-conduct" from his friend, the then Prime Minister Salim al-Hus, El-Lawzi landed at Beirut Airport in July 1978. A few days earlier, the latest issue of his paper had appeared in the Lebanese capital with a blistering attack on those Arab oil countries which, the paper said, were buying insurance from PLO terror within their own borders by financing the sojourn of the "gangs of murderers and thieves" in Lebanon. The journalist, who was 54 years old at the time, remained with his family for three days.

At the end of his visit, El-Lawzi headed for the

airport by automobile. His car was stopped at a Syrian Army roadblock, where a group of armed men from the pro-Syrian terrorist organization known as As-Saiqa dragged him out. They did not harm the driver, who was later suspected of having cooperated with the kidnappers, but El-Lawzi was taken to the notorious PLO mountain village of Armoun. There, the victim was held for three days in the torture chambers. The fingers of his hands were cut off joint by joint. He was subsequently dismembered and his remains turned up scattered about the village. Horrifying photographs of El-Lawzi's mutilated body spread terror throughout the capital's journalistic colony.

Edouard Saab, editor-in-chief of the French language Beirut daily *L'Orient Le Jour* was 46 years old when he too fell victim to an armed attack while crossing the Green Line in his automobile in the course of his daily trip from his newspaper's offices in West Beirut and his home in East Beirut. Saab, who also served as correspondent for the great Paris daily, *Le Monde,* had been systematically criticizing PLO terrorist tactics since September, 1970, calling repeatedly for liquidation of Fatahland along the Israeli border, and urging the Lebanese government to break relations with those Arab countries which were pouring hundreds of millions of petrodollars into the coffers of the PLO. Saab was murdered at one of the many roadblocks maintained by the PLO.

A terrorist fired a round into the journalist's head. Oddly enough an American friend—the Beirut stringer for an American newsweekly who was sitting beside him—was unharmed.

Over the years, the PLO terrorized into conformity, submission or silence the entire Lebanese press community, using arson, sabotage, assassination and bribery to gain its ends. On April 1, 1975, an explosion destroyed the offices of the weekly *Al Jamhoud* and killed a number of the building's occupants. The following month, similar explosions occurred in the editorial rooms of *Al Mouhared* and the printing plant called *Abi Sadr* which printed several of Beirut's many daily and weekly journals. PLO threats to blow up the offices of *Al Moustagbal* in August of that same year caused the paper's editorial and administrative staffs to move to Paris as a group.

In July 1980, Riyad Taha, president of the Beirut Publishers' Union, was shot to death in an ambush. In November, explosions destroyed the buildings of *A-Safir* and *Al-Liwa'a,* both important dailies. By the end of the year, nearly all of Beirut's 36 once flourishing daily and weekly newspapers had been bullied into acquiescence or silence.

In the meantime, according to Edouard George, a former senior editor of *L'Orient-Le Jour,* PLO terrorists killed a number of foreign correspondents based in Beirut. Among them Mr. George listed Sean Toolan, a correspondent for ABC-TV; Robert Pfeffer, who represented West Germany's *Der Spiegel* and Italy's *Unita,* official organ of the Italian Communist Party; two Italian journalists, Tony Italo and Graziella di Falco; Jean Lougeau, who represented an independent French TV network; and Mark Tryn, of the "Free Belgium" broadcasting station.

Knowledgeable Lebanese newsmen, able to speak freely after the Israelis had expelled Arafat and his trigger-happy followers from Beirut last summer, said that most of the capital's press corps—national and foreign—entered into a "conspiracy of silence" during the long occupation by "the Palestinian Mafia." The journalists tended to divide their colleagues into roughly four categories:

A large number, of whatever political persuasion, was truly sympathetic to the PLO and the leftists.

Another group simply sold out to the PLO, receiving bribes proportionate to their importance or influence, and rewarding their paymasters with sympathetic articles about "the Palestinian struggle."

A third group, fewer in number than the "sellouts," went underground. Its members emerged now and then to try to publish the truth but seldom succeeded. They met stubborn resistance from publishers and editors-in-chief who had been bribed or terrified into silence. Most simply gave up journalism and went into other less frustrating and less dangerous activities.

A last group, perhaps the largest, constituted what my informants called "The Order of the Silent Ones"—composed of Lebanese and foreign correspondents who did not have to be bribed, but were merely frightened out of their wits by a constant stream of threatening letters and telephone calls and, from time to time, severe beatings or assassinations.

It was not unusual for Lebanon's journalistic opponents of terrorist activities to find on their doorsteps human limbs in plastic containers with warnings that unless they toed the mark editorially they too would "wind up wrapped in plastic." Small wonder, perhaps, that in this atmosphere even some staunch Western correspondents became extremely wary of incurring the wrath of the PLO, and saw more merit in "the cause" than it deserved.

Despite the harassment, however, responsible Lebanese journalists compiled what they called "An Album of Terrorist Atrocities." Published clandestinely in 1978, the document was quickly suppressed within Lebanon, and never saw the light of day abroad. Thus the outside world remained in ignorance of the true nature of the PLO, and utterly unaware of Arafat's preparations for eventual *jihad* against Israel.

By the end of 1981 the PLO, with Syrian help, had virtually conquered Lebanon but the full story never surfaced in the dispatches and broadcasts emanating from Beirut. There were no articles in the

Western press—certainly not under a Beirut dateline
—about how the PLO was (1) amassing huge stores
of highly sophisticated weapons; (2) converting its
guerrilla gangs into a close approximation of a con-
ventional army of some 18,000 men fully equipped
with artillery, armor and "hi-tech" electronic communications gadgets; (3) recruiting and training more
than 2,000 mercenaries from a score of Arab (and
non-Arab) nations for service in "the cause"; (4)
honeycombing West Beirut and adjacent refugee
camps with miles of deep underground tunnels and
bunkers; and (5) placing batteries of artillery in
civilian centers, thereby creating for itself a human
shield.

Meanwhile, however, there was no lack of material in Western media—printed and visual— critical
of Israel's every move to ensure her security in a
hostile world. Much of the criticism was directed at
Prime Minister Begin personally as an inflexible and
fanatic nationalist whom the media openly disliked
despite the fact that he had made peace with Israel's
most populous and militarily most powerful enemy,
Egypt, and remained steadfastly pro-American.

The View From Beit Agron
In February, 1982, the persistent anti-Israel bias
detectable in the Western news media's reporting and
commentary of the Arab-Israeli conflict prompted
Ze'ev Chafets, then director of Israel's Government

Press Office,[1] to charge that even such eminent journals as *The Washington Post* and *The New York
Times*—as well as such important electronic media as
ABC-TV and the BBC—followed a "double standard" in their coverage. With one eye constantly on
the implications of Arab terrorism, they took for
granted and abused the freedom allowed them in
Israel's open society, Chafets said.

Interviewed in his office in Beit Agron, the press
headquarters in Jerusalem, Chafets, a bearded mild-
mannered 34-year-old American who emigrated to
Israel in 1967, explicitly charged that terror prevented
critical reporting on the activities of the PLO and
Syria in Lebanon. He cited as an example an ABC
program entitled "Under the Israeli Thumb: Life on
the West Bank" which was broadcast on February 4
as part of the network's weekly "20/20" show.
Chafets described the segment dealing with Israel as
one of the "most malicious, distorted and one-sided
programs (about Israel) shown on any American network in recent years," purposely made and transmitted in order to "pander to Arab terror."

Chafets was certain that the program had a
causal, not accidental, connection with the murder of
ABC reporter Sean Toolan in July 1981, and that by
putting it on the air the network hoped to remain free

---

[1]Mr. Chafets took a year's leave of absence from his job in September
to write a book about American press coverage of the Middle East.

of further harassment from the PLO. The network's reply was predictable. In New York, Roone Arledge, President of ABC News, dismissed the allegations as "utter nonsense."

I could NOT agree with Mr. Arledge. I saw the "20/20" broadcast in question, and having visited the West Bank in 1967, when the Israelis occupied it, and revisited it many times since, I can bear witness to the steady improvement made over the years in the economic and social conditions of the area's Palestinian Arab inhabitants. It seemed to me that ABC set out to prove that the Palestinian Arabs were, as the segment's title itself implied, suffering under the heel of the Israeli Army. In this, ABC succeeded admirably. Totally ignored by ABC reporter Tom Jarriel were the advances made since 1967 in West Bank agriculture, industry, education, housing and public health.

A point by point rebuttal of the ABC story has no place in this report, but a few observations might not be amiss. Far from having "stamped out" the Arab inhabitants' "cultural identity"—as ABC charged—four universities and three schools for advanced vocational studies have been established in a region where no such institutions existed while the West Bank was under the rule of Hashemite King Hussein. Utterly false, also, was the broadcast's contention that under Israeli administration the West Bank's rate of infant mortality has been rising. Ac-

253

tually, it has been declining sharply from 33.6 per 1,000 births in 1968 to a recent (1980) 28.3. ABC's "Under the Israeli Thumb" not only distorted truth, it compounded falsehoods into anti-Israel propaganda. It is a masterpiece of tendentious antipathy.

In fairness to ABC, however, what I saw of the network's coverage of Israel's war against the PLO in Lebanon before I left for the war zone June 22 seemed eminently balanced and objective. All the networks had a busy weekend June 4-6 with the shooting of Israeli Ambassador Shlomo Argov in London, the rain of PLO rockets and artillery fire on the towns and villages of northern Galilee, the Israeli bombing of PLO targets in Beirut and, finally, the massive movement of Israeli troops and armor across the Lebanese frontier.

Among all the misinformation about the war, one network, ABC, deserves recognition for some of its coverage. I recall anchorman Frank Reynolds' effort to put the incursion into historical perspective by remarking that "terrorism has led to tragedy" in a memorable broadcast which, if memory serves, included a piece from Bill Seamans in Israel showing the damage the PLO's rockets and shells had wreaked in Galilee, intercut with segments depicting the Argov shooting and the Israeli raid on the Beirut sports stadium, a PLO training site for guerrillas and an ammunition storage point. Some days later, ABC emphasized that the Israeli raid was aimed at eliminating "PLO bases in Lebanon" and Seamans was back on the air with a piece on how Beaufort Castle, which had fallen to the Israelis in bitter fighting, had been used by the PLO to direct rocket and artillery fire into Israeli population centers in Galilee.

In his criticism of media coverage of Israel, Chafets also alleged that late last year the Marxist-oriented PLO splinter group known as the People's Front for the Liberation of Palestine (PFLP) abducted five Western correspondents in Lebanon, held them "for 24 hours" and "threatened to kill them." One of the five, Chafets said, was "a *New York Times* reporter, and the other was a *Washington Post* man." A condition for their release, Chafets charged, was that their respective papers not mention their abduction "and the papers complied."

A member of the *Times'* Foreign Desk in New York had a somewhat different version of the "abduction." Actually, he said, not one but two *Times* correspondents were involved—William Farrell and John Kifner, both veteran Middle East hands. They were not "abducted" but were merely held for a few hours after they were stopped at a PLO checkpoint late one night while the reporters were on their way by car to investigate a tip on what they had been led to believe might be a major news story—one big enough to risk violating the PLO's curfew.

It is true, however, that the incident remained unreported for nine months. In response to Chafets'

allegations of a "cover-up," the *Times* indicated that
what happened to its reporters had not been deemed
newsworthy. The paper subsequently published a
frank piece by Kifner relating the perils of reporting
from the Lebanese capital—meaning the Beirut
before Israel launched its Operation Peace for
Galilee.

"To work here as a journalist," Kifner wrote,
"is to carry fear with you as faithfully as your
notebook. It is the constant knowledge that there is
nothing you can do to protect yourself and that
nothing has ever happened to an assassin. In this atmosphere, a journalist must often weigh when, how
and sometimes even whether to record a story. In the
Middle East, facts are always somewhat elusive. But
there is a pervasive belief among the Beirut press
corps that the correspondents should be extremely
wary of incurring the wrath of the Syrian regime..."

The Washington Post, after pondering Chafets'
charges, admitted that its Beirut correspondent.
Jonathan Randal, had in fact been arrested, but
added that so seasoned a newsman—a veteran of
wars and revolutions—could hardly be expected to
take account of so minor an incident as captivity by
the PLO.

Chafets further charged that other representatives of major Western media had fallen afoul of
the PLO and the Syrians, and had tried to cover up
the incidents. He cited a gun attack on Berndt

Debusemann, Reuters bureau chief in Beirut, who was first threatened by a pro-Syrian PLO faction which disapproved of his reporting on Syrian activities in Lebanon, then was shot in the stomach while walking home from work. Reuters played down the incident.

Even the mighty BBC, Chafets indicated, could be intimidated. The British network's Beirut correspondent, Tim Llewellyn, saw the shooting of Debusemann from the window of his office and after reporting the episode his life was threatened by pro-Syrian PLO elements. Llewellyn was rushed to safety in Cyprus, but the BBC omitted to mention the city from which he was reporting and, contrary to custom, did not replace him with a staff man in Beirut.

To what extent American reporters based in Beirut yielded to the terror tactics of the PLO or the persuasiveness of Madmoud Labadi, Arafat's spokesman in the Lebanese capital—a charmer who always carried a pistol in his belt—is difficult to gauge by anything less than an exhaustive survey of media coverage. However, the mounds of clippings from *The New York Times* that awaited me on my return from the war zone early in September reflected a fair amount of even-handedness *in the news columns*. On the *Times'* Op-Ed page, Anthony Lewis and others, among them former Undersecretary of State George Ball—a prominent exponent of the notion that practically every conflict stems from Israel's "failure" to solve the "Palestinian problem"— seemed determined to savage Israel in every printed line. However, William Safire was usually also there to do the counter-punching. I leave it to others to plumb the dark depths of the anti-Israel animus of Messrs. Lewis and Ball.

Since Arafat's expulsion from Beirut, there have been a number of analyses of American media treatment of the Israeli military operation in Lebanon. One, prepared by the American Jewish Committee, reported that press coverage, in sharp contrast to television, indicated considerably more balance than the Israeli Press Office claimed. According to the AJC's analysis, the reporting was "by and large even-handed, although consistent condemnation of particular Israeli actions produced an overall impression of pervasive censure."

Surveyed by the AJC's researchers were editorials, columns, political cartoons and letters to the editor dealing with the events in Lebanon from June 22 to August 26. Of the 167 editorials examined, the report said, 49 (29%) were clearly antagonistic, 35 (21%) were preponderantly supportive and uncritical of Israel's actions, and most of the remaining 83 were "relatively balanced."

A majority of the editorials and columns reviewed, the AJC report asserted, focused attention on three issues: (1) the urgent need to remedy the plight of the Palestinian Arab refugees; (2) the civilian casualties; and (3) Israel's offensive use of American arms in apparent violation of existing agreements.

The results were reflective of the obsession of all Western journalists with the problem of the Palestinian Arab refugees and the parallel preoccupation with Israel as the major source of turmoil in the Middle East. It has become a journalistic cliché that virtually every conflict in the Middle East is due to Israel's "failure" to resolve the "Palestinian problem." Rarely was it mentioned that if the Arabs had accepted the United Nations partition plan of 1947, the Palestinian Arabs would have had a state west of the Jordan or that a Palestinian Arab state already exists east of the river, but is called Jordan (it was once called by its true name, Transjordan). As Professor Edward Alexander put it in an article in the September-October issue of the British magazine, *Encounter,* "Israel has become the moral playground for the journalism of the world, a gymnasium in which they do ethical calisthenics designed to revitalize muscles that have grown flabby from disuse during their assignments in other countries."

The widespread focus on resolution of the Palestinian dilemma, the AJC report concluded, was "a clear harbinger of future accelerated pressure on Israel to cooperate. It was equally evident that as Israel's chief ally and supplier of (military and economic) aid, the United States was perceived as the key agent in future negotiations.''

A predominantly negative view of Israel, the AJC analysis found, was produced by the cartoons appearing in the American press. Out of 81 cartoons examined, nearly half (35) were clearly hostile. Of the latter, the vast majority dealt with civilian casualties and destruction in Lebanon.

Letters to the editor, on the other hand, the AJC said, were about evenly divided between those generally supportive of Israel (76) and those which were hostile (74). Only a very few letter writers (20) exhibited what could be called a "balanced" viewpoint.

A New Low in European Coverage

A distinctly anti-Israel bias seemed to me far more evident in the reporting by European journalists than in the work of American newspapermen. While abroad, I read with some regularity the London *Times* and the *Observer,* the Manchester *Guardian,* Paris' *Le Monde* and Milan's *Corriere della Sera.* The contrast in journalistic approach was perceptible; American correspondents tended to consider themselves simply recorders of what they saw but their European counterparts were much given to making political statements.

The European reporters appeared to be striving to make amends for their various countries' past colonial domination of native peoples by upholding the aspirations of the downtrodden populations of the Third World. In the Middle East, this means support for anyone attacked by Israel, especially the Palestinian Arabs. In the dispatches of the Europeans—with the notable exception of the pieces in the London *Observer* by Connor Cruise O'Brien—Israel invariably emerged as a morally repressive force, a threat to world peace which somehow had to be restrained. Arafat's men, on the other hand, were never "terrorists" but "guerrilla fighters," the Syrian occupying army in Lebanon was nearly always a "Syrian peacekeeping force" and Palestinian Arabs were simply "Palestinians," although historically a Palestinian nation has never existed.

Similarly, Saudi Arabia, which has consistently advocated Holy War against Israel, has bank-rolled the PLO to the tune of hundreds of millions of petrodollars ($450 million in 1981) and is without doubt the world's most racist state, rarely appeared in print as anything but "moderate." The epithet was frequently also applied to King Hussein's Jordan, whose "moderation" has consisted in having frustrated every effort since 1967 to achieve a negotiated settlement in the Arab-Israeli dispute, and in persistently refusing to talk with the Israelis about the future of the so-called West Bank.

Newspapers of record like the *New York Times* —unlike the newsweeklies which throughout the war strove for dramatic effect as vigorously as television

261

—made sporadic efforts to bring the conflict into historical perspective. Notable was a piece by David Shipler, of the *Times*, datelined Sidon, July 25, 1982, relating how Lebanese Christians and Moslems welcomed the Israelis as liberators of their country from the yoke of the PLO. Shipler described graphically what the Lebanese had suffered during the years of terrorist occupation, and inferentially justified the Israeli incursion.

But such articles were the exception rather than the rule. The words "holocaust" and "genocide" appeared often enough in most Western reporting to suggest a persistently anti-Israeli, indeed, sometimes even anti-Semitic bias that was echoed by Western leaders who should have known better but whose judgments were blurred by cowardice in the face of the ever-present threat of a curtailment in Arab oil supplies, petrodollar flows or—who knows?—fear of PLO terrorism. Generous coverage was accorded every outburst of Francois Mitterand, Andreas Papandreou, Bruno Kreisky and other leftists in high places who alleged that the Israelis were doing to the Palestinians what the Nazis had done to the Jews.

Inaccurate and imbalanced reporting obviously can have a critical impact not only on public perceptions but also on governmental attitudes and policies. A case in point was the shocked reaction of President Reagan, August 2, to a photograph distributed by United Press International and prominently published by, among others, the prestigious *Washington Post.* The photo showed a 7-month-old Lebanese baby girl swathed in bandages from head to foot. The caption that accompanied the picture said the child had lost both arms and had been severely burned in the "accidental bombing" of an apartment house in East Beirut by the Israeli Air Force. Outraged, President Reagan put in a personal telephone call to Premier Begin urging him to suspend the Israeli bombing of PLO targets in West Beirut, using the word "holocaust" in the ensuing exchange.

Israeli authorities challenged the report, made a thorough investigation, and on August 22 released a photo of the same child after treatment. The infant had *not* lost both arms, and had suffered no burns and only slight injuries to the wrists. Moreover, the baby, it turned out, was not hurt by an Israeli bomb but by a shell from a PLO battery in West Beirut. The UPI confirmed that the original caption was inaccurate and expressed regret. But whereas the original photo was splashed everywhere, the corrected version barely made the inside pages (*The New York Times* printed it on page 14).

Generally speaking, press coverage could be faulted for its omissions at least as much as for its distortions, half-truths and downright lies. There was little reporting, if any, on such subjects as: (1) the significance of the vast quantities of arms found by the Israelis in PLO bunkers and tunnels; (2) the rapidity with which the Lebanese were able to resume normal life as they returned to their homes in the liberated areas; (3) the benefits that accrued to Lebanon itself and to Western influence in the Middle East as a result of the Israeli military action; (4) the realities of the PLO as an instrument of international terrorism which was revealed in the tons of documents captured by the Israelis; and (5) the extent of Israeli help in the relief and rehabilitation of the Lebanese population, including the sizeable Palestinian Arab minority.

As Through A Tube, Darkly

But the print media, with whatever its faults, was a model of diligence and accuracy compared with the visual medium. I personally believe television is capable of great journalism. But its handling of history's first complete "TV dinner war," outclassing even Vietnam, left much to be desired in terms of fairness, balance and truthful presentation of the unfolding drama of the summer of 1982, possibly because since the days of Edward R. Murrow, television journalism has increasingly become more Show Biz than journalism.

It may be true that "a picture is worth a thousand words." It is equally true, however, that a picture can tell a thousand lies. After watching TV at home for a fortnight before flying off to the war zone, I was sure, for instance, that Tyre and Sidon had been destroyed, and most of their inhabitants killed. That was the impression produced by the highly seductive use of the TV cameras, the file footage (often undated) and the highly misleading labeling of the material shown. As I have indicated earlier, I was surprised to find both cities not nearly as badly damaged as the TV images had indicated, and to learn that civilian casualties had been minimal because the inhabitants of those towns had heeded Israeli warnings to evacuate or take adequate cover.

Television gives viewers a startling image of what is happening, when, where and to whom, but falls far short of making clear that what they are seeing is not the totality of truth, or of adequately explaining *why* the event is taking place. The total truth is not merely the 30 seconds or so of an image, but of the succession of the many, many 30-second images which preceded the event and which will follow it. Yet the picture, whatever it may be, tells the audience that what the camera has recorded is undeniable fact, absolute truth. By aiming their cameras on selected destroyed buildings in Sidon, for example, without showing the untouched neighboring structures in the vicinity or in the same street, the electronic journalists dramatically exaggerated the degree of devastation, thus deliberately failing to project a balanced scene.

The man who holds the camera, whatever his qualifications as a journalist, determines what is conveyed to millions of viewers in his home country and, often, throughout the world. He not only purveys a picture but he, and/or his director or producer, also determines what the scene shall be. By moving his camera to the left or right, up or down, he can project a totally different reality. He holds in his hands the instrument of a tremendous truth or an enormous lie. By training their cameras on the stark rubble and bloody civilian casualties, the television reporters transformed the reality of Israel's most judicious and selective use of military might into the distorted image of a brutal aggressor.

By not showing viewers PLO katyushas firing rockets and PLO artillery raining shells at civilians in East Beirut, and the agony and casualties such attacks cause, and by rarely explaining how the PLO used civilians as shields, the knights of the Electronic Cyclops failed to give viewers a balanced picture of the fighting. The conclusion is irresistible that friendship for the PLO and rage against Israel prompted much of the lopsided television coverage, and motivated the UPI misrepresentation of the notorious photograph of the "wounded child" that so moved President Reagan.

Nearly every day of the long semi-siege of Beirut through July and August, TV photographed Arafat with babies in his arms outside the entrance of one of his several bunkers in West Beirut. But I recall no single instance of a TV reporter asking him any pointed questions about his own responsibility for the carnage, or about the PLO's right to use the Lebanese capital's civilian population as hostages to his political maneuverings. There can be no doubt that favorable coverage by the media, particularly television, encouraged Arafat and the PLO to stay on in Beirut day after day, every one of which cost lives on both sides.

At the risk of being accused of "selective criticism" of TV coverage, one of the most tendentious broadcasts of the entire summer came from John Chancellor, of NBC, normally a serious, almost school-teacherish figure on his network's nightly news program. It happened during the torrid, early stages of the final battle for Beirut.

Earlier, on June 16, Chancellor had commented on "the growing feeling that Israel has turned into a warrior state," using "far more force than is necessary," and questioning Israel's "credibility." However, he did not question Israel's "legitimate security problems in Lebanon." At the time, he was speaking from New York. Later, during the first few days of August, he was in Beirut, and on August 2 aired one of the most provocative commentaries of the entire war. Speaking while silhouetted against a smoking Beirut skyline, he said:

> "What will stick in the mind about yesterday's savage Israeli attack on Beirut is its size and scope. This is one of the world's big cities. The area under attack is the

length of Manhattan island below Central Park. Five hundred thousand people live here. One in a hundred is a PLO fighter. And it went on for such a long time— before dawn until five in the afternoon. Systematic, sophisticated warfare. The Israeli planes just never stopped coming. For an entire day, Beirut rocked and swayed to the rhythm of the Israeli attack. The Israelis say they were going after military targets with precision. There was also the stench of terror all across the city. . . . Nothing like it has ever happened in this part of the world. I kept thinking yesterday of the bombing of Madrid during the Spanish Civil War. What in the world is going on? Israel's security problem on its border is fifty miles to the south. What's an Israeli army doing here in Beirut? The answer is that we are now dealing with an imperial Israel which is solving its problems in someone else's country, world opinion be damned. Nobody knows how the battle of Beirut is going to end. But we do know one thing. The Israel we saw here yesterday is not the Israel we have seen in the past.''

Chancellor asked many questions, good questions, maybe, but he was supposed to answer them, not merely pose them. He was trying hard to be Ernest Hemingway but succeeded only in being an earnest schoolmaster who had forgotten past lessons. The Israel that Chancellor described had undergone a sudden puzzling transformation into a "savage" and "imperial" state, but what puzzled me most was why Chancellor "kept thinking of the bombing of Madrid during the Spanish Civil War." Was he there at the time? The year of the bombing of Madrid by the Junkers 52s of Hitler's burgeoning *Luftwaffe* was 1936, when John was 12 or 13 years old.

Chancellor's editorializing was no worse, however, than Tom Brokaw's reference on August 4 to "what's left of Beirut" as though the entire city had been *demolished.* Despite the audible and visible bombing of West Beirut's PLO positions, this was definitely a gross exaggeration. In any case, Chancellor redeemed himself somewhat later by a thoughtful commentary from a Palestinian refugee camp wherein he observed that, although Israel bore "some of the blame" for those homeless people, it had been the Arab countries which had refused them refuge. The wretched Palestinian Arabs were "useful" he said because they helped the Arabs make "Israel look bad."

On the whole, and again with some exceptions, television tended to equate the performance of the Israeli forces in Lebanon with that of the hordes of Attila, Tamerlane and Hitler. Despite the denials of the networks' various presidents, the conclusion seems inescapable that television coverage was heavily biased against Israel. It uncritically and consistently inflated casualty figures, dwelt unduly on atrocities, and overstressed the fact of Israeli censorship which was not nearly as total as contemporaneous British censorship during the Falklands campaign. The thrust of the reporting of the new breed of electronic journalists was to depict Israel as the guilty party. The Palestinian Arabs have suffered at the hands of others, most notably Jordan's Hussein, whose Arab Legion killed an estimated 10,000 or more of Arafat's PLO "fighters" in 1970's Black September, but TV never trumpeted that particular outrage, or the Syrian slaughter at Hama in which tens of thousands died.

Television was invariably late, furthermore, in correcting mistakes whenever it was caught in error. Not until October, on an ABC *Viewpoint* program discussing media reliability, did the network's chief European correspondent, the personable Peter Jennings, acknowledge, for instance, that he himself was surprised when he visited Tyre and Sidon to find how exaggerated the earlier reports of wholesale destruction had been.

One of television's own stars, the erudite Bill Moyers, came closer than any critic or commentator to defining the shorcomings of the medium in the

270

piece he did on Dan Rather's CBS *Evening News* show on August 23, when the long-delayed departure of the PLO forces from West Beirut got under way, machine-guns blazing in air. It was a masterful summary of the situation up to that moment and worth quoting in full. Mr. Moyers:

> Watching scenes of the Beirut evacuation this weekend, I was struck by how it is possible for the cameras to magnify a lie. These Palestinian troops left town as if they'd just won a great victory. Arafat, they praised as a conquering hero. In fact, they are leaving town in defeat. And in fact, Arafat led them to this cul-de-sac where they made their last stand behind the skirts of women and among the playgrounds of children. The only victory they won was to give General Sharon an excuse for total war and so to bring upon Israel the condemnation of world opinion and to many Jews, a tormented conscience. But the world was condemning Israel even before Beirut, and will for time to come. And the anguish of Jews at the suffering caused by their own war machine comes from the bitter experience of having learned that those who die by the sword must live by the sword. Carnage, indeed, and no one's

hand too clean. But it could have been otherwise if Arafat and his allies accepted the reality of Israel, if they had not established within Lebanon a terrorist state sworn to Israel's destruction, and if Arab governments had not found it useful to nurture the PLO in the bloody illusion that Israel can one day be pushed into the sea. Argue as you might about the events leading up to the establishment of Israel. Weep as you must for the Palestinian refugees. But a fact is a fact, and Israel is a fact. Yet, the guerrillas leaving Beirut this week are vowing to fight on until victory. Well, there will be no peace in the Middle East until the Arabs stop asking their young men to die for a lie.

The Massacres: Who Was to Blame?

The departure of Arafat and most of his forces was policed—"observed" might be a more accurate word—by a small contingent of American, French and Italian troops. The terrorists gone, the Americans quit the international force soon after, two weeks before their scheduled time. Something approximating a vacuum was created by September 1, when Begin, aware that the PLO quite probably had left at least 2,000 armed men among the population of West Beirut, ordered the Israeli army to enter that portion of the city.

The decision had a tragic aftermath in mid-September when Lebanese Christian militiamen entered the Shatila and Sabra camps of Palestinian Arab refugees and massacred several hundred men, women and children. The episode was a climactic agony and moral trauma for all men and women of good will, deeply felt by Israel and by people everywhere. That the mass murders took place after the Israeli Army had entered West Beirut and virtually under the noses of Israeli military personnel sent shock waves throughout Israel where an outraged, democratic people immediately demanded an accounting from Premier Begin and Defense Minister Ariel Sharon.

Sharon's insistence that Israeli commanders had stressed to the leaders of the Lebanese Christian militia that their military action was to be solely against the many terrorists still hidden in West Beirut, not against civilians, failed to abate the Israelis' sense of dismay and guilt. Instead, it provoked massive demonstrations in Israel itself against the Begin-Sharon government for apparently having disregarded the possibility of a continuation of the feudal Moslem-Christian cycle of vengeance that had tormented Lebanon for decades. Only a week before the massacre, Christian President-elect Bashir Gemayel and more than a score of his followers were blown literally to bits by a mysterious explosion in their Phalangist party headquarters. It was foreseeable, or it should

273

have been, that the Christians, who had lost not hundreds but tens of thousands of their men, women and children over the years of PLO occupation, would seek revenge. The Christians' "pogrom" against the Palestinian Arabs, rather than Israeli failure to foresee or deter it, was a *cause celebre* that cried out for a proper moral response.

A moral response did not come from the Vatican, certainly. Arafat, who had caused the murder of tens of thousands of Christians in Lebanon—and of hundreds of Jews in Israel and elsewhere—was received by Pope John-Paul II and was photographed with the peripatetic Pontiff of that Holy Roman Church which has not seen fit to recognize Israel's existence by exchanging diplomatic representation.

Meanwhile, the Soviet reaction to the tragedy at Shatila and Sabra was an official statement, issued by Tass, accusing Israeli troops of carrying out the massacre. Not one Arab witness of the killings had seen even a single Israeli soldier in the camps. Actually, there were reports that Israeli troops had fired upon Christian militiamen in an eleventh-hour attempt to end the blood-letting when the truth finally dawned on the Israeli commanders. But Moscow made no mention of the fact that Christian militiamen had entered the camps to wreak bloody vengeance on Palestinian Arabs. Tass villified Israel alone and concluded by making the predictable comparison of the Israeli "atrocity" to the Nazi massacres at Babi Yar outside

Kiev during World War II.

This time, Western journalism backed away from such comparisons, but it did rival the Soviets in the venom, even distortion, that moved Premier Begin to cry "Goyim kill goyim, and the Jews get the blame." In democratic Italy, political leaders from far Left to the neo-Fascist Right heaped vituperation on Israel. A statement from the office of Prime Minister Spadolini in Rome distorted the truth almost as effectively as the Soviets had done: "The Italian government expresses herewith the strongest condemnation and the most indignant censure for the bloody actions perpetrated or at least concurred in by the Israeli Army."

Even China joined the chorus. In Peking, the *People's Daily* echoed Moscow, its ideological enemy, in describing the murders at Shatila and Sabra as Israeli crimes. Israel, and only Israel, was once more at the center of calumny, and the Jew once again cast in the role of the genocidal Nazi.

Also disturbing was an NBC newscast immediately following the Beirut massacre wherein a PLO spokesman claimed that Israeli soldiers actually had killed thousands of innocent persons in the two camp hospitals. NBC's newscasters never challenged the PLO representative's statement or asked him for proof of his allegations; they merely looked properly somber and nodded as though assenting to his outrageous fabrications. To the best of my knowledge, the false information was never retracted or corrected.

Prime Minister Begin, truth be told, did not help matters by refusing at first to institute a thorough independent investigation of the tragic episode. The impression abroad was that he only relented after some 400,000 Israelis took to the streets of Tel Aviv to demand an inquiry.

The fact remains, however, that when Christians murdered Moslems for having slaughtered Christians, the world immediately began denouncing the Jews who were at the very worst only indirectly responsible for what happened. Many Jews, at home and abroad, blamed Israel's leaders for their blindness to the possibility of Christian revenge in Lebanon. But is the rest of the world totally blameless? Would the massacres have occurred, for instance, if the U.S. Marines of the international force that "polices" the PLO's departure remained in place instead of going home two weeks earlier than had been agreed upon?

To this day, incidentally, the real killers have not been found. No serious investigation of the incidents has been mounted by President Amin Gemayel, Bashir's brother and successor. Nor have the Western media pursued the story with the intensity with which they slammed Israel during the fighting in Lebanon.

TV News Credibility

Israel was the darling of Western journalism

while it remained the underdog of Middle East politics. It only started having trouble with the media when, to paraphrase the late Golda Meir, Israel refused to die so that the world could speak well of it. This process continued in the wake of the quasi-disastrous Yom Kippur war, when Israel, out of sheer necessity, became a formidable military power fully capable of defending the country and its people, and of pursuing peace on its own terms rather than those dictated by the PLO and its masters in the Kremlin.

Outrages continue in Lebanon among the diverse ethnic and religious groupings as well as by the remaining PLO and Syrian occupation forces. Yet this is simply the world's "business as usual," not containing the same interest for the electronic media. Rather, what was of interest in 1982 was Israeli (read "Jewish") rain of destruction on the PLO, especially if this could be capsulated as Israeli destruction per se. How facile to switch "dog" and "underdog" to suit picture-board fads, while relegating PLO and Syrian massacres over a period of seven years to "never-ever land." How easy to overlook Israel's remarkably pinpointed bombing and shelling of PLO facilities—better sustained targeting in urban areas than that displayed by any other military in modern times—when images of screaming women can have more media shock value.

The true horror is when dog bites man, not vice versa, yet this is not news. It surely doesn't play as well in America's living rooms and Nielsen ratings. The electronic media's rewriting of history in the Lebanese summer of 1982, when one small long-suffering country was finally liberated from radical and Soviet control (without, by the way, the loss of a single American life), is a warning to us all that "1984" and "News-speak" may not be far off. Let the American viewer beware, especially when it is the public credibility of a U.S. ally which is at stake.

NBC'S WAR IN LEBANON: THE DISTORTING MIRROR

by Edward Alexander

Introduction

A word fitly spoken is like apples of gold in pictures of silver.—Proverbs XXII, 11.

It probably took several centuries from the time printing was invented for the belief to die out that "whatever is in print must be true." Now, in the age of television, we face a parallel danger in the widespread belief that "pictures don't lie." In fact, as I shall frequently have occasion to suggest in the following pages, pictures, like words, can and do lie, for pictures, like words, are created and manipulated by men, whose reputation for probity has been open to question since the expulsion from Eden. The injunction to "hold the mirror up to nature" sounds sensible enough until we remember that mirrors may be dirty or clean, concave or convex, cracked or whole; and that everything depends upon which portion of nature you choose to reflect, how often you reflect it, and how much you reveal of the history of the reflected images. Not the least danger of distortion in the use of the mirror is the tendency of the owner to hold

Reprinted by permission of AMERICANS FOR A SAFE ISRAEL
*(c)*1983 Americans for a Safe Israel.

it up to himself and make it into the deceiving mirror of self-love, a mirror that reflects not life but the spectator.

If, as James Billington argued in his book *Fire in the Minds of Men* (1980), the press, once known as the Fourth Estate*, has now "in many ways replaced the First [Estate], the Church," we are under the most compelling obligation to ask whether journalists are using their enormous power for good or for evil, responsibly or recklessly. Americans have long assumed that their press, unlike the British and European, will clearly distinguish between news and editorial opinion. Even in the wake of the war in Lebanon we may still take some comfort from the fact that American journalists generally lagged far behind their European and British colleagues in the art of cloaking naked partisanship in tendentious reporting. But the tendency of our television news media to flout the conventions of balance, fairness, and accuracy in the interests of political ideology is growing, not receding. NBC's disregard for these conventions (and, in the case of fairness, federal regulations) was by no means *sui generis*; but I have chosen to analyze NBC rather than its competitors because the malpractices common to the three major networks were drawn out

---

*In contitutional law, an "estate" denotes an organized class of society with a separate voice in government such as the clergy, nobility, and commons (knights and burgesses) were in Europe starting in the thirteenth century.

into extreme or radical form by NBC. Neither of the other networks, for example, allowed so complete a monopoly on the expression of editorial opinion on the war to one set of biases as NBC did in making John Chancellor its sole editorialist. (The closest NBC came to acknowledging that there might be a side to the question other than the anti-Israel one that Chancellor expressed several times a week, was on August 4. In the wake of Chancellor's intemperate outburst against "imperial Israel" on August 2, Tom Brokaw read from three letters disagreeing with Chancellor's views. But he took care that the three selected were all by people with names readily identifiable as Jewish, and added that in any case reaction to Chancellor was about evenly divided between those who agreed with him and those who did not.) NBC also outdid the other networks in its relentless insistence (e.g., on June 24, 28, and August 2, 4, 12, 13) that American public opinion was turning against Israel. Since NBC is one of the principal shapers of public opinion, this insistence (based on the flimsiest of evidence) could only be construed as a self-serving exercise. NBC was also the only network that consistently refused to acknowledge the existence of PLO censorship.

My discussion of NBC-TV's coverage of the war in Lebanon extends from the period of June 4 through August 31, and is based on videotapes of every night of evening news during that period. My observations touch on six major subjects or problems in NBC's reporting and commentary: 1) The Subject of Censorship; 2) The Question of Civilian Casualties; 3) Deliberate Falsifications; 4) The Terminology of Bias; 5) The Missing Background of the War; and 6) Selective and Tendentious Interviewing.

Finally, a distinction is in order. On this subject as on most others, generalizations about an organization cannot authoritatively render the whole truth about every individual who works for it. Not everybody who reported the Lebanon War for NBC was engaged, as Mudd, Chancellor, Brokaw, Mallory, and Reynolds appeared to be, in a private war against Israel. Whatever objections one may have to particular reports and even the surrender to shared media clichés by Bob Kur, Rick Davis, or Martin Fletcher, it would be unfair to impute to them any such will to deceive as moved many of their colleagues. These men acquitted themselves, under very trying conditions, honorably; but their efforts in the direction of seeing clearly and telling what they saw in a plain way were nearly lost in the plethora of calculated distortions that comprised NBC's overall approach to the war in Lebanon.

I. The Subject of Censorship
In Lebanon, Palestinian commanders permitted camera crews and correspondents to move freely into areas under attack, but not to photograph military tar-

282

gets hidden among civilian offices and apartments.— John Martin, ABC News.

No theme, not even that of civilian casualties, was more relentlessly pursued by NBC-TV than that of censorship: that is to say, of Israeli censorship, for censorship by Israel's adversaries was blithely accepted by NBC as an aspect of the natural order of things. The opening salvo in NBC's campaign against Israeli military censorship came on June 5 and established the pattern that would be followed throughout the summer. Jessica Savitch, introducing a report by Vic Aicken from northern Israeli "settlements and villages," sternly warns that "It's censored by the Israeli military." Aicken himself stresses at the outset of his report that he can only show pictures "allowed by the Israeli censor," and concludes the report with these words: "Vic Aicken with a censored report from northern Israel." Then Savitch, who believes in nothing so much as incessant repetition, remarks: "His report was heavily censored by the Israelis and half of the pictures he wanted to send out were cut." Then, presumably for the benefit of those viewers who can understand nothing unless it is repeated five times, NBC places next to Savitch a large placard saying "ISRAELI CENSORSHIP," at the same time that she most audibly and visibly inhales her scarcely controllable outrage at this violation of NBC's inalienable rights.*

---

*Readers interested in Miss Savitch's techniques of demagoguery applied to a wholly different subject should consult Dorothy Rabinowitz, "Lesley and Jessica: TV demagogues," *N.Y. Post,* 27 May 1983.

In the days and weeks to follow it became clear that NBC was determined to retaliate whenever possible the injury inflicted upon its "right to know" by Israeli censorship. Not only would reports from Israel and from southern Lebanon begin and end with graphic and oral references to Israeli censorship, but reporting of the war would be periodically punctuated with entire program segments devoted to the subject of Israeli censorship. Thus what might have begun as a piece of valuable information about the difficulties of reporting the war soon became a means of editorializing, almost unceasingly, against Israel. The venomous tone and compulsive repetition suggested that people at the upper echelons of NBC News had allowed their sense of outrage to determine editorial policy.

The anger was much in evidence in Roger Mudd's remarks of June 18 about Israel having censored two cassettes of interviews with PLO prisoners, and "refusing" to say why, and in the furious outburst of June 23 and 24 by Brokaw and Chancellor. Brokaw started the program of June 23 with the ritualized announcement of Israel having broken yet another cease-fire, then switched to Steve Mallory, whose voice came out of a blackened screen, against which were boldly superimposed the words: "PICTURE CENSORED." Since NBC had decided (perhaps, even from its own point of view, unwisely) that no amount of repetitious haranguing on this subject

284

can be excessive, Brokaw followed up with a separate story on the Israeli refusal to transmit pictures of injured children, damage and casualties in a Beirut neighborhood. The visual backdrop showed an Israeli flag, cassettes, and "Israeli Censorship." Then, in high dudgeon, Brokaw declared that the story had nothing to do with Israeli national security, and, in a voice dripping with sarcasm, noted that Menachem Begin had complained of "corrupt media."

The fury against Israel over the censorship spilled over on this evening into a particularly egregious distortion of facts by Roger Mudd. Trumpeting what sounds like a spectacular revelation of yet more Machiavellian skullduggery by Israel, he "reports" that this war in Lebanon has been coordinated with a "campaign" against Palestinians in "Jordan's West Bank, which is occupied by Israel." When we switch to Martin Fletcher in said "West Bank" however, we get nothing more than a reasonably sober account of Israeli troops quelling demonstrations by Arab university students in favor of the PLO. Mudd's revelation proves to be mere wind. Mudd tried a similar stunt on the following evening, June 24, in his introduction to Steve Mallory's typically sensational report of blood, chaos, filth, and fire in West Beirut, caused by the explosion of powerful carbombs of unknown origin. Since not even Mallory was about to assign the blame for these to Israel, Mudd took it upon himself to do so by insidious juxtaposition:

285

"The Reagan White House revealed today that Prime Minister Begin promised President Reagan on Monday that Israel would not try to capture Beirut. By making Israel's pledge public...the White House was bringing pressure on him to live up to it. But as we will see in a moment...sending in an army is not the only way to destroy a city. It can be shelled to death from without and within." But just in case there are viewers who do not fall into the Mudd trap, Brokaw is ready with yet another blast at Israeli censors for allowing such scenes (which might reflect unfavorably on the PLO) to be transmitted while deleting material that has nothing to do with Israel's national security. Now that its anchorman has on two consecutive nights editorialized against Israeli censorship, one might suppose that the subject has been for the moment exhausted. But no, NBC's resident sage John Chancellor must add a long, sweaty editorial on the matter.

Chancellor begins with the astounding remark that "Censorship in the Middle East is getting to be a real problem, and it sometimes makes it hard to cover a story." Chancellor did not remind his audience that Israel is the only democratic country in the Middle East, the only one in which there has always been a free press, or that censorship, ranging from authoritarian to totalitarian, and employing methods ranging from persuasion to coercion to murder, has, time out of mind, prevailed in the Middle

East. Had he done so, viewers might have wondered why Middle East censorship never became a "problem" for Chancellor and his colleagues until practiced, in the midst of a hard-fought war, by Israel. He does, in the course of his diatribe, mention that although Syria helpfully transmitted the tape that Israel had intercepted, Syria "enforces a total ban on stories about its own military." Yet Syria's far more stringent censorship is mentioned only casually and "incidentally": it does not, for Chancellor, constitute a "problem." Exactly why this should be so is not clear, especially since Syrian censorship had earlier in 1982 effectively kept television cameras away from the Syrian city of Hamma (the fifth largest in the country) while the Syrian army ruthlessly massacred, with tanks and artillery, between 15,000 and 20,000 of its own unarmed citizens, who had been guilty of refractory behavior towards the regime. Where then was Chancellor's concern for the American public's right to know, and for NBC's right to film? Was he not then, and is he not now, troubled by the "problem" that very little, if any, attention is paid by the news media to slaughters that cannot be photographed although they are known to have happened? We know that his employer, Reuven Frank, is not. For when the head of NBC news was taxed with this question, he responded with his characteristic moral tact: "There isn't interest in the Copts or the Kurds, or the massacre in Burundi...so you don't cover them." To talk of what "should" be covered is impermissible because it suggests *moral* criteria, with which his profession is unconcerned. "You cover what you think is interesting for the viewers. I can't imagine anybody getting upset about the Copts." As if it had never occurred to Mr. Frank that the absence of "coverage" explained the absence of "interest."

Although Chancellor acknowledged that Syria's censorship policy left something to be desired, he expressed no misgivings about PLO treatment of journalists and even went out of his way to remark that "There is no censorship in Beirut..." This must have come as a stunning revelation to the countless journalists who in recent years have testified to what the *Guardian* of London (one of the most fiercely anti-Israel papers in the world) called the "censorship by terror" that prevailed in Beirut, and the *Economist* named the phenomenon of "publish and perish." On February 22, 1982, John Kifner, *New York Times* correspondent in Beirut, wrote:

> To work here as a journalist is to carry fear with you as faithfully as your notebook. It is the constant knowledge that there is nothing you can do to protect yourself and that nothing has ever happened to any assassin. In this atmosphere, a journalist must often weigh when, how, and sometimes even whether, to record a story....
>
> There is a pervasive belief among the

Beirut press corps that correspondents should be extremely wary of incurring the wrath of the Syrian regime of President Hafez al-Assad.

In February 1982 Ze'ev Chafetz, then director of Israel's Government Press Office, charged that substantial segments of the western news media follow a double standard in reporting and commentary on the Arab-Israel conflict because they fear and respect Arab terror, but take for granted and abuse the freedom allowed them in Israel's open society. He explicitly charged that terror prevented critical reporting on the PLO and Syria, and that ABC's wide-ranging attack on Israel (in the program "20/20") had a causal connection with the murder in Beirut in July 1981 of Sean Tolan, ABC-TV's correspondent there. (Toolan's sin had, apparently, been his contribution to a program by Geraldo Rivera on PLO terrorism.) Chafetz also claimed that five US journalists had in 1981 been held for almost 24 hours by Palestinian Arab terrorists without the incident being reported in their newspapers for over six months. (They had been released after their lives were threatened and their employers promised not to report on the episode.)

Over a period of five years a series of threatening letters, assassination attempts, explosions, and murders by the PLO intimidated the Lebanese press to the point where, according to Edouard George, senior editor of Beirut's French language daily

L'Orion Du Jour, "not one of them dared to write or broadcast the truth." Peter Mayer-Ranke, Middle East correspondent for Germany's Springer chain of papers, said he had personally observed "self-censorship, self-restriction, and silence," by his colleagues in Beirut. Among those who, because they did not silence themselves, were silenced forever by the PLO are: Salim Lawzi, owner of the weekly *Al-Hawadit,* arrested at a PLO checkpost in July 1978 and tortured to death in the village of Aramoun, after which photos of his body were distributed among Beirut's journalists as a warning; Edouard Saeb, editor-in-chief of *L'Orion Du Jour* and local correspondent of *Le Monde,* shot to death in September 1976 while crossing Beirut's Green Line; Riadh Taha, president of the Lebanese newspaper publisher's union and part of an effort to form an anti-PLO front with Bashir Jemayel, murdered by the PLO outside the Carlton Hotel in Beirut. George listed* several foreign journalists murdered by the PLO in West Beirut between 1976 and 1981: Larry Buchman, ABC-TV cor-

---

*NBC has questioned the accuracy of George's list, claiming that not all of these journalists were killed by the PLO or Syrians. George told us in a telephone conversation that his sources were articles in his newspaper *"L'Orion du Jour"* as well as other journalistic sources in Beirut. The murder of Pfeffer has been generally acknowledged by journalists, but it is impossible for us to independently confirm the cause of the other deaths. It is well known, however, that many foreign journalists were forced to leave Beirut because of threats from the PLO. According to press reports, these included Larry Pintak of CBS, *Le Figaro*'s J. Stocklin, BBC's Tim Llewellyn and Jim Muir. Reuters correspondent Bernd Debussman was shot in the back after receiving threats from Syrian officials. *Editors.*

respondent; Mark Tryon, Free Belgium radio; Robert Pfeffer, correspondent for *Der Spiegel* and *Unita*; Italian journalists Tony Italo and Graciella Difaco; ABC correspondent Sean Toolan.

Where, during the years when these outrages were perpetrated in Beirut by the PLO, was the voice of John Chancellor and NBC to decry censorship? Why is it censorship beomes a Middle Eastern problem only when it is practiced (and hardly in a manner even remotely resembling the instances just cited) by Israel? No one with a passing acquaintance with human nature ought to have been surprised that the intimidation and terror with which the PLO censored journalists before June 1982 continued, *a fortiori*, once it came under direct attack by Israel. Countless witnesses told how PLO commanders—in the words of John Martin of ABC News—"permitted camera crews and correspondents to move freely into areas under attack, but not to photograph military targets hidden among civilian offices and apartments." In other words, the television reports coming from PLO-occupied West Beirut were indeed censored, contrary to what Chancellor alleged, and censored in such a way as to remove from sight precisely the evidence used by Israel to justify its siege. "What's more," observed the *New Republic*, "you weren't even told that you weren't seeing something important. So while television relentlessly repeated that dispatches from the Israeli side were censored by Israeli authorities, it didn't tell you of the PLO's censorship—which of course made the censorship that much more effective." Ann Medina, of the Canadian Broadcasting Corporation, showed the rare courage to film PLO censorship with a hidden camera. Her film proved, beyond any possibility of contradiction, how a PLO censor accompanied reporters in Lebanon "everywhere we go." This may help to explain the intriguing way in which *Newsweek*, in a rare burst of candor, sought to justify the "anti-Israel tone of many dispatches from the front" by disclosing that "many correspondents based in Beirut developed warm relationships with PLO leaders." Is it conceivable that fledgling reporters are taught in their journalism courses that cozy relationships with terrorist combatants afford indispensable aid in impartial reporting of wars in which those terrorists become involved? If so, perhaps they should be warned that in the business of war reporting, "warm relationships" may be a self-deceptive label for anticipatory compliance with terrorist censorship.

The extent to which television became, in the words of Ted Koppel of ABC, a war-weapon in PLO hands, even forced two of the major networks—CBS on July 9 and 12, and ABC on July 12—to acknowledge the existence of PLO censorship; only Mr. Chancellor and his colleagues at NBC maintained their stony silence on this subject. They maintained it even in the face of what an observant viewer of their own pictures might well have construed as evidence to the contrary. Thus, on June 12, just after Mallory's standard report on bombing in Beirut, we are shown several PLO fighters retreating into central Beirut. One of them points his gun menacingly at Mallory's cameraman, prompting the remark that "they *don't* like to be photographed." In advertently, NBC thus reminds us that the PLO is very much in the censorship business, but that its favored instrument for keeping camera crews from photographing military installations is the gun rather than the pen. By a peculiar coincidence, which perhaps only a Viennese doctor could satisfactorily explain, this very same film sequence was again used, with typical unscrupulousness, and without comment (or any explanation of the gross falsification involved) as part of Jack Reynolds' report of events allegedly taking place on June 29, and as a prelude to a Roger Mudd harangue against censorship—Israeli censorship, that is. By some subterranean psychological process, the fact of PLO gun censorship insinuated itself into the minds of the NBC news staff but came out to the American public as an attack on Israeli pen censorship. And wherein lay the Israelis' offense against free expression? Jack Reynolds' signoff words— "West Beirut" —were "inexplicably removed by Israeli censors." This, but not the PLO threats against reporters' lives, was yet another "problem" for Chancellor, Mudd and company.

Following the line taken by Brokaw on June 23, Chancellor in his commentary of the 24th generously allowed that "every journalist can understand when censorship is used by a government to protect the lives of its troops. But increasingly, in the Lebanese story, censorship has been used to protect Israel's image and to serve its political goals." NBC's commentators always know what is or is not relevant to Isaeli national security, for which—so it is implied—they have the gravest concern; but no other form of censorship is permissible. At least it is not permissible for Israel, for it is well known that the British blackout of television coverage of the war in the Falklands, a war that, whatever might be said in its justification by the British, could hardly be said to have been fought in the protection of British national security, did not stir Chancellor, Brokaw, and Mudd to the rage they vented whenever Israel refused to transmit film over satellite. Rarely is the arrogance which Reuven Frank recommends as the *sine qua non* for ambitious journalists so much in evidence as in NBC's lectures to Israel on its enemies in wartime. First, even the most careless viewer, watching NBC's relentless barrage of anti-Israel stories, must be struck dumb by Chancellor's temerity in saying Israeli censors won't pass stories "that make Israel look bad." Secondly, is Israel any more under a moral obligation to transmit from its Tel Aviv satellite interviews with Yasser Arafat or other PLO spokesmen than the United

294

States in World War II would have been to disseminate interviews with Hitler conducted by foreign journalists sympathetic to his "cause"?

When Reuven Frank, the president of NBC News, was asked about the vendetta his staff had carried on against Israel over the issue of military censorship, he replied that "Basically, the Israelis are treating the foreign press better than most of the other countries. We are picking on them." This is a typical reply from Mr. Frank, who is fond of parading his general cynicism, which diverts attention from his particular responsibility for NBC's misdeeds and from his own entire indifference to self-correction.

Throughout the summer, NBC continued to hammer away at Israel over the issue of censorship. Always the stress was on the political nature of Israeli censorship, sometimes qualified by a fleeting reference to Syrian censorshhip, but never any at all to PLO censorship by terror. The program of August 1 appeared at first to give some semblance of balance by using background graphics referring to Syrian censorship in Rick Davis' report from East Beirut, and background graphics referring to Israeli censorship when John Hart appeared before a map of Lebanon, and informed his viewers that during the preceding eight weeks many scenes had been "missing in the war reports from Lebanon...Reports from West Beirut sent from Syria, subject to Syrian censorship; reports from East Beirut sent from Israel are restricted by Israeli censors." But all this was merely prelude to yet another report, very detailed, on Israeli censorship, with the Syrians forgotten altogether. Bob Kur, a far more scrupulous journalist than Chancellor, made some attempt to explain Israel's rationale for what Kur condemned as "purely political" censorship: "Israel does not want to generate sympathy for the PLO or, some say, with good reason, provide a stage for its spokesmen." Kur also admitted that "Israeli censors never tried to hide the damage in southern Lebanon, nor did Israel try to hide its unprecedented anti-war demonstrations," and that "a degree of censorship during wartime is not unusual for any country, and some have been more restrictive than Israel." But any credit that might redound to Israel from these acknowledgements was quickly erased by Kur's conclusion that there was so much criticism from abroad of Israel censorship that "Israel could not easily have increased censorship." In other words, here as in all other respects, Israel was just as mischievous as the world allowed it to be. Why "the world" allows Israel's adversaries to be so much more mischievous, with impunity, Kur did not bother to explain. Perhaps the answer is, as R. Emmett Tyrrell, editor of *The American Spectator,* alleged: "Not all our allies are...diabolized. The diabolizing comes down only on those who actually oppose America's enemies."

II. The Question of Civilian Casualties:
   "No Military Targets Here"

Israel, by aiding Lebanese Christians since 1975, has saved more civilian lives than have been lost in this war. But a television screen is easy to fill... Television in war is bound to suggest more generalized destruction than has occurred. Furthermore, had there been television at Antietam on America's bloodiest day (Sept. 17, 1862), this would be two nations. Americans then lived closer to the jagged edges of life, but even they might have preferred disunion to the price of union, had they seen the price, in color in their homes in the evening.—
George Will, *Newsweek*, August 2, 1982

On August 2, a photogaph, published throughout the world, showed what was described as a severely burned baby girl, with her arms amputated, who had been wounded during an Israeli bombardment in West Beirut. The photograph came to symbolize Israel's allegedly indiscriminate bombing of civilians. On August 14, NBC's Fred Francis reported Secretary of State George Shultz's endorsement of Ronald Reagan's view that the "symbol of this war" was this same "picture of a baby with its arms shot off." It was a symbol in more ways than Reagan and Shultz understood, for by August 20 it had been conclusively proved that the photograph had been deliberately misrepresented in the news media in order to smear Israel. Doctors who suspected the veracity of the photograph sent a special team to find the baby, and discovered it to be a healthy boy (Reagan, Shultz, and NBC even had the sex wrong) with a broken left arm still in a cast, but otherwise healthy and intact. He was released from the Beirut hospital five days after his picture as a moribund girl made front pages around the world. NBC did not think it worthwhile, after Francis had reported the "story," to correct the misrepresentation, or, for that matter, to correct the impression given by the complementary supporting story of the August 14 news, by Steve Delaney in Beirut. This told of a West Beirut home for retarded children in which—allegedly as a result of frequent Israeli shelling—the children were found starving, and lying in their own excrement. Mother Teresa was photographed carrying one of the skeletal children from the home. But Mother Teresa, unbeknownst to NBC viewers, said in a later television broadcast that the children had been kept in these wretched conditions for a very long time, and that those responsible for the conditions, since long before the Israelis came, not only got off scot-free, but had the additional satisfaction of seeing their hapless victims used for their own propaganda purposes.

The doctored photograph and the stage-managed hospital visit of Mother Teresa were thus "symbolic" of the uncontrollable desire of many in the news media to depict Israel as a brutal power intent mainly on the destruction of Palestinian Arab civilians. That civilians were uprooted, injured, and killed in this war, as in all wars, no one can doubt; but they were not up-

298

rooted, injured, and killed to anything like the extent or with anything like the callous indifference or evil intent alleged by the journalists, NBC's reporters foremost among them.

Almost from the outset of the war, NBC's field reporter in Beirut, Steve Mallory, made it his special duty to insist, day in and day out, that Israeli bombing raids did not merely cause civilian casualties as a by-product of military missions, but were directed at civilian targets and areas. On June 4 Mallory reported the Israeli attack on a sports stadium in southern Beirut used by the PLO as an arms depot; the attack, said Mallory, was "deadly accurate" and "officials said most of the casualties were civilians." Who these helpful "officials" were Mallory did not say. On June 5 he reported the Israeli bombing of "a school bus: 15 died in the bus." He thus conveyed the impression to his innocent audience that those inside the bus were school children. In fact, nearly every other report on the incident said that the bus was not a schoolbus, and that its occupants were adults, not children. Some reports, crediting PLO claims, identified the men as construction workers, but Mallory suppressed even this half-truth lest it dilute the image of an Israeli massacre of young innocents. As for the larger attack on the "major coastal highway" linking Beirut to Southern Lebanon, Mallory claimed that "Bystanders asked, 'Why? No military positions here.'" On June 11, Mallory reported that "As the cease-fire was taking effect, Israeli warplanes streaked over Beirut. One dropped a bomb on a predominantly Moslem side of the city, hitting a civilian area. There are no military targets here." On June 12, Mallory reported crews "looking for casualties or survivors of yesterday's Israeli bombing of civilian areas of central Beirut." On June 17, Mallory described Israel's attack on Beirut International Airport and then sounded his standard refrain: "no military positions here." It was perhaps at this point that those viewers of NBC who had ever been in a war, or read about one, or been endowed with even the most modest portion of common sense, must have wondered whether there was anything that Steve Mallory did consider a military target, since he had already ruled out major airports and highways (so long as they were under Arab control). No matter how often he reported on Israeli attacks, it was the identical story. June 21: "An Israeli round hit...in Central Beirut— primarily a civilian area" (and to show just how "civilian" it is, NBC follows the pictures of Israeli shelling with one of Arafat dandling a baby); June 25: "no military positions here" (residential area of West Beirut); June 26: "Most casualties were civilians"; June 28: "It's been...*civilians* who've lost the most."

The pattern of reporting the war from West Beirut established by Mallory was continued by Jack Reynolds, with the addition of strongly tainted political rhetoric and lurid emotionalism. On July 9, one

of the rare occasions when NBC allowed that somebody else besides the Israelis was firing, Reynolds
noted that when "the Israelis responded—people
were hit. On July 10 he gave his typically florid account of the day's shelling, followed by invocation of
the Mallory refrain: "There are no Palestinian fighters here, they said." In this instance, "here" was the
area of the foreign embassies, an area which published reconnaissance photos showed to be replete with
tanks, mortars, heavy machine guns, and anti-aircraft positions; yet NBC saw no need for correction,
retraction, or apology.

James Compton, who replaced Mallory in West
Beirut in mid-summer, seemed torn between repetition of the Mallory-Reynolds formula and glimmer-
ings of awareness of what virtually every disinterested
observer of the PLO "defense" strategy had known
for many years: namely, that the PLO always places
its troops and its weapons in and around schools,
hospitals, and apartment houses, deliberately seeking
to maximize civilian casualties in the event of an Israeli attack. (In many cases, PLO fighters hid behind
rows of women and children when firing on Israeli
forces.) As David Shipler wrote in *The New York
Times* of July 25:

> The P.L.O. was not on a campaign to win
> friends among the Lebanese. Its thrust was
> military. The huge sums of money the
> P.L.O. received from Saudi Arabia and

301

other Arab countries seems to have been
spent primarily on weapons and ammunition, which were placed strategically in
densely populated civilian areas in the hope
that this would either deter Israeli attacks
or exact a price from Israel in world opinion for killing civilians. Towns and camps
were turned into vast armories as crates of
ammunition were stacked in underground
shelters and antiaircraft guns were em-
placed in schoolyards, among apartment
houses, next to churches and hospitals.
The remains could be seen after the fighting, and Palestinians and Lebanese can still
point out the sites.

Whether from ignorance, obtuseness, or craven-
ness, Mallory and Reynolds failed to mention any of
this while expressing continuing wonderment and
outrage at Israel's bombing of what they confidently
declared to be "civilian" targets.

Compton began in the established NBC style.
On July 27 he reported a hit on an apartment house
"at least a mile from any Palestinian military concentration." On July 29 he reported on a hospital hit by
six artillery shells because Israel was "trying to get at
an already-destroyed tank that sits nearby." On
August 1, however, complications arose. As usual, it
is alleged that Israeli "artillery (shells) fell in a seemingly random way in congested central neighbor-

hoods," yet we are also told that "whole neighborhoods that held concentrations of Palestinian forces have now been reduced to rubble by the Israeli bombing." This must have come as something of a shock to viewers who had been assured, by Mallory and Reynolds, for week after week, in the wake of Israeli shelling of these very neighborhoods, that "there are no military targets here." Then, in yet another paradoxical turn, Compton remarks on "the assumption here...that the PLO forces will now pull back into neighborhoods that hold concentrations of Lebanese civilians, forcing the Israelis to come after them in door-to-door fighting. . . ." On August 5 he was back to the formulaic post-bombing refrain—"We could not find any Palestinian military targets"—but followed it with an apparently contradictory reference to the "tragic" situation in which PLO fighters have moved out of "camps" and into "civilian" neighborhoods, inviting Israelis "to come and get them."

Not all of the confusion here is innocent. At no point did NBC ever bother to inform its viewers of what this little word "camp" may mean in the Lebanese context. In the context of the phrase "refugee camp" it evokes the image of post-war DP camps and the miserable hovels in which the first wave of "displaced persons" the world over takes refuge. But very few PLO camps fit into that description. What NBC referred to as "PLO camps" should have been called "armed bases," which were additionally "protected" by maintaining the close presence of Palestinian Arab civilians and their families. They were also, as *The Times* of London reported on August 21, "military training camps:" "members of the Italian Red Brigades and the West German Baader-Meinhof gang were trained at the so-called 'European base' at the Shatila refugee camp in Beirut. The camp is one of those subject to recent heavy Israeli bombardment." Many of the "refugee camps" were in reality whole urban neighborhoods, with highrise apartment buildings, and not a tent or mud-hut in sight. It was as if Mallory, Reynolds, and Compton were to have called General Custer's Indian-fighting camps, or the Wild West's Fort Bravo, "trading posts." This became abundantly clear, even despite what might be called NBC's own censorship system, on August 11, when Compton reported Israeli raids on the refugee camps. A woman resident, sounding very much as if she'd been coached by Steve Mallory, steps forward to express the predictable denial: "there are no fighters here." But James Compton, to his credit, declares that this isn't the whole truth, for no sooner had she spoken than three PLO fighters emerged from hiding: "the truth is the Palestinian forces are mingled with civilians everywhere in this refugee camp," a truth it took NBC ten weeks to divulge.

The false testimony of this Palestinian Arab woman, testimony of precisely the kind so eagerly sought after, and so uncritically regurgitated by Mallory and Reynolds week after week, should make us pause to re-

304

flect on just how innocent are the "innocent" adult civilians injured in bombing raids on PLO concentrations. The PLO constitution, or "National Covenant," spells out, in 33 variations on a single theme, its members' commitment to the destruction of the state of Israel. No matter how diligently certain journalists seek to deceive themselves and others on this fundamental point, every Palestinian Arab is aware of it and no Palestinian Arab bothers to deny it except when whispering into the ears of journalists in cafes. Palestinian Arabs in Lebanon are not innocent of the PLO's merciless plans and procedures for the erasure of Israel from the map. How could they be, when they saw the wholesale deployment of PLO armaments in houses, and hospital grounds? The degree of culpability of a person who harbors a killer is not the same as that of the killer; but it is not the same as innocence either. Even in the "normal" circumstances of war, it has traditionally been assumed that the immunity of noncombatants must be qualified if military operations are to be made possible at all. Should the fact that the PLO went to such lengths to mingle itself with the civilian population have made it as immune to attack by Israel as it made it immune to attack by the reporters at NBC?

Chancellor, reflecting and then magnifying the reactions of NBC's Beirut reporters, consistently damned Israel's siege of Beirut as exacting "a terrible human... cost" (June 7), "savage" (August 2), "horrifying" and "brutal" (August 5), and "inhuman" (August 6). Yet there is abundant evidence that Israel made greater, not lesser, efforts than most attacking armies to avoid injuring civilians, and increased its own casualties by doing so. Robert Tucker, professor of International Relations at Johns Hopkins University and a careful observer of modern warfare, has stated that "The places attacked were almost invariably known or long-suspected PLO military positions. Civilian casualties were incurred in the immediate vicinity of such objectives. Moreover, from all that is known, these casualties were of an incidence to be expected when an attacking force is taking even more than reasonable precautions to spare the civilian population from injury." He also noted that even the severest bombardments of the war, those of August 4 and 12, resulted in civilian casualties which, even if we accept the figures given out by PLO officials—not famous for their probity in such matters—"bear no real comparison in their magnitude with the indiscriminate bombings of cities in World War II" and "compare quite favorably with measures taken by American forces against civilian centers in the Korean and Vietnam wars." On August 12, NBC reported thousands of tons of bombs dropped on West Beirut. But the military historian U.S. Colonel Trevor N. Dupuy, Retired, stated that "on that day I spent about five hours observing this bombardment. During that time, it was apparent from my observation that no more than 150 bombs, probably 200 to 500 kilograms each, were dropped on Beirut. . . . To any veteran who has been under air or artillery attack in 'normal' combat situations, this was relatively modest harassment.''

The truth of the matter, of course, is that for those who articulate NBC's foreign policy *any* damage wrought by Israeli air attack in Lebanon would have been deemed disproportionate in relation to the value of Israel's enterprise, for it is NBC doctrine that Israel (unlike Britain, for example) may not go to war unless its very existence is at stake. Former Secretary of State Henry Kissinger wrote on June 22 about the war that ''No sovereign state can tolerate indefinitely the buildup along its borders of a military force dedicated to its destruction, and proceeding by periodical shellings and raids.'' But on August 6 Chancellor said that although Israel might have had a ''genuine'' concern about PLO actions from Lebanon, it was in ''no mortal danger'' and therefore had no right to go to war. NBC also laid it down from the outset that, whatever Israel or the Lebanese people might claim to the contrary, the sending of Israeli military forces across the Lebanese border was an invasion by what Chancellor on August 2 called ''an imperial Israel which is solving its problems in someone else's country.'' The notion that Israel entered Lebanon, as the allies entered France in World War II, to liberate the country from a brutal conquering regime received no countenance from NBC's policy-makers.

When people in Christian neighborhoods of Beirut had the temerity to inform Steve Mallory (June 15 broadcast) that they were happy to see the Israelis arrive, he heaped scorn on those who "welcome the invaders as liberators." Clearly, it is the reporters and not the inhabitants of Lebanon—after all, they just happen to live there, and are not "Palestinians"— who are entrusted with the task of deciding whether the Israelis are invaders or liberators. No wonder that one journalist, shocked by the behavior of many of his colleagues in Lebanon, expressed the view that not the Jews but the journalists consider themselves the chosen people.

III. Deliberate Falsifications

If the reporter has poisoned our imagination by his version of the truth, he brings us back to reality by his lies.—Karl Kraus

The propaganda battle against Israel during the Lebanon war began with the invention by the PLO of the figures of "600,000 homeless civilians" and 10,000 civilians killed in the portion of southern Lebanon taken by Israel. On June 10, Roger Mudd reported that "the Red Crescent, which is Lebanon's Red Cross, is quoted as estimating that more than 10,000 civilians have been killed or wounded since Friday." This statement did not merely transmit a wildly exaggerated figure, it contained a double falsification. The Red Crescent is *not* Lebanon's Red

Cross but a branch of the PLO, something any conscientious reporter would have known and said; and
—a fact that Roger Mudd chose not to share with his
audience—the Palestinian Red Crescent organization
is headed by Yasser Arafat's brother, Fathi Arafat.
Although on June 16 John Chancellor announced
that "The Red Cross said today that approximately
300,000 may have been made homeless," Jessica
Savitch on June 19 proclaimed that favored PLO figure of 600,000 without going to the trouble of invent-
ing a "source" for the figure: "It is now estimated
that 600,000 refugees in south Lebanon are without
sufficient food and medical supplies." The real Red
Cross had on June 18 already refused to endorse the
600,000 figure, but this did not trouble the intrepid
Jessica Savitch, any more than she was troubled by
the fact that her colleague Bob Kur had on June 17
said that 70,000 had been left homeless by the war.

The figures that NBC disseminated so eagerly
were of course ludicrous. 600,000 refugees amounted
to more than the total population of southern Lebanon under Israeli control. If, as was alleged by the
PLO and its publicity agents in the news media,
10,000 had been killed, primarily in Tyre and Sidon, it
seemed odd that the Mayor of Tyre reported to *The
New York Times* that only 62 persons had died there,
while the Bishop of Tyre said only 50 civilians had
been buried as a result of the war operations. The official figures released by the local authorities in Sidon

indicate that about 100 were killed. In his story of July 15 in *The New York Times,* David Shipler (certainly no great friend of Israel) said that "it is clear to anyone who has traveled in southern Lebanon, as many journalists and relief workers now have, that the original figures of 10,000 dead and 600,000 homeless, reported by correspondents... during the first week of the war, were extreme exaggerations." When he was asked why NBC had knowingly disseminated these PLO-invented fabrications, Israel Bureau Chief Paul Miller replied petulantly that it is "not the job of the media not to report the figures" bandied about by various parties, so long as the sources of the figures are also given. We have already seen how scrupulous Roger Mudd and Jessica Savitch were in identifying their "sources." What Paul Miller did not even attempt to explain was how his reporters could have been so ignorant of the country they were covering as to blithely pass on a figure of 600,000 refugees for an area whose total population, the vast majority of whom never left their homes, was less than 500,000; or so contemptuous of their audience that even after it became, as Shipler wrote, "clear to anyone who has traveled in southern Lebanon" that the original figures were lies, they never retracted the figures or corrected them. In fact, they gave PLO supporters every opportunity to recite these bogus figures (see, e.g., Steve Delaney's report of June 28 and Jack Reynolds' of July 2) without their accuracy being challenged.

310

The figure of 600,000, a patent absurdity on the face of it, was irresistibly attractive to journalists hostile to Israel for the same reason that it was invented by the Arabs in the first place: it began with a 6 and facilitated the licentious equation of 600,000 Palestinian Arabs with the 6 million Jews who had been murdered by Hitler. At least since 1967 the PLO has made it a consistent practice to ride on the coattails of the Jewish experience of discrimination, exile, oppression, and murder by stealing the Holocaust from the Jews, presenting themselves as the "Jews" of the Middle East and the Israelis as their Nazi oppressors. Although NBC went to nothing like the lengths of von Hoffman, Cockburn, Oliphant, and other inhabitants of the dirtier sections of Grub Street in alleging that Israelis were doing to Palestinian Arabs what Nazis had done to Jews and others, their reports and commentaries were certainly tainted by this practice. John Chancellor, musing autobiographically on the bombing of August 2, confessed that he "kept thinking yesterday of the bombing of Madrid during the Spanish Civil War." ("Was he there at the time?" asked Frank Gervasi. "The year of the bombing of Madrid by the Junkers 52s of Hitler's burgeoning *Luftwaffe* was 1936, when John was 12 or 13 years old.") James Compton artfully described the Israelis (July 30) as "prepared to force a final military solution." Steve Mallory was always ready at hand when Yasser Arafat

311

had something to say about Beirut's being the Arabs' "Stalingrad," and Jack Reynolds— true to form— went a step further by endorsing the equation (June 29).

Reynolds had already demonstrated his high respect for historical accuracy on June 13 in a report on the rush to volunteer for action among Palestinian Arabs in Jordan, where they have, according to Reynolds, been living in camps "since Israel took over Palestine in 1948." What inflames these would-be fighters "is inevitable. . . anger at the Israelis who pushed them out of Palestine." Not even Reynolds' most tendentious colleagues, during three months of broadcasting the war, had the temerity to go quite this far; but Reynolds is NBC's most devout believer in Oscar Wilde's dictum that "the one duty we owe to history is to re-write it."

By 1948 four-fifths of the territory known as Palestine under the British Mandate was already under Arab control, in the country known as Jordan. The United Nations had voted to partition the remaining section—western Palestine—into two countries, one Jewish, one Arab. Israel recognized the Arab part as the Palestinian Arab state, but no Arab country did or ever has done so. Instead, the Arab countries declared war on the Jewish state and attempted to destroy it. The attempt was unsuccessful, but Jordan did succeed in occupying eastern Jerusalem, which the United Nations had intended to be an "internationalized" city. And this was how Israel "took over Palestine in 1948." Reynolds' version of why many Arabs left Palestine in 1948 is exactly the PLO version, but no reputable historian would endorse it. Even the anti-Zionist historian Christopher Sykes wrote that "there is no evidence of a long-standing and agreed Jewish policy to evict the settled population; on the contrary in the first half of 1948 there is considerable evidence that the Jews tried to prevent the fight. . . When the war was over, Arab journalists and broadcasters asserted on several occasions that the exodus was a planned Arab maneuver the main object being to clear the land and thus give freedom of action to the invading armies." *(Cross Roads to Israel)* It is anticlimactic to note that, having uttered these boldfaced lies, Reynolds also failed to ask, as any normally curious reporter would have done, why these refugees of 1948 have for 35 years been kept in such wretched conditions by their brother Arabs. Even John Chancellor was willing to admit (August 9) that "when Arabs attacked Israelis they [refugees] ran away" and that their present plight was more the fault of the Arab countries than of Israel. To anyone who wonders why Jack Reynolds' every broadcast from Lebanon was a condemnation of Israel and an exoneration of the PLO, the broadcast of June 13 is a revelation, the key to an enigma: PLO "anger" at Israel is, according to Reynoldsian psychology, "inevitable"; if it is inevitable, then no moral blame can possibly be attached to the actions

313

that it brings in its wake, however merciless and bloody they may be.

As this discrepancy between Chancellor and Reynolds suggests, the re-writing of history appears to be a freelance affair at NBC; reporters are free to distort as they like, so long as what they like is not what Israel likes. Roger Mudd, for example, has taken it upon himself to refuse recognition of Jerusalem as Israel's capital city. NBC's staff is in general chary of locating events in Jerusalem which happen merely to have taken place there. Paul Miller and Martin Fletcher are usually "in Tel Aviv" even when the scenes they describe and the stories they narrate are recognized to be in Jerusalem by anyone who has ever been there (June 6, 7, July 25, 30, etc.). But at least they can justify this practice by claiming that they are transmitting their reports from a Tel Aviv office. With Roger Mudd, however, we are dealing either with spectacular ignorance or the attempt to distort facts to fit policy. On June 29, Bob Kur reported on a debate in Israel's Knesset, which meets in Jerusalem, and concluded with "Bob Kur, from the Israeli Knesset," specifying no location. Roger Mudd promptly helped out by locating it in Tel Aviv, saying "While Tel Aviv Debates, Beirut Waits." On July 19 he announced that the "focus of the Middle Eastern crisis shifted from Tel Aviv and Beirut to Washington today." The Lebanese seat of government is Beirut, the American seat of government is Washington, and the Israel seat of government is Jerusalem. Why then Tel Aviv? On August 5 Mudd introduced Jim Bitterman, reporting "from Israel's capital"; perhaps by this time somebody at NBC had told Mudd that it was unseemly to adjust geography so blatantly to fit bias, but that if he felt so strongly about the matter, he should rest content with blank ambiguity. (When Shakespeare's Macduff asked his countryman Ross, upon the latter's return to England, "Stands Scotland where it did" was he really worrying about his country's suffering or fearful that some eleventh century Roger Mudd had relocated Caledonia in Wales?) Although NBC did not go so far as explicitly to consign Jerusalem to the rule of those who are daily proclaiming their resolve to "liberate" the city, it did refer over and over again (see Savitch, 31 July, or Mudd, 23 June) to "Jordan's West Bank" and it is hardly a secret that the city of Jerusalem is included in the Arab definition of "West Bank." It was as if NBC had decided, on its own, to assign sovereignty over this disputed area to the country that invaded it in 1948, a sovereignty not even Arab nations have ever granted to Jordan.

Some observers believe that such falsifications result from ignorance. Thus Martin Peretz of *The New Republic* wrote in October 1981 that "NBC can't persuade its 250 affiliates to air one hour of network news instead of the present half-hour. Thirty minutes is preferable to sixty, since TV news comes to

315

us from men and women who know little and understand even less. But if you haven't seen them improvise, you have not really seen ignorance in full flower.'' This seems to me an overly charitable interpretation. Those who believe that Roger Mudd, for example, blundered innocently into his falsifications and misrepresentations should pay particular attention to the broadcast of July 2, a typical example of NBC's double standard in conveying statistics to the unwary viewer. A Lebanese American doctor who gained international fame for her fiery flow of anti-Israel rhetoric in interviews by most television reporters in Beirut recites to Jack Reynolds the by now standardized PLO estimates of civilian deaths (those "extreme exaggerations" referred to in *The New York Times*) while the respectful reporter obediently nods his head in agreement. Mudd, entering the ring to deliver the second part of the regular NBC one-two punch against Israel, then announces:

> Prime Minister Begin claims the Israeli army has picked up 66 children aged 12 to 13 and armed with submachineguns who were recruited into the PLO. . . . Later, however, a spokesman for Begin said that he had made a mistake and read from the wrong paper, and that the correct number was either two or twenty-two child soldiers.

NBC, suddenly very conscientious in sifting the evidence for statistical claims, was doing its best to suggest that Begin was a liar or a fool. Nevertheless, in subsequent days it became irresistibly clear that, as *The New York Times* reported on July 25: "An extensive PLO conscription program drafted Palestinian boys as young as 12 and mobilized all male students for one to three months of duty a year, according to some Palestinians. During the invasion, Israeli soldiers said they found themselves in combat with 12-year and 13-year-olds shooting rocket-propelled grenades. More than 200 youngsters from 12 to 15 were captured and have been released. The PLO's draft apparently stirred resentment, for Rima Shabb told of checkpoints being set up to catch young Palestinians who were trying to run away. . . . Sister Alisse Araigi, headmistress of a Maronite school in Nabatiye, said, "Families came to us and asked for certificates that children were sick and couldn't be drafted." That Begin's statement of July 2 was essentially true, and that he had erred on the side of caution rather than exaggeration was a fact rigorously concealed from NBC viewers. Showing up Menachem Begin clearly had a higher priority for NBC News than telling the truth about the PLO's short and ready way of exploiting Arab children.

As if this were not enough skulduggery for one evening, NBC also gave an account of "a growing feeling of anti-Americanism" in West Beirut because of injury caused by U.S.-made cluster bombs and shells, dutifully displayed for the cameras. But, as

Joshua Juravchik pointed out in *Policy Review* (Winter 1983), NBC neglected to point out that the "story" was written from a PLO press conference at which the shells were displayed. "In contrast, one of the other networks ran the same footage with the simple announcement that it was a PLO press conference. There was a remarkabe contrast between the abundant cooperation that NBC gave to this PLO public relations effort and the deep skepticism that it showed to Israel's slightly bungled public relations effort the same night." (Another aspect of the cluster bomb"story" not made public by NBC is that its chief non-Arab disseminator was Franklin Lamb, a certified fraud with a criminal record who had earlier invented out of whole cloth the horror story about the Israeli "vacuum bomb," a type of bomb that does not exist.)

NBC was often so eager to impute monstrous, destructive evil to Israel that it disregarded even the visual evidence it placed on the screen and so fell into ludicrous self-contradiction. On July 5 Reynolds reported Beirut "slowly reduced to rubble" and said that "almost all the civilians here have fled" except the few who had no place else to go. Yet on July 6, one day later, because he is eager to unify his report under the heading "amazing resiliency" of the people in West Beirut, Jack Reynolds shows Beirut returning "to its own sense of normalcy [sic]." By July 8 Reynolds had effected a miraculous transformation and resurrection of a city that three days earlier was little but "rubble." "Almost overnight," he exclaims, West Beirut has begun to change for the better and things look fine now. People are crowding into supermarkets. On July 9 Reynolds continued his rapid repopulation and rebuilding, but not without some uneasy suspicion that some viewers might wonder whether total evacuation and nearly total destruction can be fleeting temporary phenomena. He therefore hastens to explain that "parts of West Beirut are still deserted and destroyed." (!) Reynolds' antics provide a shocking example not merely of how selective camerawork can be used to support virtually any assertion, but of how journalists can persuade themselves that destruction is an arbitrary invention of the camera, and that cities can be emptied and filled, destroyed and resurrected, by tendentious reporters more readily than by the mightiest historical forces or the most powerful machines.

NBC repeated the same cycle at the end of the month. On July 31 Jessica Savitch, with characteristic hyperbole, says "You've got to wonder what is left in West Beirut to be destroyed." If the photographs of Beirut that flashed across the screen two minutes later, showing a city essentially intact, did not raise several million eyebrows, then surely John Chancellor's commentary of August 2 must have done so. For Chancellor speaks against a background showing a majestic city of brightly shining high-rise buildings stretching as far as the eye can see. Apparently, NBC's reporters, by a judicious turn of phrase and an opportunistic direction of the camera, can destroy and restore cities at will. Whether they can also restore our confidence in their honesty, having first destroyed it by such unscrupulousness of statement and slight of hand methods, remains to be seen.

IV. The Terminology of Bias

And let us bathe our hands in. . . blood / Up to the elbows, and besmear our swords. / Then we walk forth, even to the market place, / And waving our red weapons o'er our heads, / Let's all cry "Peace, freedom, and liberty!"—Julius Caesar, *III, i, 106–110.*

More pervasive, more effective, and more insidious as an instrument of persuasion than outright attack upon an object of the journalist's dislike is the repeated use of biased and highly charged language. As the English novelist Arnold Bennett once wrote: "Journalists say a thing that they know isn't true, in the hope that if they keep on saying it long enough it *will* be true."

A listener attuned to the subtleties of language could recognize in the early days of June the tendentious drift of NBC reporting. Mudd began by referring (on June 4 and again on June 7) to Israeli action taken after the shooting of Ambassador Argov in London as "an eye for an eye and a tooth for a tooth," thereby implying not merely that Israeli ac-

320

tion against terrorist bases was taken solely in response to the shooting, but that it was morally equivalent to it, and that the whole nasty business was an atavistic irruption into the modern, civilized world of unredeemed, "Old Testament" Jewish ferocity. References to PLO shelling of Nahariya on June 4 and 7 depicted it as a "settlement south of the Lebanese border." Nahariya is a town 50 years old; one might as well refer to Bellingham, Washington as a "settlement" because it is south of the Canadian border. The choice of this ludicrous label is not innocent error, for it has the effect of suggesting that Nahariya and other northern Israel towns that come under PLO fire share the questionable and disputed status of the "settlements" in Judea and Samaria (the "West Bank") of which Americans have heard so much (and none of it good) in recent years.

On June 6 Paul Miller referred to the approximately 40,000 Syrian troops in Lebanon as the "Syrian peacekeeping army in Lebanon," an expression Senator Daniel Moynihan called "an Orwellian triumph." On June 7 NBC referred to the "PLO coastal town of Sidon," but by June 26 it had become "Israeli-occupied Sidon." In fact, no sooner did Israeli troops take over an area than it was referred to as "Israeli occupied Lebanon" (thus Martin Fletcher in Tyre on June 19). At no point in its three months of covering the war did NBC find it necessary to inform its viewers that Syria, in addition to having

321

had those 40,000 troops occupying half of Lebanon, including half of Beirut, for seven years, has never in its history had an ambassador in Beirut because it does not recognize Lebanon as a sovereign country but considers it part of Syria. Whereas Syria's troops, which had made very substantial contributions, through savage shelling of Christian population centers, to the figure of 100,000 people killed in Lebanon between 1975 and 1982, are for NBC a "peacekeeping army," Israel's soldiers are part of a "war machine" (Mallory, June 15, Brokaw, June 16) representing "a warrior state" (Chancellor, June 16).

NBC developed certain fixed epithets which it applied throughout the war with a mechanical illogic and unsuitableness far exceeding anything that we find in Homer. Its reporters attached the label "moderate" to Saudi Arabia, for example, so regularly that many Americans watching NBC must have come to think it a geographical term. On June 13 John Hart said that despite King Khaled's death no change was to be expected in Saudi Arabia's "reliable" supply of oil and "stable" prices, and Marvin Kalb prognosticated that the "Saudis may now encourage moderation in Lebanon." On June 14 Paul Miller reported the Mubarak-Fahd meeting as one of "moderate Arab states," adding that Fahd is "known for his peace proposal to recognize Israel" (a disingenuous piece of puffery which disguises the fact that Fahd's proposal did not mention recognition of Israel at all).

On June 27 Miller was finding more evidence in London of Saudi moderation and desire for "diplomatic solution" in Lebanon. On July 16 Chancellor expressed fear that Iran might turn its guns "on its moderate Arab neighbors." These endless hymns of praise sung by NBC to Saudi moderation may have gone far to make NBC's viewers forget that this is the same Saudi Arabia that consistently advocates *"jihad"* (holy war) against Israel; that massively supports the PLO; that holds the oil cartel together; that practices public beheadings; that rejected the Camp David accords, the Reagan peace plan, and the Lebanese-Israeli accord worked out by the United States in 1983. Nevertheless, it is an article of faith at NBC that King Fahd is always busily working behind the scenes for "moderation" and peace.

Jordan's King Hussein had his "moderation" credentials and label conferred upon him by NBC and most of the news media long ago, but it seems to have taken the Lebanese war for NBC to transform Yasser Arafat himself into a moderate. Although Jillian Becker, the English writer on terrorism whose study of the Baader-Meinhof gang *(Hitler's Children)* gained world renown, has said that "to speak of international terrorism without mentioning the PLO would be like describing the circulation of the blood without mentioning the heart," nobody at NBC dared to use the word "terrorist" in connection with Arafat and the PLO. It was as if nobody at NBC had been looking when the PLO murdered Israel's Olympic athletes (1972) or invented the fine art of hijacking by blowing up all 47 passengers in a Swissair plane (1970), or slaughtered Christian pilgrims arriving at Tel Aviv airport from Puerto Rico (1972), or murdered the U.S. ambassador in Khartoum (1973), and the Egyptian diplomat in Ankara (1979), or attacked the kibbutz nursery of Misgav Am (1980). An organized ignorance or else a collective amnesia seemed to have taken hold of Reuven Frank's staff, so that none of the hundreds of outrages committed by Yasser Arafat's organization against innocent human beings of every nationality (including the Arab nationality) could be allowed to cast the slightest shadow over NBC's idyllic picture of "guerrillas" fighting for their homeland and freedom and (this above all) "honor" in Lebanon.

On June 20 Steve Mallory reported that Arafat was "trying to work out a compromise peace settlement." On June 22 Chancellor worries solemnly over the danger that as a result of Begin's "success" in Washington Arafat "will lose out to the extremists." (This is said by Chancellor against the background of NBC's picture, already used on the previous day, of Arafat kissing a baby.) NBC's reporters not only insisted on the term "guerrilla" and refrained from using the term "terrorist" for Arafat and the PLO; they were forever suggesting the bias, if not downright bigotry, of those who did call them terrorists.

324

Judy Woodruff reported from Washington on July 12 (on the basis of evidence yet to be uncovered) that the administration was threatening to deal directly with the PLO, "which *Israel* considers a terrorist organization." Tom Brokaw, interviewing Israeli Foreign Minister Shamir on August 6, refers to "the PLO, or the terrorists as *you* call them." In a later report, August 16, Brokaw allowed by implication that some members of the PLO might be less devoted to moderation than Arafat when he said that "even hardline factions of the PLO are willing to leave."

Whereas NBC classified Arab nations and the various factions of the PLO according to their greater or lesser moderation, Israelis were classified ornithologically, as hawks or (less frequently) doves. Typical was James Compton's (July 17) reference to Ariel Sharon as popular with the "hawky sector of Israeli society." For Roger Mudd even this epithet was not strong enough: on June 9 he averred that "Israel's decision to go after the Syrian missiles undoubtedly means that superhawks are now in the ascendancy in Tel Aviv" (to which city, we recall, Mudd had moved Israel's seat of government). Since nearly all Israeli factions in and out of government were in agreement on the necessity to destroy these missiles, we must conclude that Israel is a society made up of these predatory aggressors, an impression frequently reinforced by NBC's automatic references to "Israel's aggressiveness" (Brokaw, August 12).

325

The gentlemanly reticence about using the term "terrorist" when Yasser Arafat and the PLO came into view naturally disappeared altogether when NBC went after Israeli leaders. On July 19 Martin Fletcher reported on documents Israelis captured in Lebanese camps, several of which "Israel hopes" will show that the PLO was the center of internationally supported terrorism. But John Chancellor, determined that NBC's viewers will remember who is the *real* terrorist in the Middle East, introduces, in the midst of a commentary having nothing to do with the war at all, the following: "Menachem Begin, a terrorist in Palestine, went on to become Prime Minister of Israel." NBC's Israeli reporters showed remarkable diligence in transmitting those speeches by Communist members of the Israeli Knesset which referred to Begin and Sharon as "terrorists." This was no doubt one reason why Chancellor on August 13 recommended to the U.S. Congress that it emulate the forthrightness of the Knesset in speaking out against Israel's role in the war. (Christian leaders opposed to the PLO fared little better than Israel with Chancellor: Bashir Gemayel was identified in Chancellor's August 24 commentary as "this bloodthirsty young Christian.")

The connotative epithet most frequently applied to the PLO in the course of NBC's reporting of the war in Lebanon was "honorable." On June 25, Kemal Jumblatt, the leftist Druze leader who became

326

one of NBC's favorite interviewees, claimed that Israeli bombing didn't allow time to talk or the chance for an honorable solution. Steve Mallory, acting as the dutiful puppet of Jumblatt's intention, then asserted that "without some honorable solution" the "Palestinians" would continue to fight. Two days later, June 27, Mallory bridled at the notion the PLO should leave Beirut without some *quid pro quo*, because "the Palestinians want to leave with some honor." (He claimed that "Israelis have rejected the compromise" agreed to by the PLO and the United States, an agreement that seems to have existed exclusively in Mallory's head, for no evidence of it could ever be discovered.) On July 11 Jack Reynolds (sounding very like a PLO spokesman) declared that "the PLO will resist unless an honorable withdrawal can be arranged." On July 13 Reynolds again pleaded that "what he [Arafat] wants most is an honorable withdrawal and a continuation of the struggle for a Palestinian homeland." In June and July, PLO "honor" was constantly invoked by NBC as an argument against the continuance of Israel's siege of Beirut. Such "honorable" men could hardly be expected to agree to negotiations for their withdrawal so long as the siege continued. (No attempt was made to explain why Israel should continue the siege if the PLO was ready to leave, or why, if the PLO had showed not the slightest sign of willingness to leave until the siege had commenced, it should be more willing to leave once the siege had been lifted.) In August, PLO "honor" was as sacred as ever; only now it was the bombing that prevented these honorable men from negotiating their withdrawal. It seems never to have occurred to anybody at NBC that a main reason why the quickly defeated PLO forces stayed in Beirut during the many weeks of Philip Habib's patient efforts was not their "honor" but the fact that the Arab states refused to take them in, and therefore they had nowhere to go. Both Lebanese and PLO officials have stated that the bombardments of August 4 and 12 had the effect of persuading the Arab states to change their mind and of dissuading Arafat and his followers from holding out for political victory in spite of military defeat. Nevertheless, on August 16, Brokaw asserted that now, having fought the Israelis for two months, "they can leave with honor: they believe the world is more sympathetic to their cause (as well they might, given the efforts made on their behalf by NBC and like-minded journalists).

V. The Missing Background of the War:
The PLO in Lebanon

I rather choose/To wrong the dead, to wrong myself and you, /Than I will wrong such honourable men./
—Mark Antony (on the assassins of Julius Caesar)
Shakespeare, Julius Caesar, *III, ii, 127-29*

Who, then, were these honorable men and why was Israel going to such lengths to expel them from

Lebanon? NBC had short and ready answers to these questions. Homeless "Palestinians" (in NBC lexicon, only Arabs, not Jews, can be Palestinian, an excellent linguistic means of implying that Palestine belongs exclusively to the Arabs), out of desperation, had organized themselves in Lebanon into fighting units that sought to regain a usurped "homeland." Their "chairman" Yasser Arafat is a beloved leader (see, e.g., Reynolds, July 16) who spends much of his time kissing children, and proclaiming that "We resist to protect the children, the next generation." NBC followed this vignette on its July 12 broadcast by freezing the picture of Arafat kissing a little boy, as if this were the image of him that it wished forever to keep before our mind's eye, although on July 16 he was kissing adults for NBC cameras.

NBC's frequent glimpses of PLO members showed them as devoted to their families, eager to avoid destruction, given to volunteering to clean up neighborhoods in their spare time, and having no desire to kill Jews. The weakness and essential "powerlessness" of Arafat's forces were constantly stressed in NBC battle reports. "Sophisticated Israeli warplanes" are always going " too high, too fast" (June 23, July 22, 23). One could never have guessed from this relentless stress on PLO powerlessness that its forces had in fact amassed gigantic quantities of weapons: rocket-launchers, anti-aircraft guns, tanks, thousands upon thousands of light arms plus ammunition supplied from nearly every arms merchant in the world, and enough from the Russians to equip an army of three to five divisions. NBC viewers rarely saw pictures of PLO weapons being fired from the midst of civilian life because pictures of anti-aircraft batteries and tanks within apartment houses or hospitals would have seriously damaged NBC's portrait of the Israeli attack as an onslaught against civilians.

Ironically, the only time in NBC's version of the Lebanon war that we saw an impressive display of fire-power by the PLO was during the last week of August, when they daily "celebrated" their withdrawal from Beirut. Even these fiery occasions, so lavishly covered by NBC, were deceptively presented. When "salutes" are given "with everything from small arms to tank fire" (Vic Aicken, August 22) one is curious about where the bullets and shells land. NBC yielded to its curiosity so far as to note (August 23) that two people were killed by these salutes. NBC's stress had to be, however, on PLO "rejoicing" and on the universal devotion of Arafat's men to their leader, a stress that must have left many viewers puzzled when in 1983 violent mutiny against Arafat's leadership broke out.

Israel, on the other hand, was presented as an imperialist power "solving its problems in someone else's country" (Chancellor, August 2). Its prime minister Menachem Begin was usually pictured with a scowl on his face and a *Never* under his chin in a photograph placed alongside a smiling Arafat (see, e.g., July 27) forever searching for "peaceful settlement" (July 3) and tirelessly "signaling...willingness to leave Beirut" (July 30). Israel's leaders were nearly always "hardened," "defensive," and "militant" (Brokaw, August 11), its Minister of Defense "boisterous," "uncooperative," "intransigent," and also appearing with a *Never* under his photograph (Fred Francis, August 27). Israel's stony intransigence and unwillingness to compromise found expression in its reliance only on force. Rick Davis, to the sound of blasting guns, declared on July 31: "This is the tactic of persuasion—Israeli style." This already powerful imperial "war machine" was, moreover, supported by the mysteriously "powerful Israeli lobby" (Mudd, June 28) in the United States, where the Congress' reluctance to take a bold stand against Israel may well be due to "the influence of Jewish voters" (Chancellor, August 13). It is even possible, according to NBC, that "the power of the American Jewish community" has been responsible for a long-standing "pro-Israel bias" in news coverage. Since this particular sentiment has been expressed by none other than NBC News' own president Reuven Frank (interviewed August 9, 1982), it comes as no surprise that Roger Mudd should imply sympathy with those Arab-Americans who hope to persuade the news media to be more "fair" to them (June 28).

NBC's reporters often sounded as though they were under instructions to assume that Israel was guilty until proven innocent, and that all utterances by Israeli officials were to be treated with a caution and circumspection nowhere in evidence when Arabs were quoted. Brokaw (June 30) warns that Rick Davis will report from Sidon on how Israelis presented 'what *they* called evidence'' of an international terrorist ring'' that the PLO operated. Judy Woodruff (July 12) has the U.S. administration threatening to deal directly with the PLO, ''which *Israel* considers a terrorist organization.'' Martin Fletcher (July 19) reports on ''documents Israelis say they captured'' in Lebanese camps. On August 1 the cautious Fletcher says that ''Sharon produced aerial reconnaissance photos he *said* showed PLO tanks and heavy machine guns near Western embassies.'' In itself, such caution about accepting official pronouncements is admirable, but NBC's caution, like its morality, was very selective. NBC invariably took at face value condemnations of Israel by unnamed U.S. government ''sources,'' that convenient formulation that provides license for every tendentious speculation of the journalist. More to the point, it invariably assumed the PLO to be innocent until proven guilty—or rather, even after proven guilty, for when PLO casualty statistics, for example, were shown to be utter fabrications, NBC continued to allow pro-PLO Arabs to repeat them without challenge or correction. NBC in-

332

variably accepted PLO claims that Israel had broken the cease-fires, though even President Reagan blamed the PLO for this. On August 1, one of the extremely rare occasions during the entire war that NBC show-ed civilian casualties in *East* Beirut, Rick Davis said: "One report said Palestinian mortar hit two apart-ment buildings. . . . But some of the people here say it was a misplaced Israeli bomb."

In order to arrive at this conception of the adver-saries in this war, still more to persuade their viewers to share the conception with them, NBC's news staff had to conceal from view both the immediate background of the war and much of the history of the Arab-Israeli conflict. An American citizen who had been so unfortunate as to rely on NBC News for his information about Lebanon between 1975 and 1982 would have known little, if anything, of the PLO oc-cupation of southern Lebanon, of the Syrian occupa-tion of half of the country, and of the bloody civil war that had raged there for seven years. In June of 1982 NBC exposed this viewer to pictures of spec-tacular devastation and damage in Tyre, Sidon, Damur, and southern Beirut, but rarely bothered to tell him that a war had been going on in these places for seven years. Television cameras zoomed in on damage, but television reporters were not overly scrupulous about specifying when the damage had occurred. John Chancellor's first "history" of the conflict leading to the 1982 war (June 7) included not

a single word on the seven years of PLO-Syrian occupation and civil war; viewers were simply told that
"Israel is trying to buy a few years of peace at a *terrible* human and political cost." If you had just been
watching pictures of devastation in Damur, filmed as
Israeli tanks passed through, Chancellor's anger
might seem justified. Similarly, if the news media had
begun their coverage of World War II on the day of
the allied invasion in June 1944, and not taken the
trouble to recount what the Germans and the other
axis powers had been up to since 1939, the landing in
France and the ensuing carnage would have seemed
monstrous acts. The truth of the matter was that
Damur had been a Christian township whose population had been massacred and its survivors exiled by
the PLO in the fighting of 1976-77.

The PLO, generally pictured by NBC as power-
less, besieged, idealistic freedom fighters longing for
a land and state of their own, had in actuality for six
years "had something closely approaching an independent state" in southern Lebanon. These were
the words of *New York Times* reporter David Shipler
in a lengthy dispatch from Sidon on July 25. The
PLO "had an army, a police force, a crude judicial
system. . .a civil service and a foreign policy. Those
who lived within its rough boundaries said they were
too terrified then to describe it to outsiders. Now, for
the first time, they are describing what it was like,
telling of theft, intimidation and violence." NBC

viewers who took time away from their screens to read Shipler's report must have been stunned to discover that "the major tool of persuasion" of this organization whose yearning for peace NBC regularly contrasted with Israel's aggressiveness "was the gun." NBC's idealistic "guerrilla" fighters looked very different to those who lived under their reign of terror. "Both Lebanese and Palestinians describe...outright theft as a common practice of the P.L.O. ....They often took things from shops without paying, Miss Raad and others complained. Youssef Alifreh, a young Palestinian resident of the Burj al Shemali camp, near Tyre, confirmed it. 'Now we are happy because the armed P.L.O. left,' he declared. 'When somebody wanted to buy something, he would take it and not pay, and if someone would complain, he would shoot him.'" Although NBC's reporters were mightily impressed by Arafat's devotion to children, many Palestinian Arab refugees in camps took a dimmer view, and told Shipler: "Our children were working in the lemon groves, and then the P.L.O. forced them into service!" For the majority of Lebanese under the PLO rule, NBC's honorable men were, precisely, terrorists and thugs: "'Life was terrible,' said Khalil Hamdan, who owns a gas station in Harouf, a Shiite village near Nabatiye. 'They never used their brain. . . . They used their Kalashnikov. Even in the car, they used a machine gun to open the road for them.'"

This aspect of the Lebanese picture was not confined to *The New York Times.* David Ignatius, reporting from Damur for *The Wall Street Journal,* described how, on the night of January 17, 1976, "Palestinian guerrillas and their Lebanese Moslem allies attacked the northern part of the town...crying 'Allah-u-akhbar'—God is great—as they stormed into the houses of Christian civilians. The screams of the attackers and the victims could be heard a half-mile away.... About 300 of the people of Damur were killed." Martin Peretz, writing in *The New Republic* (August 2) related that "Lebanese of all persuasions and origins have expressed—I heard it myself dozens of times—gratification at their liberation from the PLO." John Laffin, writing for the *Catholic Herald,* described (September 10, 1982) how "White flags are beginning to show on many a house in southern Lebanon—but not the white flags of surrender. In this region the flags indicate that the family has an unmarried daughter—and naturally a virgin. The Lebanese found that the traditional signal was merely an invitation to rape by the PLO and the custom went into abeyance. Whatever the PLO were defending it was not the sanctity of the Lebanese home." Nevertheless, Roger Mudd on July 28 lamented that the "war has rekindled old hatreds" between Christians and Moslems. (If so, this was a classic case of carrying coals to Newcastle.)

It is scarcely necessary to remark that some

awareness of the fact that, in the words of *The New York Times,* "The P.L.O. established a de facto capital in west Beirut" or that "the camps became the P.L.O.'s political and military centers, where they shared control with the Syrian Army," would have given NBC's innocent viewers a very different impression of Israel's bombing of west Beirut and of the "camps" than the impression they very likely received from NBC's presentation. There were exceptions to the rule among NBC reporters. On June 13, June 17, and June 21 Bob Kur transmitted reports from southern Lebanon that included interviews with Arabs thankful to Israel for liberating them from the PLO's reign of terror, and he also once mentioned (June 21) that the PLO habitually positioned their guns near schools and hospitals. But for every such report by Kur there were two dozen by Mallory, Reynolds, and Compton that reiterated the PLO version of past history and present events, which also was the version accepted and propagated by Chancellor, Mudd, and Brokaw on the home front. (On occasion one could sense the conflict between sense impressions—the witness of one's eyes and ears—and ideology, as when Martin Fletcher, on July 28, reported from Damur how returning Christians were trying to restore homes and lives ravaged by the PLO and then—in a jarring *non-sequitur*—asked "How hard will it be for Christians to shake off Israeli patronage, and for Christians and Moslems to learn to live in peace again?")

337

If NBC viewers got little of the immediate Lebanese background of the war, they got nothing at all (apart from Jack Reynolds' grotesque travesties) of the larger background of the Arab-Israeli conflict since 1948. They were never told that the neighboring Arab states, with the exception of Egypt since it signed the peace treaty in 1979, have been formally at war with Israel since 1948. In that year the state of Israel was established, the Arab states declared war against it, and sent five armies across its borders. This act of aggression, recognized as such by many Security Council resolutions adopted between 1948 and 1951, continues down to the present day, so that the Lebanon War is but the latest in a series of six major battles (1948, 1956, 1967, 1969-70, 1973, 1982) of a prolonged war. Israel, confronted with a permanent state of war for 35 years, in 1982 decided that if the Arabs wanted a state of perpetual war, they could no longer expect Israel to wait for a time of attack convenient to the Arab rulers and commanders.

The PLO too has a history. In 1964 the Arab League created it in order to carry out terrorist attacks against Israel (Israel, of course, in its pre-1967 borders). Although rent by factionalism—Syria, Iraq, Algeria, and Libya financed their own factions within the PLO—and at the service of Saudi, Soviet, and Syian foreign policies, it was united by a "covenant." The PLO National Covenant stipulates in article 6 that no Jew who arrived in Palestine after the

"Zionist invasion" (dated by Arafat from 1882) has the right to live there. Article 19 declares that "the partitioning of Palestine and the establishment of Israel are entirely illegal." Article 20 denies any "historical or religious ties of Jews with Palestine" as "incompatible with the facts of history." Arafat declared in January 1980 that "Peace for us means the destruction of Israel." In May of the same year his Al-fatah organization announced, in Damascus, that its purpose remained "the complete liberation of Palestine, the liquidation of the Zionist entity, politically, militarily, culturally, and ideologically." Although the cold-blooded murder of infants and children figured very prominently in the record of PLO exploits—the Avivim school-bus ambush in 1970, the abbatoir at the Maalot school in 1974, the machine-gunning of the babies at Kiryat Shemona in the same year, the smashing of the head of 3-year-old Galit Haran of Nahariya against a rock in 1979—NBC did not shrink from presenting Arafat as specially attached to children.

NBC's presentation of the PLO as a valiant band of "guerrillas" seeking to regain their "homeland" resulted either from organized ignorance or the will to deceive. Is it conceivable that nobody at NBC recognizes the distinction between "guerrilla" actions, which inflict injury upon an enemy by whatever means possible and result in innocent casualties, and PLO terrorist actions, which do not even recognize the concept of innocence among the Israeli population but assume that every man, woman, child, or infant, regardless of occupation, place of residence, or personal history, who happens to be in any street, bus, marketplace, or building where a PLO bomb goes off or PLO members attack, is deserving of death? Is it conceivable that nobody at NBC wondered why, during the nineteen years when Jordan controlled what Jessica Savitch and Roger Mudd call "Jordan's West Bank," there was not only no call for an independent "Palestinian" state in that area but no peace in the Middle East? Is it conceivable that nobody at NBC wondered how an apparently rational man like John Chancellor could present the Lilliputian state of Israel as a predatory Brobdingnagian warrior extending its imperial reach over an Arab world composed of twenty states sprawled over 14 million square kilometers and controlling resources beyond the dreams of Croesus?

During its three months of broadcasting the war in Lebanon, the closest NBC came to an acknowledgement that it might have blotted out the background essential to an understanding of the conflict came on August 6. Tom Brokaw, now in Israel, mentioned, in a bemused fashion, that some Israelis had asked him, "Where were you when the PLO was killing thousands of Lebanese over the past seven years?" But since NBC's willingness to admit error is non-existent and its belief in its infallibility unshakeable—"the press," says Reuven Frank, "ought to be arrogant"—no pro-

340

gram of self-correction was ever undertaken.

Predictably, NBC lingered uncritically, admiringly, even affectionately over the PLO's riotous departure from Beirut and the arrival of its various factions at their several destinations. The evacuation was the ultimate "media event" of the war, for it is not difficult to imagine how different it would have looked if the cameras had not been there. Vic Aicken was specially touched by the "pride as well as sorrow" of George Habash's men, and offered mournful threnodies over the wounded, and rhapsodic accounts of tearful farewells, and of Arafat on yet more kissing sprees. (His tone turned acerbic, however, when he noted that U.S. Marines "got lost" because their maps included places that had been wiped out by Israeli aerial bombardment.) Tom Brokaw did say that although "Arafat left Beirut today like an Arab head of state at the height of his glory...in fact he was being driven out of Beirut by a massive defeat." Yet none of NBC's resident sages could bring himself to name the real truth that was concealed by this masquerade, as Bill Moyers did on CBS (August 23):

> Watching scenes of the Beirut evacuation this weekend, I was struck by how it is possible for the cameras to magnify a lie. The Palestinian troops left town as if they'd just won a great victory. Arafat, they praised as a conquering hero. In fact, they

are leaving town in defeat. And in fact, Arafat led them to the cul-de-sac where they made their last stand behind the skirts of women and among the playgrounds of children. . . . It could have been otherwise if Arafat and his allies accepted the reality of Israel, if they had not established within Lebanon a terrorist state sworn to Israel's destruction, and if Arab governments had not found it useful to nurture the PLO in the bloody illusion that Israel can one day be pushed into the sea.

VI. Selective and Tendentious Interviewing

Jack Reynolds, NBC: "Is the American attitude toward the PLO changing?" Yassar Arafat: "We hope so. I began to touch it through the mass media. . . I began to touch it."—(July 16, 1982)

On July 30 NBC's Roger O'Neill offered a special report on what was alleged to be a "spirited and bitter debate" within the American Jewish community over the war in Lebanon. Yet it soon became apparent that this was a debate in which, so far as NBC was concerned, only one side was permitted to speak. By way of showing its readers the substance of this debate, NBC offered its viewers two people at a synagogue commenting, from identical positions, on "Israel's wrong path to peace"; this was followed by glimpses of the anti-Israel protests of "New Jewish Agenda," an extreme left, pro-PLO fringe group;

after which O'Neill commented that "to make sure voices of dissent don't get too loud Israeli military commanders are now speaking to American Jews about the war." Apparently these military commanders despatched to stifle dissent have not done a very good job, since Roger O'Neill *appears* to have been unable to locate a single Jewish voice to speak *for* Israel. He concluded this survey of the "bitter debate" with the observation that the "war has split the American Jewish community like no issue before" and quoted an unidentified rabbi who (bravely defying those Israeli military commanders sent to silence him) told the interviewer that "If we forget about Palestinian humanity, we may soon lose our own." If there exists anywhere in America an articulate Jewish voice that supports Israel's action in Lebanon, NBC has taken special care that nobody shall hear it.

On the next evening, Rick Davis interviewed three officers of a relief organization called World Relief about the Israeli blockade against supplies going into West Beirut. They expressed anger against Israel because, they insisted, their food went only to civilians. Also, by happy coincidence, these dispensers of charity (and strong opinion) had met with an Israeli officer who, just like the American rabbi interviewed by Roger O'Neill the night before, alleged that Israelis were losing their own humanity because of their inhuman treatment of the Palestinian Arabs. "The three men said they asked an Israeli officer where his humanity was, and he said 'I left it behind when I came to Lebanon.'..."

Two nights later, Roger Mudd interviewed Israeli Foreign Minister Shamir in Washington. He asked Shamir whether President Reagan would pull Habib out of his negotiating role "if you don't lower the level of violence," an expression Mudd was so taken with that he repeated it a few seconds later: "also, if you don't lower the level of violence, won't President Reagan force you to negotiate with the PLO?" Mudd also took it upon himself to suggest—as if he himself had already replaced Habib as the chief negotiator—that Israel pull back five or ten miles as a "sign of good faith." As if this were not enough to indicate NBC's powerful disapproval of Israeli policies, Mudd followed the interview by saying, "Shamir would not acknowledge that Israel is having a credibility problem in the United States, but he also said that if there was one, it was not justified, because, he said, Israel tells only the truth." Mudd's arrogance, hostility, and rudeness towards Shamir must have come as a surprise to viewers who remembered his manner in the previous interview he had done (July 20), with the Saudi Foreign Minister, Prince Saud al-Faisal, a manner that can most charitably be described as one of oily sycophancy. On that occasion Mudd not only kept putting into the prince's mouth the idea that "The Middle East crisis can't be solved unless Palestine is recognized" (whatever this means) and that

344

Syria dare not take in the PLO for fear this will give Israel an "excuse" to attack Syria; he also interjected engaging laughter by way of tacit approval whenever the prince referred to Israel's malignant designs upon the region.

These three interviews, coming within a period of four days, were only too representative of the way in which NBC sought to buttress its hostile view of Israel's actions in Lebanon by an artful selection of hostile witnesses and a double standard of behavior in cross-examining them. One could watch NBC for weeks on end without hearing a single pro-Israel voice, while Arafat and such fervid supporters of Arafat as Saeb Salam and perfervid Israel-haters as Walid Jumblatt performed day after day. It was not merely that they were interviewed and interviewed frequently (more than seven times as often as anti-PLO Lebanese) but always in a manner respectful, admiring, even affectionate: no hard questions, no abrasive challenges, no snide remarks, all of which were standard in interviews with Israeli officials. To watch an NBC reporter interviewing an Arab official was to be reminded of Swift's adage that crawling and climbing are done from the same posture. A particular egregious example of oleaginous fawning on PLO spokesmen was James Compton's interview with Arafat on July 21. In response to Arafat's indicating that in addition to already-existing UN resolutions on Palestine he would like "a new one," Compton helpfully proposes a Madison Avenue formulation: "If America will say yes, Palestinians have legitimate rights, is that everything you need?" and is mightily pleased by Arafat's sweet reasonableness in replying, "Oh, yes." On none of the many occasions when Arafat was interviewed by NBC did any of the network's reporters dare to ask him what his own responsibility might be for the civilian dead of Beirut and other places. As a *Wall Street Journal* writer remarked on the very next day, July 22: "The American media still has the sense not to glorify a gunman who uses hostages to shield himself from the police, but everyday they are making Yasser Arafat out to be a plucky little hero, even as he hides behind the innocent civilians of West Beirut." And who can know by how much Arafat prolonged this hiding (and multiplied the attendant casualties) because of the favorable publicity NBC's reporters and their colleagues were giving him? If by July 16, as he told Jack Reynolds, he had begun "to touch" American hearts "through the media," was it not plausible for him to believe that he might eventually capture those hearts entirely?

Everywhere a double standard was in evidence in the selection and treatment of interviews. On July 14 Bob Kur reported on Israeli soldiers refusing to serve again in Lebanon, and interviewed an Israeli soldier who urged his countrymen to "talk" with Palestinian Arabs instead of fighting them, after which Yitshak Rabin, also interviewed, criticized Israel's "political" goals in Lebanon as illegitimate. On July 17 James Compton mentioned that a rally reported to be twice the size of the anti-war rally so lavishly covered by NBC on July 3 had taken place in Tel Aviv, but in this case none of the people involved was interviewed. While Jumblatt and Salam appeared so regularly to castigate Israel that it was easy to believe they had been salaried as NBC field reporters, Bashir Gemayel, the Lebanese Christian leader soon to be elected president of the country, was interviewed only twice, and since, as noted above, John Chancellor had tagged him with the label of "bloodthirsty young Christian" it didn't much matter what he said. PLO representatives were interviewed fourteen times in July and August, but Major Sa'ad Haddad, whose forces now controlled southern Lebanon, was not considered worthy of NBC microphones and cameras. When he was referred to, it was invariably as leader of a right-wing "Christian army" (Fletcher, July 28), although 60% of his militia is Shia Muslim.

In July several U.S. congressmen visited Lebanon. One was Representative Charles Wilson, a Texas Democrat who had voted for the AWACS sale to Saudi Arabia and intended to vote for the Jordanian arms sale, and nevertheless brought back from Lebanon impressions of "the universal enthusiasm with which the Lebanese welcomed the Israeli army.... I mean it's almost like a liberating army...it was astonishing. I expected this, somewhat, from the Christian population. But I didn't expect it from the Muslim population. . . . And in talking to a group of people, some of whom had lost their homes, some of whom had lost relatives, they said it was awful. But they said that all in all, to 'be free of the PLO was worth it.'" This was a remarkable and newsworthy eyewitness American reaction to the Lebanese war, but it did not appear so to NBC, which never reported it to its viewers. But when five U.S. congressmen, led by the anti-Israel crusader "Pete" McCloskey, called a press conference to announce (falsely, as it turned out) that Arafat was ready to accept Israel's right to exist, the story (or non-story) dominated NBC's Middle East news for three consecutive nights and brought a Tom Brokaw interview of McCloskey on July 26. Congressman McCloskey's announcement that "Arafat accepts all UN resolutions relevant to the Palestinian question" was a transparent farce that has been performed a hundred times in the past decade. Arafat did not, of course, specifically recognize UN resolutions 242 and 338, which do not refer to the Palestinians or the Palestinian question at all; he said nothing about Israel's right to exist; he spoke in full awareness that the totality of UN resolutions dealing with "Palestine" is a contradictory hodgepodge that includes condemnations of Zionism as the greatest evil ever visited upon this planet. Nevertheless, Tom Brokaw, exhibiting NBC's characteristic amenability to PLO balderdash, not only failed to ask McCloskey any hard, skeptical questions, but noted irritably that "debate" over the meaning of Arafat's statement "didn't keep Israel from pounding West Beirut for the fifth straight day." How unreasonable of the Israeli air force not to be as impressed as, say, Roger Mudd by the familiar PLO masquerade! At no point did NBC provide identification of McCloskey as an anti-Israel activist who has long worked to cut off U.S. aid to Israel and been a regular performer on the PLO lecture circuit.

During its three months of reporting the war, NBC never succeeded in discovering a single interviewable American who supported Israel or opposed the PLO. It never interviewed any Lebanese Americans who opposed the PLO, and indeed went out of its way to give the demonstrably false impression that Lebanese Americans supported the PLO against Israel. (The most casual reader of American newspapers would likely have known that the American Lebanese League publicly castigated the PLO for holding much of Lebanon and West Beirut hostage and asked them who gave "the PLO authority to insist that Lebanese civilians die with them?") Also, by a remarkable coincidence, every one of the ten Americans (not counting government officials) NBC interviewed condemned Israel and supported the PLO. Although over 200 U.S. generals and admirals signed their names to newspaper advertisements stressing the "extraordinary significance" of the defeat of the most advanced Soviet arms by "Israel-modified American weapons and tactics," NBC, despite the fact that it consistently took the view that Israeli action had damaged U.S. policy and interests in the Middle East, felt no obligation to interview a single one of them. Had it done so, of course, its constant reiteration that Israel had destroyed U.S. policy and weakened U.S. influence in the Middle East (thus Chancellor starting on June 7, 1982 and continuing without let-up through July 14, 1983, when he still insisted that in Lebanon the "only winners are the Soviets") would have had a hollow ring. For the truth of the matter, as the generals and others pointed out, was that Israel's action had given the U.S. the foothold it had sought in Lebanon for a decade, shattered the Soviet reputation as the world's leading arms supplier, and demonstrated that Soviet clients (Syria and the PLO) can be defeated by an American ally. For the first time since 1975 the opportunity existed as a result of Israeli action, for Lebanon to be reconstituted as a quasi-democratic nation allied to the West. Are we nevertheless to assume, along with John Chancellor, that this was an occasion for rejoicing in Moscow? Apparently the American government and American people do not think so. Throughout the war, NBC's Chancellor, Mudd, Brokaw, and Francis relentlessly insisted that Israel's action had permanently alienated the American government and the American people. Yet public opinion polls taken during the war showed substantial numbers of Americans supporting Israel and condoning Israel's actions in Lebanon. Moreover, in the late summer of 1983, as I write, public opinion polls show a higher rate of approval of Israel than existed before June 1982. Was NBC's failure to find and interview any of the people who make up this "public opinion" perhaps a result of wishful thinking about the possibility of driving a wedge between Israel and America?

Conclusion

It is not easy, nor is it the aim of this essay, to say what is the underlying cause of the deplorable lack of self-critical professionalism in NBC's reporting of the war in Lebanon. We know that just before the Six-Day War of 1967, when the Straits of Tiran were closed and Arab armies were advancing toward her borders, and Nasser and Shukairy were promising to turn the Mediterranean red with Jewish blood, Israel was the recipient of a good deal of sympathy, including journalistic sympathy. But after the war, Israel discovered that the price she would have to pay for winning a war that, if lost, would have meant her destruction, was the universal loss of the sympathy Jews had been collecting since 1945, when discovery of the Holocaust became general. All those statesmen and journalists whose eloquence had for twenty-two years gushed forth on the subject of the dead Jews and of their vanished civilization now fulminated with rage and resentment against a people and a state that preferred life to death and even to the rhapsodic eulogies that might be bestowed on dead Jewish martyrs and the glory that was Israel. Since 1967 this rage and resentment have taken a variety of forms, some of which may have found expression in the reporting of the war in Lebanon. Jay Bushinsky, Cable News Network's man in Jerusalem, described the foreign press as "enraged, bitter and resentful" towards Israel; and David Bazay (CBC) referred to a "get Israel" attitude among his colleagues. Another possible explanation, one of more immediate relevance to citizens of a democracy like America, is that precisely because Israel, unlike any of its neighbors, is an open, democratic society with a free press, it is peculiarly vulnerable to the depredations of a press which has perverted liberty into license. With 1984 only a few months away, it is pertinent to recall that the totalitarian Oceania depicted in Orwell's *1984* rests mainly on the assumption that, given modern technology and a contempt for moral tradition, anything is possible, anything can be done with the human mind, with history, above all with language. Orwell understood that a free press is indeed a guarantor of democratic freedoms, but that a press which plays fast and loose with facts, which attempts to destroy memory, which uses language to render spite and incite hatred, which sacrifices traditional standards of fairness and objectivity to sectarian passion, may well be undermining precisely those principles of freedom, democracy, and tolerance which justify its existence.

352

LESSONS OF THE LEBANESE CAMPAIGN

by Marvin Maurer and Peter E. Goldman

The shocking treatment by the media of the Israeli campaign in Lebanon during the summer and early fall has long since become unchallengeable. The reporting of the war from June through October made it clear that the media—including *The New York Times,* the *Washington Post, Newsweek,* ABC, CBS, NBC, the Associated Press (AP), and the United Press International (UPI)—sought to undermine the moral legitimacy of the State of Israel and its democratically elected leaders while simultaneously idealizing the PLO.

The media war against Israel is difficult to understand. The Israel Defense Forces (IDF) vanquished Syria and the PLO, two Soviet clients notoriously inhospitable to human rights. The IDF success in Lebanon gave that war-torn nation another chance to become independent and even democratic. The media

Marvin Maurer is a Professor of Political Science at Monmouth College and a member of the Academic Advisory Committee of Americans for a Safe Israel.

Peter E. Goldman, former director of the Center for International Security (Washington, D.C.) and of the Denmark-Israel Association (Copenhagen), is director of Americans for a Safe Israel.

Reprinted by permission of MIDSTREAM(c)1983 Midstream, Inc.

did not, however, see it that way at all. They transmuted Israel's success into a major moral defeat. Its leaders were pilloried as mass murderers, its foes became folk heroes.

Were the proverbial man from Mars to rely on the media's coverage of events last summer he would have to conclude that Menachem Begin and Ariel Sharon were the world's most evil men and the State of Israel was writhing in agony for its acts of mass-murder against women and children. He would also conclude that Yasir Arafat was a well-meaning, avuncular, ever-smiling fellow who when not hugging children is being received by the Pope and other world leaders.

Yet while most observers were deeply disturbed by the statistical fantasies served up to the American public as facts, what was far more pernicious, in our view, was the emotional bias persuasively communicated by the sensationalization of the news stories that made up the basic thrust of the media. This was especially striking in the United States because most Americans believe in the media. Hence the vilification of Israel was transmitted to the American public on many levels; the effect was the erosion of support for Israel, as shown by reactions in polls. Thus the emotional framework of the lies about Israeli atrocities, false civilian casualties, and outright slanders undercutting Israel's reasons for launching a preemptive military campaign could not be offset by an occasional dry denial from a selected spokesman.

354

Sensationalized portrayals of Israel's use of indiscriminate force (with American supplied weapons) or dramatic photos of infants with their limbs blown off by Israel's made-in-U.S. bombs leave indelible impressions on Americans who were kept uninformed about the realities of the Middle East over the years. A belated confession by a media pundit that he lied or used tainted data cannot offset the original damage, especially as the corrections are hidden in the folds of a paper or reported in off-prime-time hours. (How many pundits are just now confessing they lied on behalf of Hanoi some 10 years after the damage was done?) Nor can one OP-Ed piece supporting Israel make up for a half dozen or more attacking Israel. Of 30 such pieces to appear in *The New York Times* in June, only three supported Israel.

A laconic statement that "we goofed" about the crippled infant cannot undo the initial propaganda. Years of ignoring Syrian and PLO brutality in Lebanon cannot be undone by brief comments—especially when the media persist in describing Israel's actions as Hitlerian in scope. A technical analysis of the siege of Beirut cannot offset searing portrayals of Israel destroying whole cities and populations. Television interviews of "objective" observers such as Professor Edward Said, in political affairs an ardent apologist for the PLO, cannot be offset by presenting the pleas of some Israeli official. The vitriolic distortions of an Anthony Lewis cannot be countered by an objective refutation. The very fact that the media present propagandists as serious analysts legitimizes their views, while at the same time a pro-Israel spokesman is identified as a partisan.

It is obvious that the media would not permit sexists, racists, etc., to hawk their wares on prime time or use headlines as if they were telling the truth. They know perfectly well that providing space or time to a colorless functionary from the aggrieved group would be useless. The media moguls and news producers are well aware, as we shall show, of the techniques they used to report the war to Americans.

It is apparent that democracies are vulnerable to their media. No institution is exempt—save for the media—from exposure. Michael Novak, an observer of the American scene, argues that elite media intellectuals have a power not available to other elites, namely the power to control "visibility, charisma, decency, virtue" and to determine what is *moral.*

One thing that is not viewed as moral by the media, according to Kevin Phillips, a long-time media critic, is the exercise of "effective military-diplomatic power." From a different vantage, Walter Cronkite agrees by observing that the media changed in the 1960s in that "most newsmen have come to feel very little allegiance to the established order. I think they are inclined to side with humanity rather than with authority and institutions."

The economies of the media complement their

356

biases. They thrive on sensational and negative news. Exposure of evil in America (adverse journalism) attracts readers and viewers. An old journalistic formula sums up the media need: "Good news is no news, bad news is good news." A *Wall Street Journal* editorial concludes that the media are protected by, and thrive in those very societies that they so zealously delegitimize. Media righteousness makes it increasingly difficult for democracies to defend themselves against determined foes, especially those foes that are free from media exposure at home, and, as we shall show, even abroad. America's inability to stay the course in Vietnam is attributed to the mass media's relentless exposure of the conduct of America's armed forces. The media coverage in Lebanon was very similar to the techniques developed in reporting the Vietnam War. This is no surprise as today's generation of journalists learned their profession and absorbed their prejudices during the Vietnam War and its aftermath, including Watergate.

The media succeeded in turning around significant American victories into defeat (such as the 1968 Tet offensive). American policies were described in the harshest superlatives as being immoral and criminal. While destroying President Johnson's moral credibility, the media canonized the late Communist dictator Ho Chi Minh. A *New York Times* editorial described Ho as an admirer of America's most noble principles, and even though he turned Communist it

357

was only to "achieve his lifelong goal of freedom and unity for his country." (Cited by Norman Podhoretz, "J'Accuse," *Commentary*, September, 1982.)

Robert Elegant, a foreign correspondent, concluded that the media made "it impossible for Washington to maintain even the minimal support...for continued resistance" in Indochina. He predicted "the Vietnam Syndrome" will occur again since some democratic nation "could again be forced to operate most precariously in an environment dominated by a hostile press." The media will become "the war scene" while the actual struggle for the democratic state will be hidden from the public's view. ("Vietnam: How to Lose A War," *Encounter*, August, 1981). His anticipation was realized one year later in Lebanon.

Those aware of Israel's need to preempt in Lebanon were appalled at the media coverage of the war, especially their use of tainted and false data plus the use of emotive terms drawn from the Nazi era. ABC (June 28) for example, and CBS (July 1) equated the siege of Beirut with the battle of Stalingrad. Having access to the PLO's inner enclaves, Western reporters and photographers literally functioned as its public relations arm.

Casualty and death reports attributed to the IDF suggested that it launched a major blitzkrieg to obliterate Lebanon. Both *Time* and *Newsweek* sensationalized the action as "Israel's Blitz." Compilations of photos and reports left the impression that Israel, acting out of some biblical fury, was an avenger leaving a swathe of destruction and death. *The New York Times*, NBC, etc. reported that 10,000 civilians were killed, 40,000 wounded, and 600,000 made homeless. These casualties were attributed to the IDF's advance in Sidon, Tyre, and other PLO bases in southern Lebanon. Citing these data, columnist Anthony Lewis, in hyperbole reminiscent of his Vietnam diatribes, stated that Israel has made *every* Palestinian Arab a suitable target for extermination.

The media failed to report that the refugee flow was toward Israeli controlled areas.

Ironically *The Times* accused the Begin government of having "lied about . . . the civilian casualties it has caused." Bent on rushing to judgment, the media uncritically presented and accepted data from the Palestine Red Crescent, an agency headed by Arafat's brother. The fabricaton became apparent when it was revealed that the population of the area was about 500,000: the media had accused Israel of creating more refugees than there were people! Unfortunately, long after the tainted data were exposed, *The Times* and television news repeated the PLO data. (See log of television news by Anti-Defamation League, *Television Coverage of the War in Lebanon*, October, 1982.)

In spite of any embarrassment that might have been felt over using the phony PLO data, the media continued their relentless campaign of bombarding the American public with selected and one-sided material. In order to sustain the image that Israel was destroying a people, fabricated data were presented as straight news, as the following suggests.

ABC News (August 1) aired an interview with an Arab doctor who, as an eye-witness, accused Israeli soldiers of brutalizing and torturing wounded Palestinian Arab prisoners. This was indeed a serious charge. To provide a semblance of balance an Israeli official was pulled in from somewhere and perfunctorily denied that any such incident had occurred. No effort was made to verify the doctor's charge and no independent evidence was presented, nor was there any subsequent follow-up. The report failed to mention that Israel reacts harshly to any abuses by its troops. One could say that this report was an example of "creative" reporting, i.e., a form of journalism free from the encumbrances of verification.

Similarly, the phony picture of an infant reported to have been crippled by Israeli bombs was a potent image. It was so effective that President Reagan put a copy of the photo on his desk. A Reagan aide insisted that "that picture of the baby with the burnt arms had more impact on him than 50 position papers." (*Times*, August 16) When the picture and the caption were proved to be false, the UPI merely stated it "regrets the error." (*New York Times*, September) The failure to give this piece of vicious mendacity the coverage it originally received exemplifies the media's intent.

Throughout the summer the media produced an unending stream of photos of civilian casualties, mourners, and destroyed structures which were invariably linked to Israel. Lurid techniques were employed to buttress the rush to judgment. Headlines included "Destroying Beirut: Israel Tightens the Noose." (*Time*, August 16)

Though examining government responses lies outside our scope, it is relevant to observe how the media treated information favorable to Israel. On occasion President Reagan strongly defended Israel. The media buried, omitted, or undermined his statements. Reagan was asked, on August 13, for example, how he felt about the horrible bombardments and his continuing to send weapons to inflict more. He replied that "the image has been rather one-sided because of the Israeli capability at replying, but in...most...instances the cease-fire was broken by the P.L.O. attacking those Israeli forces." (Text of the news conference, *New York Times*, August 14)

ABC news ignored his remarks and other outlets gave it brief notice. In short, the media deemphasized a major statement on behalf of Israel.

While campaigning in New Jersey, Reagan commented on the Israeli move into Beirut as follows: "It is true that what led to the move in was the attack after the assassination of the elected President

[Gemayel], the attack on its forces by some of the leftist militia who are still there in west Beirut.'' He went on to affirm that America's and Israel's views coincided on Lebanon's future. *The Times* ferreted out unidentified "officials in Washington" who were "stunned" at the President's statements (September 18). Thus a statment on behalf of Israel was torpedoed.

Another media device was to make extensive use of the Israeli press and Knesset debates, and to cite assorted Jews in order to suggest that Begin and his government were moral lepers. The Knesset is, of course, the world's most open and uninhibited legislative body and even Israel's military personnel are free to speak out. (The Syrians and the PLO prevent the slightest hint of dissent.)

All too often the media cite extremist Israeli publications and politicians whose views do not reflect Israeli public opinion. *Time* quotes *Al Hamishmar*, a left wing paper, as follows: "This slaughter has made the war in Lebanon the greatest disaster to befall the Jewish people since the Holocaust." No reason is given why this paper was selected, and *Time* fails to indicate that Israel, too, has an adversary press.

The embellishment and fabrication in the media had become so prevalent by the 1970s that Lester Merkel, a retired *New York Times* editor, expressed his concern that in the process of trying to create an

impression, journalists applied techniques used in fiction, including the use of unsubstantiated psychological imagery (*New York Times*, October 31, 1972). Similarly NBC news chief Reuven Frank unabashedly stated that television news sought to leave emotional impressions rather than impart cold, factual materials.

The Beirut massacre of September 18 and 19 gave the media new fuel for frying Israel. Judging by the headlines and reporting, it would appear the media hired psychologists to do their work. *Time* and *Newsweek*, for example, included these gems (October 4): "Israel: A Shaken Nation," "Israel in Torment," "The Anguish of American Jews," "After the Massacres Can Israel Survive?" The *Newsweek* cover showed a bloody dove on a Star of David. (Perhaps, a sharp investigative reporter might check with the World Council of Churches and the National Council of Churches to see if their leaders are quivering in "shame" and "writhing in torment" inasmuch as the massacres were carried out by Christians.)

Israel is an ideal target for psychological imagery since it is vulnerable to such emotive terms as "holocaust," "genocide," etc. Media the world over tossed about the words "Warsaw Ghetto" to describe Israel's efforts to get PLO forces out of Beirut. Deathcamp imagery was freely used. On September 27, the *Asbury Park Press* (New Jersey) reprinted a

syndicated cartoon showing two wraith-like inmates behind barbed wire to which a sign is attached reading "Auschwitz." The balloon above one inmate asks, "Wasn't it Begin who condemned others for standing by while a slaughter took place?" *The San Francisco Chronicle* (October 1) portrays an exaggeratedly ugly Begin staring at the tattooed numbers "9/17/82" (the date of the massacre) on his arm. Every imaginable effort was made to link Begin and Sharon to the killings, which were equated with the Holocaust.

Shortly after the massacre the media began to exclude "Christian" from their accounts thereby linking Israel to the massacre. A headline reads, for example: "Israel to Pull Out [of Beirut] as Outrage Builds." The accompanying AP story (September 25) reads: "Outrage in and outside Israel intensified yesterday as that nation's alleged role in the slaying of hundreds of women and children became the subject of more attention." Whenever "Christian" was used it was linked with Israel's perfidy in letting the massacre take place. The Christians are likened to a "gun," but Israel is the "trigger."

Generally, the media ignored the PLO's role in the massacre except for its protests. The media failed to emphasize that the PLO introduced the chain of massacres in Lebanon and invited assaults against its own people by using their homes as bases. In a two-inch column, *The Times* (October 7) reported that the

Lebanese army found "an elaborate network of concrete-lined tunnels to the three refugee camps—Sabra, Shatila and Burj al Brajneh...Reporters taken on a tour saw huge bunkers packed to the ceiling with explosives...and shells...." Why did not the media hold the PLO accountable for such flagrant abuse of their own people? Instead of trying to locate Israel's role within the context of what occurred, the media elevated Israel to the center of the tragic massacre.

Massacres, unfortunately, are not uncommon in war. Some are spontaneous, however, others are well-planned. As with the My Lai massacre in Vietnam, the one in Beirut came close to being an unauthorized display of Christian hatred. On the other hand, the massacre in Hama, Syria, a few months earlier, resulting in some 25,000 deaths (50 times more than in Beirut), was planned and systematically executed by the Syrian government as an object lesson to their citizens. By virtually ignoring the Syrian massacre the media were able to concentrate on their chief target—Israel.

The media went to great lengths to demonstrate that the "civilized" world condemned Israel for its alleged actions in Lebanon. An ABC report (September 17) tried to link the U.S. and the USSR in a common front against Israel. First, a Soviet official is filmed giving an eye-witness account of the damage the Israelis allegedly inflicted on the Soviet Embassy.

365

The next frame reports that the Israelis fired at a U.S. Marine atop the American Embassy. An American official says the attack was inexcusable. Then Ambassador Dobrynin appears and warns that his country will not tolerate aggression. The ABC commentator concludes by asking, what can the U.S. and the USSR do with an Israel that takes on the big boys?

Several newspapers sought to show the U.N.'s hostility toward Israel by using photos of a Begin pathetically addressing a near-empty General Assembly. There was a failure to remind the public that the U.N. invariably boycotts any Israeli speaker. In this vein, *The New York Times* (August 25) reports, with no critical qualifications that the "Austrian leader calls Israel 'Morally Naked, " and just below we learn that a very concerned "Castro offers to take in Palestinian orphans." By the time the media imagery takes its toll there is not much left of the reality of a small democratic state struggling against totalitarian foes who repeatedly vow its destruction. The media intent is clear. It seeks to impress upon Americans that the whole "civilized" world looks upon Israel as a criminal state—a major barrier to world peace.

Pursuing the Israel-versus-its-victim theme, the *Washington Post* accused Israel of excessive brutality, of "lording" it over the Syrians and of obstructing justice for Palestinian Arabs on the West Bank.

The *Post* accused Israeli soldiers of looting and desecration and carried a vivid account of an Israeli soldier defecating in a mosque. (The Israeli newspaper *Ha'aretz* said that the looting and desecration reports were without foundation; it is well-known that Israeli soldiers are punished for looting.)

The irony of such reporting about an army second to none in correct behavior is that these descriptions could very well be descriptions of the PLO, whose personnel robbed the Lebanese and desecrated churches during its seven-year reign of terror in Lebanon. Columnist Jack Anderson (August 22) accused the media of blurring the true picture of a tyrannical, greedy PLO. Very few media outlets carried, let alone highlighted, for example, the massacre of 65 Lebanese by the PLO in a church in Hayshi, the bloody PLO massacres in Damur, or the desecration of churches in many parts of Lebanon. (An exception was David Shipler's account of PLO barbarity and vandalism in *The New York Times* June 21).

Similarly, Francis Ofner, dean of the foreign press corps in Israel, related in the *Jerusalem Post* (July 25) how foreign TV crews deliberately ignored scenes of Lebanese welcoming Israeli soldiers in order to seek out "victimized" Palestinian Arabs. Such tendencious selectivity in the media led the Canadian Broadcasting Corporation correspondent David Bazay to state (September 26), in a rare burst of candor, that there is a "kind of get Israel attitude" among his colleagues in the international press.

The influential *Washington Post*, read by all branches of the U.S. government, has for many years stood at the forefront of Israel's abusers, praising its enemies and misrepresenting the Arab-Israel conflict. The *Post* (along with most of the media) has deliberately censored the repeated statements by PLO leaders that in conformity with their Charter they would accept no solution short of Israel's liquidation. Instead, the *Post* has promoted the fiction that a West Bank Palestinian Arab state (which the PLO rejects as a solution) would provide the Arab-Israel answer. However, the scope of the *Post's* imbalance and distortions during the Lebanon war was disquieting.

A central focus of the *Post* was the canonizing of the PLO and its leadership. A *Post* article (June 24), for example, entitled "Arafat's Dilemma—a Martyr's Death or Banishment" goes on to describe this "guerrilla chief"—"smiling and unbowed"—as the "miracle man of Palestinian politics." The *Post* bemoaned the "loneliness of [the PLO's] course," but admired its "grim determination to die with honor" in Beirut "as an inspiration to future generations of Palestinians." Nowhere in this article by David Ottaway was there mention of the PLO's aim of destroying Israel or the brutality inflicted on Lebanese, dissident Palestinian Arabs, and numerous men, women, and children around the world.

On the same day, the *Post* asserted that unless Israel were prevented from destroying the PLO, terrorism would spread and the U.S. would be made to pay for Israel's excesses. The *Post* accused Israel of holding the U.S. "hostage," and preparing to destroy a "good part" of Beirut with "the massive firepower used on Tyre and Sidon." (Reliable eye-witnesses have reported that Tyre and Sidon were left relatively unscathed.)

To impress upon its readers America's abhorrence with Israel's behavior, the June 24 *Post* is replete with anti-Israel quotations from members of Congress.

If the PLO was not the guilty party, who was? One need only turn to the same day's editorial page where a member of the newspaper's writers group, Edwin Yoder, points to Begin's "Old Testament mysticism," which rationalizes his quest for a "Greater Israel." Begin, along with "hardline" supporters—the Sephardim—are turning Israel into a "Middle East Prussia, ruling subject Arab populations by blood and iron." Impressionable readers must marvel, in the words of Edward Alexander, at "the prodigious energy which enables so tiny a people to commit so many Brobdingnagian misdeeds."

Transforming criminal terrorists into heroes and martyrs with commendable goals was not confined to the *Washington Post*, but was spread throughout the media. *Newsweek* (August 16) (owned by the Washington Post Co.) published a seven-page panegyric to

the PLO and Palestinian Arabs in an article entitled
"Where do They Go From Here?" The reporting
team tells how the Palestinian Arabs lost their "green
paradise" and share a "common dream. . . of returning home." Israeli "expansionism" is at the root of
the problem, and Israel's ultimate goal is "to do
away" with the Palestinian Arabs. (*Newsweek* might
then have asked why do some 600,000 Palestinian
Arabs stay in Israel?) The PLO's atrocities are attributed to "the surpassing sense of grievance and injustice" inflicted by the Israelis after the Six-Day
War. (Why did the PLO and its terrorism begin
before the Six-Day War?)

To further solidify the Palestinian Arab case,
Newsweek falsely claimed that prior to Israel's existence the Arabs of Palestine owned 95 percent of the
land. (They owned 20.2 percent, according to official
figures.) Obviously uncomfortable with the fact that
the PLO Charter calls for Israel's destruction, *Newsweek* downplays this problem by insisting that 95 percent of the Palestinian Arabs would accept part of
present-day Israel as a state. Though the PLO has re-
confirmed its Charter at every meeting of the Palestinian National Council, committed acts of murder
against Israel and Jews, built up an army in Lebanon,
and has repeatedly insisted that its aim is the liquidation of Israel, both *Newsweek* and the *Washington
Post* portray the PLO as a social organization willing
to live in peace next to Israel, having long ago given up

370

its "dream" of removing the Jewish state from the map.

After transforming PLO terrorists into brave fighters in a noble cause, the media's next step was to present this Soviet client organization as an ally of the United States. ABC's Bill Redeker on *Nightline* expounded the myth of a long time U.S.-PLO cooperation including PLO efforts to negotiate the Iranian hostage crisis. Since there is ample evidence that the PLO was involved in the embassy takeover, trained Iranian "students," and has often called the United States a bigger enemy than Israel, ABC's mendacious broadcasting simply rewrites history to suit the present bias.

The media have persistently placed the Palestinian Arabs and the PLO (terms used interchangeably) in the underdog role. For the media, Israel's actions in Lebanon were so heinous that it led CBS's Dan Rather, for example, to exclaim that with the arrival of the U.S. Marines in Lebanon there was now "at least an army that does not massacre children."

This is not news, it is warfare.

Media studies reveal that television is the main source of news for the American people—hence its potency during the Lebanon war. TV's awesome role has not been tempered by a sense of balance or responsibility as exemplified by NBC's John Chancellor setting the tone for NBC news. Describing Israel's raid over Beirut as leaving a "stench of terror all across the city'' as the Fascists did in Spain in the 1930s, he asserted:

> Nothing like it has ever happened in this part of the world. I kept thinking of Madrid during the Spanish Civil War. What in the world is going on? Israel's security problem on its border is 50 miles to the south. The answer is that we are dealing with an imperial Israel which is solving its problems in someone else's country— world opinion be damned.

Media coverage of the various peace plans offered by President Reagan and the Arab League depict an ever-scowling Begin saying ''no'' to peace. Evidence of ''hints'' and ''leaks'' culled by the media at the Arab League meeting in Fez suggest the Arabs were receptive to Reagan's peace proposal. King Hussein gave the impression that talks with Israel were a possibility.

Yet aside from posturings before the media, the Arabs offered nothing new. The old code-words were used at Fez, including ''the right of return'' for all Palestinian Arabs and ''the inviolable rights'' of the PLO to recover all of Palestine. Contrary to media implications, at no time did the Arab League recognize Israel's right to exist.

Attempting to foster an illusion of moderation, the media gave wide coverage to Congressman Paul McCloskey's erroneous assertion that Arafat recognized Israel's right to exist. Repeatedly *The Times* and other sources look and almost discover that magic concession by Arafat—that Israel has the right to exist. Deliberately excluded are the repeated affirmations by PLO leaders of the Palestine National Covenant calling for Israel's demise.

Some media moguls acknowledge that their reporting is governed by distinct prearranged biases. In an interview conducted by Leon Hadar of the *Jerusalem Post* (August 8-14), NBC news chief Reuven Frank admitted that the television media hold long-term biases which impart a distinctive tone to the news. Frank explained that between 1949 and Sadat's visit to Jerusalem the media were pro-Israel because of the sympathy for the Holocaust victims and because of "the power of the Jewish community." The Palestinian Arabs then "took over...that underdog image." According to Frank what is seen in the media now is only "a reduction in the pro-Israel bias." When asked why television failed to report the Christians' agony at the hands of the PLO, or for that matter the suffering of the Copts in Egypt or the Kurds in Iraq, Frank replied, "You cover what you think is interesting for the viewers. I can't imagine anyone getting upset about the Copts."

Frank was asked why the media did not compensate for their presentation of one-sided, sensationalized material by providing context and background material. He replied that "political context is only rationalization'' for the destruction and violence committed by the Israelis. What counts are action scenes, he insisted; the only one in Lebanon that lets the media perform freely are the Israelis.

Frank, in effect, is revealing two points. First, the public's faith in the objectivity and reliability of the media is not warranted. Second, he is arguing that the pro-Israel interests—as he referred to them—can only *hope* for media fairness: they cannot persuade the media to adhere to the canons of objectivity and balanced reporting.

In part, the PLO was able to dole out the news they saw fit to print because of the media bias. Pictures of PLO members with their families gave the world the impression that hometown boys were leaving Beirut to prevent their neighborhoods from being destroyed. No emphasis was given to their being illegal occupiers. The almost daily diet of Arafat posing with children belies the fact that these children and hundreds of thousands of others were PLO hostages. Had the media been willing to place the war in context they would have had to stress that the PLO, as Eliahu Saltpeter pointed out, "systematically used schools, mosques, and public buildings for gun placements and training bases, as well as shopping centers and apartment buildings for command posts and ammunition dumps." ("Lebanon: The Good, the Bad, the Misleading," *The New Leader*, June 28.)

In addition to the widespread media bias against

374

Israel, the media are duly restrained and influenced by Arab intimidation. While making the recent murders of our reporters in El Salvador a major issue, and rightly so, the media have permitted only the barest hints revealing gross intimidations by the PLO in Lebanon. (See John Weissman, "Intimidation," *TV Guide*, October 23 and 30 for an overview of totalitarian pressure on the media.)

Aaron Dholev, writing in *Ma'ariv* (August 20) describes the systematic terrorizing of the entire international and Lebanese press by the PLO, which included the murder of eight foreign correspondents including two from ABC. Based on interviews with Beirut journalist Edouard George and other Christian and Muslim Lebanese journalists, Dholev relates how the entire press was made to do the bidding of the PLO, which used a combination of fear and bribes. What is most remarkable about the Dholev article is not that these things occurred, but the systematic cover-up by the media. The media have not indicated that their reports on the war reflected PLO intimidation.

Thus, much of the PLO's favorable press is attributable to the harassment and murder of Western reporters.

Time (June 2) briefly reported that correspondents in Beirut were so frightened they "stick together, do not go out at night and never photograph Syrian troops." According to Edward Alexander, both the

Washington Post and *The New York Times* acknowledged their journalists were harassed and illegally detained by the PLO but chose not to make an issue of it. ("Israel in the Dock," *Encounter*, September-October, 1982.) The media, however, made a cause-celebre of restrictions imposed on reporters by Israel during the early days of the war. Only later did some in the media concede, grudgingly and briefly, that Israel was generally cooperative in letting the press do their business. Apparently, the media silence over PLO intimidation did not clash with their anti-Israel, pro-liberation biases.

On June 25, John Chancellor joined the media attack on Israel's censorship in an inflammatory style. He said this censorship "is an outrage coming from an ally which fights with American weapons, a country which has received almost $13 billion in American aid the last five years." (He was not even factual: most of the money was interest-bearing loans.) Chancellor did not display such wrathful righteousness over the total British censorship during the Falkland war or the refusal of either the Iraqis or the Iranians to allow foreign journalists to cover the war. Nothing was said about the Syrians' cover-up of the destruction of their own city of Hama. In short, these omissions lead to only one conclusion—Chancellor is waging war, not analyzing events for the public.

Chancellor's cry of Israeli censorship is the

height of chutzpah because the same evening's NBC news reported the war in great detail in a manner unfavorable to Israel. NBC reported the Israeli assault on Beirut in terms of a massive attack against civilians, daily filling the screens with pictures of maimed women and children. NBC reporters went out of their way to state that the Israelis were aiming at non-military targets. "Israeli gunboats pound residential areas in central Beirut. No military targets here," reported Steve Mallory. He was followed by Ed Kellerman, who stated, "They are hitting all these residential buildings. They are not hitting anywhere the Syrians are." Not only was the Israeli version not reported, NBC ignored readily available information that the PLO persistently housed their guns and weapons in civilian areas. In short, the PLO used civilians, including Palestinian Arabs, as hostages.

The NBC onslaught suggests one conclusion— the PLO and its allies were the source of its information—even though it was presented without such acknowledgements. NBC (June 14) presented erroneous civilian casualties and failed to retract them when they were disavowed by the Red Cross. Lebanese "public opinion" turned out to be the voice of the pro-PLO Walid Jumblatt. It is no secret that the bulk of the Lebanese factions and religious groups were relieved to see the PLO depart. These views were almost never included. NBC made it clear it was going to foster perceptions that Israel seeks territory and dominance rather than peace and security.

Since the late 1960s the media have increasingly succumbed to advocacy. The more compelling the "cause" the more a journalist is encouraged to abandon norms of objectivity.

A column written by Anthony Lewis during the Vietnam War demonstrates how the process works.

Lewis contends that when "there is no longer any question of moral ambiguity," supporting what is just is more important than one's professional commitment. He urged that all professional codes and standards be violated (save for the use of violence) to oppose the war and get America out of Indochina.

Thus he contends that the journalist's calling is not to inform but to forge his tools into a weapon and even to prevaricate when the cause merits it (*New York Times*, May 13, 1972). On a recent ABC *Nightline*, Lewis told host Ted Koppel he saw no difference between the U.S. in Vietnam and Israel in Lebanon, thereby conceding that his emotive columns are dedicated not to the truth but to war on Israel.

It is no accident that the war in Lebanon dominated the media. A report on media budget allocations (*New York Times,* July 15) stated that the wars in Lebanon, El Salvador, and the Falklands were straining media budgets. With the latter two shunted aside it takes minimal effort to see that the media budget

378

goes toward covering Lebanon. It could be argued that budget resources should go toward covering the far more important, as well as ruinous and murderous, wars in the Middle East—including those in Iran, Ethiopia, and Afghanistan. These wars, which will decide the fate of the Middle East, and have a greater bearing on U.S. strategic and economic interests than Lebanon, receive at most brief attention. For Americans these wars, compared to the one in Lebanon, are virtually non-events.

In an analysis of the reporting of the Iraq-Iran War and West Bank clashes just before the Lebanon war, David Sidorsky, a professor of philosophy at Columbia University, demonstrates how *The New York Times* space allocations distorted the meaning of these two events ("Balance and Responsibility in the Media," *Midstream*, June/July, 1982). He notes that in a given week (March 22-27, 1982) over 1000 lines were devoted to the clashes in the West Bank culminating in the arrest of one Arab youth. The front-page stories were accompanied by evocative and sensational photos. The Iraq-Iran War, however, involving thousands of troops inflicting massive casualties and destruction was buried in *The Times* and reported in only a few lines. Thus, *The Times* resource allocation turns a relatively minor event into a major one and the major one into a virtual non-event. The allocation of funds buttresses the media theme that Israel alone is responsible for the turmoil in the Middle East, and that it alone holds the key to peace and stability.

The basic contention of the media with respect to the motivation of the Israeli campaign in Lebanon arose out of the general hostile analysis of Israel: there was no queston of a preemptive attack; Israel invaded Lebanon because Begin is fired by biblical fantasies to conquer and wipe out the "Palestinian people." The motive stems from Israel being an imperial state.

Yet the media systematically disregarded evidence justifying Israel's fears. This evidence included the thousands of foreign terrorists being trained in PLO camps, the vast quantity of Soviet war materials stored in PLO enclaves, and captured documents revealing future war plans against Israel. Had the public been made aware of the dismemberment of Lebanon by the PLO and Syria as well as the immediate threats faced by Israel, the latter's preemption would have been more understandable.

According to the London based newsletter *Arab-Asian Affairs* (July, 1982) the Soviet Union was militarizing the Levant. The Israel Defense Forces captured enough weapons to arm five brigades, including 1,320 armored combat vehicles. The PLO was in the process of being transformed by the Soviet Union into a mechanized army of three divisions which would have placed a new and dangerous burden on Israel's defense when added to Syrian, Iraqi, and Jordanian units.

380

Had the media bias not predetermined its selection of information, captured PLO documents would have had the value of a huge news item on the scale of the Pentagon Papers. They would have also alerted Americans as to Soviet intentions and shown that U.S. and Israeli interests were very close. This means the documents would have to be exposed in a meaningful way via prime-time and front-page coverage.

Preliminary examination of the captured documents suggests it would be impossible to sustain media charges that Israel preempted without sufficient reason. The documents (partially summarized in *Arab-Asian Affairs* and the London *Economist* for July 10) reveal the following: Soviet plans to store even more war supplies in Lebanon, plans for a major assault against Israel in the near future, the training of thousands of Palestinian Arabs by the Communist powers in the use of Soviet armor, and "neutral" Yugoslavia's training of PLO forces in command skills and in the use of chemical warfare.

These documents from Fatah and the PLO military command reveal plans to destroy Israel's northern population areas. Fatah reaffirmed its dream of destroying "the Zionist entity" in all its forms. Fatah revealed how the PLO occupied and organized Sidon: "The built-up areas in Sidon and the villages surrounding the city are excellent cover zones. The trees provide camouflage, and perfectly conceal vehicles and personnel." By excluding meaningful exposure of these revealing data and by not stressing the presence of thousands of foreign terrorists being trained by the PLO the American public was denied access to a major dimension of the causes leading to Israel's preemptive campaign.

It does not require hours of content analysis to conclude that the media reversed reality. They cast the PLO's image as "wholesome" and that of Israel as "arrogant and ruthless." How many Americans are aware that the Lebanese cheered the Israelis as liberators? Buried in the media, as noted, there were hints that the PLO "state within a state" was a cruel dictatorship. Churches were desecrated as they were turned into warehouses and garages. People were arbitrarily arrested; abuses of the PLO went unpunished. Children of 12 were conscripted, homes and businesses confiscated. By virtually ignoring PLO behavior (TV was far more negligent than the press) in Lebanon the public was denied important clues as to how the PLO would actually govern a Palestinian Arab "democratic state."

An October 14 *Newsweek* poll revealed a large drop in American support for Israel. It would be more accurate to conclude that the poll data recorded the effect of the media's campaign against Israel. Not only did the media turn Israel's preemptive attack into a moral defeat, but it damaged American interests. With the PLO enjoying a media victory, the Arab states will continue to promote the PLO as an irritant. For a while the Arab states were near relinquishing the PLO as a tool; this was in evidence by their refusal to aid the PLO during the war. Arafat's command of the media has changed that.

The media bias against Israel is also a bias against America. It is as if Israel did nothing to thwart Soviet plans in Lebanon or demonstrate the superiority of American military technology. In the media's eyes the United States has no enemies, therefore, it needs no allies. R. Emmett Tyrrell, Jr., an editor and media critic, concludes the following about the media bias towards Israel: "Thus, the defaming of another American ally picks up steam... Not all our allies are so...diabolized. The diabolizing comes down only on those who actually oppose America's enemies." (*New York Post*, August 9)

The media elites, as Walter Cronkite conceded, are universalist and humanity oriented, which translates into support for Third World totalitarian Marxism at the expense of Western and American security. The U.S., they believe, need only free itself of its troubles by abandoning its so-called friends, who are exploiters and oppress their subject masses in the Middle East and elsewhere. America would gain by supporting the people of the Third World, i.e., their liberation movements. Tyrell disagrees with the media intellectuals and warns that there is no middle ground between our allies and the liberation fronts, between the PLO and Israel. "The PLO aids, trains and applauds every anti-American force on earth... including the thugs of the Salvadoran bush."

The media's version of the news has stirred many Jews in America as they discovered how it was applied to Israel. They are outraged that the media have made Israel into an outlaw state. Most shocking is the realization that *The New York Times* has joined in the effort to destroy Israel as a moral entity. *The Times'* stand is particularly alarming because it carries the message into the heart of the New York metropolitan area. Its approach is cleverly packaged, as a variety of materials are squirreled away to give off the aura of fairness. It also subscribes to a higher form of morality as the summary of the following editorial of July 1 suggests.

The Begin regime is accused of lying "at the start when it said it wanted only a 25-mile cordon sanitaire .... [It] has lied about or at least suppressed the civilian casualties it has caused.... [It] has seemed obvious from the start that the slaughters in Lebanon were clearly disproportionate to any immediate threat." Stressing its evenhandedness the editorial continues: "Critics of the civilian bloodshed in Lebanon now fail to remember the much greater slaughter of civilians by which the P.L.O. and Syria took over the country. By remaining indifferent until the Israeli intervention, the world has created a double standard."

How clever! *The Times* stands above the fray. It criticizes all parties, but the operative feature of the editorial is to describe Israel falsely as being as criminal and inhumane as its foes.

In order to undermine the Begin administration further, *The Times* and other mainline media rely on what Edward Alexander calls "display Jews." These people have never reconciled themselves to the fact that in order to survive in the hostile Middle East, Israel must resort to arms and project power. Instead, these display Jews write, as Ruth Wisse noted in *Commentary*, as if it were Israel's moral behavior and not its existence that is the cause of its troubles in the Middle East. Readers and viewers are not made aware that many of these "resources" have opposed Israel's strong military for years and some are in reality party partisans opposed to Begin and his coalition. These views are useful to the media in that they buttress their assertion that Israel's immorality threatens vital U.S. interests.

The media tapped a group whose own feelings of doubt about Jews using military power to defend themselves coincides with the media's bias not to countenance, in the words of *Times* military analyst Drew Middleton, "a peaceful, unaggressive people who under the pressure of continued Arab enmity" were compelled to organize militarily.

To appreciate Jews only as victims is a vicious form of stereotyping. Holding Israel to standards of behavior not required of others, as *Commentary* editor Norman Podhoretz writes, is to raise anti-

Semitism to the nation-state level. Media moralists agonize over Israel's "soul" while virtually ignoring the powerful alignment seeking to extinguish it.

In savaging a small democratic nation that vanquished America's foes, the media, as Tyrell observes, reveal themselves to be more isolationist than the media of the 1930s. In the name of "humanity" the media are isolating America from valiant allies. If this trend prevails America will be alone with its totalitarian enemies.

The media have forged a weapon to expose the faults and failings of a democratic state while overlauding a "liberation organization." Savage use of front-page and prime-time cannot be offset by occasional pretenses. to provide alternative critical materials. Basically the media formula unfolds as follows:

An advanced nation allegedly oppresses a Third World people. The latter rise up under the leadership of what is identified as an indigenous liberation front whose leader, some investigative reporter "discovers," is an admirer of Thomas Jefferson. The people, i.e., the liberation front, resort to terror because the oppressor will not grant justice, i.e., turn over power to the front. Should the oppressor respond with force the media flays its behavior as evidence of excessive and unwarranted power. Today Israel is the newest victim of this adversary syndrome.

Some lessons can be gleaned from the reporting

of the Lebanon war this past summer. A military action, for example, that is not quickly executed enables the liberation front to "milk" an all-too-willing media. Because of the openness of Israel and the clever control exercised by its foes the media output have become structured against Israel.

The media have failed to live up to the strictures of honest and balanced reporting. Not since the Vietnam War has a democratic nation been subject to a major media onslaught. Adversary journalists are all too committed to the premise that in prompting the "cause" anything goes. The media have forgotten that the survival of free nations, such as Israel, and now perhaps Lebanon, are crucial to their freedom.

THE RECORD:
'TIME' vs. REALITY
by Rael Jean Isaac

The Foreign Broadcast Information Service is among the most reliable of sources for information on the Middle East. Its *Report on the Middle East and Africa*, one of eight such regional reports available through the Department of Commerce, appears five times a week. During the five-week period between August 29 and October 3, 1977, the Carter administration was trying to find a way to reconvene the Geneva Conference (Sadat did not make his famous trip to Jerusalem until late in November); the Arab states insisted on PLO representation and Israel refused to attend if the PLO attended. *Time's* coverage was sharply and consistently at odds with FBIS reports during this stage (and most other stages) of the peace process.

Time, August 29: While Israel's Menachem Begin was digging in deeper on the West Bank issue, off in Beirut his Palestinian foes last week took a big if unheralded step

Rael Jean Isaac is the author of *Israel Divided* (Johns Hopkins) and *Parties and Politics of Israel* (Longmans), and is a member of the Executive Committee of Americans For A Safe Israel.

Reprinted by permission of THE NEW REPUBLIC, (c) 1980 The New Republic, Inc.

toward peace. *Time* has learned that after extensive negotiations... the so-called Palestinian 'rejectionists' have decided to end their defiant stand against peace on any terms with Israel and agree with the larger Palestine Liberation Organization on the goal of securing an independent state on the West Bank and in Gaza.... The deal was crucial.... [T]he continuing holdout of the rejectionists, notably the Popular Front for the Liberation of Palestine, headed by hard-lining George Habash, had muddled the Palestinian position.... [O]ne of the rejectionists explained 'We feel this is the time for the Palestinians to stand together.'

FBIS, September 12, Algiers: Interview with George Habash, leader of the Popular Front for the Liberation of Palestine. 'We reject it [242] because the Palestinian struggle is based on the premise that Palestine is an Arab country afflicted with Zionist colonialism. The armed Palestinian revolution will continue until the complete liberation of Palestinian soil is achieved.'

Time, August 29: 'We're not blocking peace,' says a PLO spokesman, 'Israel is.' To press that point Yasser Arafat plans... to push for a new UN resolution... [which] will meet Carter's injunction by explicitly accepting 242, but it will also include his very words on the Palestinian homeland. 'We would be very much surprised if the U.S. vetoes the President's own language.'

FBIS, September 26, Algiers: Abu Hassan, PLO representative in Algeria, asked about the PLO attitude to 242 said: 'The PLO says no. Israel is an alien body in the Arab sea. This body is bound to disappear given the effective medicine – a united Arab front.'

Time, September 19: In a rare show of unanimity 21 Foreign Ministers of the Arab League adopted in Cairo what one Western diplomat called 'the last hurrah of the moderates.' He meant an eight point working paper. . . . Significantly the document distinguishes between territory occupied after the 1967 war and Israel's 1948 boundaries – a tacit admission that Israel has a right to exist as a state.

FBIS, September 7, Riyadh: Arab Foreign Ministers approved an eight point working paper prepared by the Arab League Political Committee. . . . It called on all states to give no aid to Israel and to halt immigration to 'the occupied Palestine and Arab territories.' [This call to countries to forbid emigration of their citizens to Israel obviously does not distinguish between Israel's boundaries before and after the 1967 war. – R.J.I.]

FBIS, September 8, Riyadh: Saudi Arabia's Information Minister Muhammad Yamani reaffirmed Saudi Arabia's position on the Palestinian question referring to foreign press campaigns casting doubt on the kingdom's position. Crown Prince Fahd had underscored to President Carter the kingdom's support for 'the full rights and demands of the Palestinians written with their own hands.' [This is a reference to the Palestinian Covenant, 13 of whose 32 articles call for the destruction of Israel.—R.J.I.]

Time, October 3: One bar to PLO participation [at Geneva] is Washington's insistence that the organization endorse United Nations Resolution 242, which calls for 'secure border' for all nations in the area—an implicit recognition of Israel's right to exist. The PLO has refused to accept the resolution since it refers to the Palestinians as refugees rather than as a nation with rights.

FBIS, September 12, Algiers: Interview with George Habash. 'Our rejection [of 242] does not stem from the consideration that 242 only talks of refugees but that it talks of recognition of Israel and secure borders.'

FBIS, September 12, Cairo: Zuhair Mohsen [head of military operations for the PLO] again rejected 242 because according to him 'it recognizes Israel's right to exist.'

R.J.I.

THE HIJACKING OF FLIGHT 847: THE MEDIA BLAMES ISRAEL

by David Bar-Illan

The deterioration in U.S.-Israel relations in the year following the June 1982 invasion of Lebanon was the steepest ever. It reached an unprecedented low point when an American marine waving a pistol at an Israeli tank was commended for "heroism" by the Pentagon, as if he had repulsed the armor of a hostile army about to cross a DMZ.

One example of the extent to which television coverage encouraged such attitudes in high places came to light in December 1984, when a prominent senator confessed to a Jewish group that the reason he had recommended sanctions against Israel in 1982 was that he had been convinced by television commentators Israel was perpetrating a holocaust in Lebanon. Nevertheless, toward the end of 1983, the mood seemed to change. The

David Bar-Illan is a founding member of "Writers & Artists for Peace in the Middle East," a member of the board of the "Committee on the Present Danger" and of "Americans for a Safe Israel," and former chairman of the Executive Committee of the "National Committee on American Foreign Policy." Mr. Bar-Illan is the host of the weekly public affairs television program, "International Dateline."

A version of this essay is published in the September, 1985 issue of **Commentary Magazine.**

bloody, hopelessly irresolvable sectarian conflicts in areas evacuated by Israel; the bombing of the American embassy and marine barracks by suicidal Shiite fanatics; the Lebanese abrogation, under Syrian pressure, of the American-sponsored agreement with Israel; and Syria's refusal to honor its pledge to withdraw from Lebanon, all served to effect a rapprochement between Israel and the U.S. In the face of Arab enormities, Israel-bashing lost much of its appeal.

Not that the media—particularly television reporters in the field—ever stopped trying. Whenever gorier-than-usual massacres occurred, they would swoop down on the survivors and, with unswervable tenacity, cajole, solicit and prod anti-Israel statements from them. There was an almost symbiotic reciprocity in the transaction: the traumatized, homeless and bereft would blame Israel's 1982 invasion for all the evil in Lebanon (a far safer exercise on camera than bad-mouthing a rival sect) and the journalists would discreetly refrain from questions about the preceding 12 years of Arab atrocities and bloodbaths.

A particularly inflammatory flurry of media activity occurred just before Israel's final withdrawal. In response to sniping, car-bombing and suicide attacks by the Shiite militias seeking credit for "forcing" Israel out of Lebanon, Israel implemented a "strong hand" policy. The measures included arresting men caught carrying weapons, and blowing up houses in which arms caches had been found. These proved highly effective; but the media, in a *deja-vu* depicted Israel's actions as indiscriminate attacks on civilians (none of the guerrillas wore uniforms, of course) and even mistranslated the name of the operation from "strong hand" to "iron fist," to convey brutal, ruthless repression.

The anti-Israel campaign reached a climax with the accusation that two Lebanese cameramen serving as CBS part-time employees had been deliberately murdered by an Israeli tank crew. This was later retracted, without apology, when it became obvious that the Israeli troops had mistaken the cameramen for combatants. But the hyperbolic, hysterical tone of the accusation, the rush to judgment on threadbare evidence, the irresponsible repetition of a patently preposterous story, and the ill-concealed rage of virtually the entire communications industry betrayed a deep-seated hostility in the media for the State of Israel. Characteristically, only one newspaper in the whole country—the Boston Globe—published a widely distributed wire service photograph showing that even from a distance of ten feet it was difficult to discern the difference between a TV camera and a shoulder-held anti-tank weapon used by the guerrillas. It was later proved that the Israeli tank was approximately one mile away.

In the aftermath of Israel's withdrawal from the area south of Beirut, the Shiite Amal militia, in an attempt to establish hegemony over the area, attacked the Palestinian "camps" (really suburbs) of Sabra and

Shatila. The atrocities were, as usual, unspeakable. Children were shot dead point blank; men and women were dragged out of hospital beds and ambulances to be killed; Red Cross convoys were kept out of the area while the sick and injured were left to die in the streets; families huddling in shelters were slaughtered in their sleep. But the reporting of these atrocities was underplayed and understated, providing a striking contrast to the coverage of the 1982 massacre in the same "camps," when Christian Arabs allied with Israel killed 450 men of military age and 35 women and children. The latter received more air time and more inches of print in the American media than all the atrocities and massacres throughout the world since World War II combined.

Still, despite the efforts of the media, it was difficult to sustain the notion that this time all blame could be laid at Israel's doorstep. As one of the hosts on CNN's talk show CROSSFIRE put it, there was a growing consensus that the Arabs in Lebanon were "into killing."

***

All this changed overnight with the hijacking of TWA flight 847. From the very beginning, the networks pounced on *one* of the hijackers' demands—the release of 766 Lebanese detainees in Israel—to the exclusion of all the others. Ignored was the demand for the release of 17 Shiite prisoners held in Kuwait, even though Kuwait's refusal to release them in the preceding December caused the murder of two American passengers by Shiite terrorists on a Kuwaiti plane hijacked to Teheran. Ignored was the fact that the release of these Shiite prisoners in Kuwait was also the stated purpose for kidnapping seven Americans in Beirut over the preceding 16 months. Ignored, indeed, was the fact that this was the only demand which made sense, since the detainees in Israel were in the process of being released anyway. Completely disregarded were the hijackers' other demands: the release of their cohort, held by Greece, the release of two Shiite terrorists held by Spain, the reversal of America's policies in the Middle East, the termination of aid to Israel, and the overthrow of President Mubarak of Egypt and King Hussein of Jordan. When Israel's ambassador to the U.N., on ABC Evening News, pointed to these demands as a clear indication of the theatrical nature of the hijacking and its propagandistic purposes, anchorman Peter Jennings cut him short and insisted on knowing if Israel would release the Shiite prisoners to save the hostages. Clearly, from the point fo view of the media, the only "viable" demand was the release of the detainees.

The hijackers and their supporters—whose sensitivity to media techniques and moods has been a source of amazement to communications experts— were quick to recognize this as a public-relations bonanza. Realizing that if they stuck to this demand alone, television networks throughout the West would act as their mouthpiece, and the round-the-clock services of the world's most influential opinion-molders would be at their disposal, they dropped all other demands and concentrated on Israel. At the same time Israel, innocently assuming that the President of the U.S. rather than the media represented American opinion, took its cue from official pronouncements. Prime Minister Shimon Peres announced that his country would not release the detainees under terrorist threats.

So the all-too-familiar scene was set: on one side persecuted Arabs, "understandably enraged" by horrible injustices, making "reasonable" demands (after all "they were entitled to the release of those prisoners," said American arbitration experts paraded before the cameras), and on the other side intransigent Israelis cold-bloodedly oblivious to the fate of the innocent hostages. Over and over again, as they alternated subtle hints with blunt accusations, television commentators, anchormen and reporters, assuming the roles of negotiators, arbiters and moralizers, portrayed Israel as an ungrateful ally who would release 1150 convicted murderers in return for three *Israeli* soldiers, but would not release 766 innocent Lebanese ("not charged with any crime") to save the lives of 50 innocent *American* tourists. Thus, Bryant Gumbel of NBC's *Today* Show, in a June 27 interview with Georgetown University Fellow Jeoffrey Kemp asked, "Will Israel compromise on the TWA hostages or play fast and loose with American lives?" and, "Is Israeli international politics going to take precedence over the well-being of the hostages?"

To buttress this campaign the media, with the help of leaks from anti-Israel officials in the American government, invented a "split" between the two countries. On June 17, three days after the hijacking, CBS Evening News reported a "diplomatic standoff" between the U.S. and Israel. On the same evening, NBC News reported that the U.S. was "frustrated" with Israel and that Secretary of State Shultz was "annoyed." On June 21, CBS Evening News reported that "Israel is trying to ease tensions with Washington" and ABC's *Nightline* reported that Israel was trying to smooth over "ruffled feathers." On July 1, host Ted Koppel wondered aloud on *Nightline* if the U.S. "will begin to move away from Israel as an ally as a result of the hostage crisis?" Throughout the crisis, Prime Minister Shimon Peres, Defense Minister Yitzhak Rabin, Minister Without Portfolio Moshe Arens, Ambassador to the U.N. Benjamin Netanyahu and Member of Parliament Ehud Olmert all flatly denied any differences between the two countries on the subject of the hostages. But the networks persisted, apparently oblivious to the fact that by pressuring Israel to release the Shiites, they were asking it to contravene the publicly and privately stated wishes of the President, the Secretary of State and the National Security Advisor of the United States.

Ironically, journalists who for years had excoriated Israel for refusing to talk with the PLO, suddenly made a startling discovery: Israel's long negotiation with a PLO faction which produced the release of 1150 terrorists was the root cause of all subsequent acts of terrorism not only in Lebanon but throughout the world. Ignoring the endemic nature of terrorism in the Middle East, the anti-American thrust of world terrorism, and the eight hijackings in the months preceding the TWA drama—all perpetrated by Shiites and none connected to the detainees in Israel—Robert Novak, co-host of CROSSFIRE on Cable News Network, averred that the killing of the six Americans in El Salvador, the bombing of the Air India flight over the Atlantic and the explosions at the Frankfurt and Tokyo airports were all triggered by Israel's release of the 1150 PLO terrorists. Throughout the 17-day ordeal, hardly a word was uttered by TV newsmen about the possibility that America's ''fist-shaking warnings and tiptoeing backdowns after Embassy bombings and the massacre of the marines,'' as columnist William Safire put it, might have encouraged terrorists to believe that they could hijack an American plane with impunity. On the contrary. They persistently parroted the Shiite line that retribution for the murdered marines had been exacted when the battleship New Jersey shelled

"Shiite villages," and that the "indiscriminate slaughter" caused by the shelling created bitter anti-American feelings which brought about the hijacking. In fact, as every newsman must have known, the New Jersey shelling was directed at the Druze militia and its allies who were advancing on the presidential palace in East Beirut and threatening to overthrow the legitimate government of Lebanon.

This was not the only Shiite interpretation of events adopted by the newscasters. The Shiite spokesman contended that the plane was hijacked by men desperate to free "their relatives" held hostage in Israel, thus creating a parallel with the families of the American hostages who wanted freedom for *their* relatives. Allyn Conwell, the hostages' chosen spokesman (George Will of ABC called him "an active collaborationist" and William Safire of the New York Times referred to him as a "quisling") said, "If my wife and children were abducted and taken illegally across the border, I guess I too would have resorted to anything at all to free them." Not a single reporter in Lebanon questioned these absurd statements. Surely even the most ignorant among them knew there were no "wives and children" in Israeli custody. Only young men of military age, all caught in actions against Israeli troops during the late phases of withdrawal from Lenanon, were incarcerated. Even the inference often made on television, that they had been taken as "insurance" against further attacks was

401

absurd. Had the Israelis wanted such "insurance" they would have arrested village elders, religious leaders and sheiks. But with the exception of Ted Koppel and George Will of ABC, and perhaps one or two others, no one protested this spurious parallel.

It should come as no surprise that the scenario of hostages on one side of the border and hostages on the other, conjuring a moral symmetry between the Arab hijackers and the Israeli army, would prove irresistible to the media. It is, after all, a pattern they often follow in describing the United States and the Soviet Union, portraying both as committing parallel crimes in the pursuit of hegemony. The Soviets invaded Afghanistan; we invaded Grenada; they shot down KAL flight 007; we support the atrocities of the "contras." Such symmetries are obscene mutilations of fact which play into the hands of totalitarians. The use of the word *hostage* is typically applied to kidnapped innocents whose lives are threatened. To describe the Lebanese detainees in Israel this way is a travesty. They were neither innocent nor threatened.

Similarly, much was made by the media of the "illegality" of holding those prisoners in Israel and its equivalence to the "illegality" of the hijacking. Both were "violations of international law." Whether or not transferring the detainees to Israel actually constituted a violation of the Fourth Geneva Convention —leading experts in international law adamantly insist it did not—to compare this kind of infraction to the TWA hijacking is like comparing a traffic violation to murder. None of the media analysts bothered to say so, and even the more serious talk shows never bothered to invite experts to discuss the purpose of the Fourth Geneva Convention and its proper application—neither of which had anything to do with the situation in Lebanon. Nor did anyone seem to remember that the invasion of Grenada, the rescue of Israeli hostages at Entebbe, the abduction of Eichmann, the pursuit of Mengele, and virtually all the proposed retaliatory measures against hijackers (blockading the Beirut airport, apprehending the hijackers and bringing them to justice in America) were, strictly speaking, violations of international law.

Throughout the ordeal, the networks faithfully adhered to another bit of Shiite fiction: that the "bad guys" were the first two hijackers, who killed Navy diver Robert Stethem, that the dozen reinforcements who assumed command on the second Beirut stop were much more moderate and civilized, and that the Amal militias who took the hostages off the plane and guarded them until their release were kind, gentle and considerate saviors. It is one thing to hear such naive nonsense from hostages who, after witnessing a murder and expecting to be murdered themselves would consider anyone who did *not* kill them a savior, and another to hear it from presumably impartial media observers. The facts were no secret: the reinforcements, who were invited to the plane by the original two, knew them by name, gave them orders upon boarding and worked in smooth collaboration with them through the next trip to Algiers and back to Beirut. Together they stripped the passengers of all their valuables, together they randomly beat them and together they ordered the Auschwitz-like selection of those with Jewish names. The 'savior' militias who transferred the hostages to "safe houses" in Beirut also acted with the full cooperation of the original hijackers. There was no altercation among them, not a harsh word, not the slightest disagreement. During the hostages' incarceration, the original hijackers, including the owner of the silver pistol who killed Stethem, were very much in evidence among the 'savior' militias, some of whom amused themselves by using the hostages for games of Russian roulette. And, finally, after the release, the two original hijackers appeared hooded at a press conference under Amal auspices. But almost no one in either print or electronic media seemed to recognize this pattern, so similar to the modus operandi of the 1979 Teheran hostage crisis. Mark Helprin, in the Wall Street Journal of July 1, was the exception:

> "As in Iran, we have seen in the latest hostage drama the game of "hard cop/soft cop," in which the U.S. is put off balance by the alleged differences between a set of good guys and a set of bad guys. In Iran it was Bani-Sadr and Ghotbzadeh as opposed to Khomeini and the "students." In Lebanon, it was Mssrs.

404

Berri and Assad as opposed to the "hijackers" and Hezbollah. Both crimes were adjuncts to local power struggles, but if what was true in Iran was true also in Lebanon, only one set of actors was in control, and the other was merely being used. In this context, it is interesting that the hijackers of TWA 847, supposedly uncompromising Islamic militants from whom Mr. Berri and Mr. Assad were to protect us, are reported to have consumed all the liquor on the plane and badly mistreated the women. Islamic militants certainly have their faults, but they rather studiously avoid such things. If the reports are true, who hijacked the plane in the first place? The operation was a lot more secular and political than some might think and was probably planned not in a mosque but in a ministry.''

A few of the hostages were astute enough to recognize what the journalists ignored. Peter Hill insisted after the release that all the various groups were in cahoots and were no different from one another—for which hostage-spokesman Allyn Conwell called him emotionally unstable and a racist. Hill and the other real heroes of the saga—the hostages who had refused to play talking puppets in the terrorist theater and who had presented a sullen and defiant visage to the captors' cameras—were practically ignored by the media after the release. But Conwell became an overnight superstar, holding nationally televised press conferences, being interviewed on national news programs, appearing alone on hour-long talk show, and even endorsing Jimmy Carter's book on the Middle East *The Blood of Abraham*. In a Washington Post article on July 1, media critic

Tom Shales said, "The TV networks afforded Conwell the totally undeserved status of foreign relations expert: When network anchors weren't playing diplomat themselves, they were putting Conwell on the air to play diplomat from his own wildly distorted vantage point." The networks justified the numerous interviews with Conwell, before and after the hostages' release, by insisting that the American public had a right to know the viewpoint of the hostages' spokesman. They did not, however, insist on the viewers' right to know that Conwell ostentatiously carried Muslim prayer beads and the Koran throughout his captivity, and that he was a 10-year resident of an Arab country, Oman, where he represented an American company and to which he intended to return. Interestingly, when asked about his background, Conwell would sometimes refer to "working overseas" in the last ten years without mentioning Oman.

In portraying Amal chief Nabih Berri, the media again accepted the Shiite script, depicting him as a moderate negotiator, an impartial go-between trying to do his best to save both the Arab "hostages" in Israel and the Amereican hostages in Beirut. What the networks did not deem worthy of telling their viewers was that Berri was responsible for eight hijackings before the TWA incident, that he had called for suicide attacks on the withdrawing Israeli army, that he personally commanded the Amal militias that had mercilessly slaughtered Palestinian women and children in Sabra and Shatila, that during the hostage crisis his militias killed two Palestinian nurses who had stumbled on the hostages' hiding place, and that neither Amal nor any other armed group could make a major move in Lebanon without Syrian approval.

One of the most revealing incidents during the crisis, which inadvertantly exposed the inner workings of the media's anti-Israel bias, occured on Cable News Network. Again, Tom Shales of the Washington Post:

> "CNN showed its taped pictures from Beirut Saturday as an "unedited satellite feed," meaning no producers or editors had gone through the footage before it aired. Viewers may have been confused, or infuriated, at the zeal with which CNN reporter Jim Clancy baited hostages to condemn or at least implicate Israel in the crisis. He badgered the hostages on this point; he wouldn't give up until they agreed with his thesis that Israel was not justified in detaining its 735 Lebanese captives."

When asked about this episode, CNN anchorman Bernard Shaw said, "It was a mistake to show unedited material." Indeed it was, for it displayed in all its nakedness the process of masquerading propaganda as news. An edited version would have undoubtedly shown hostages "spontaneously" spouting anti-Israel statements, without any help from your friendly, objective, even-handed correspondent. (To what extent Mr. Clancy became a spokesman for the Shiites was again evident on July 4, when he stated that to obtain the release of the seven kidnapped Americans still in Lebanon, "Kuwait would have to release the 17 Shiites serving long sentences in Kuwait jails for *allegedly* bombing the U.S. embassy there." When it comes to Shiites, trial and conviction are obviously not enough for Mr. Clancy.)

The correspondents were by no means the only anti-Israel players in this drama. Anchormen and talk-show hosts served the hijackers even better. One of the primary purposes of terrorist acts is to draw world attention to their "cause." It is a known psychological truth that under emotional strain, especially when accompanied by ignorance of the facts, one tends to absorb propaganda with eager compliance. Mindlessly serving this purpose, every network invited the most virulent anti-Israel spokesmen available to "explain" the hijackers' grievances. The list reads like the Who's Who of the Arab lobby—James Abourezk, Jesse Jackson, Michael Hudson, Walid Khalidi, Clovis Maksoud, Hisham Sharabi, David Sadd, James Zogby et al, plus the obligatory appearance on practically every major program of Rajai-Khorasani, the Iranian ambassador to the U.N. Not surprisingly, they all advocated yielding to the hijackers' demands—not because they approved of the hijacking, of course, but because one had to understand their grievances. All agreed that terrorism would not end until grievances were eliminated, and that the only way to eliminate them was to stop supporting Israel. Only once did a television host, Ted Koppel, ask a guest, former Senator James Abourezk, if he thought it proper to discuss American foreign policy at such a time.

After the hostages' release, some anchormen and talk-show hosts were asked why so much air time had been given to the hijackers and their apologists. Again the reply was that the American public needed such education and that it was only fair to give the hijackers' point of view a hearing. On July 10, New York Times columnist Tom Wicker, echoing this view, wrote, "Was television 'used' by Amal? Of course, just as it is being used all the time by the Reagan administration for its own purposes." (Here we have it. The ultimate even-handedness: a "godfather" of cutthroats, kidnappers and assassins on the one hand and the democratically elected President of the U.S.A. on the other.)

One wonders how Wicker would have responded to a question asked of ABC anchorman Peter Jennings by Larry King, host of a CNN talk show: "Would you have let Hitler come on the tube in September 1939 to explain the reasons for the Nazi invasion of Poland?" Jennings adroitly evaded the question. (Unfortunately, King's burst of common sense was short-lived. Two days later he had Allyn Conwell on, alone for a whole hour, and treated him with the kind of deference that would make rest room attendants blush.)

Perhaps the most sickening spectacle was the orgy of self-congratulation during a post-hijacking program on ABC's *Nightline*, in which all the senior ABC correspondents in Beirut participated. Not only had they not done any wrong, they insisted, they had probably advanced the cause of peace and justice in the Middle East by exposing the defects of American policy there. The climax came when Charles Glass, the journalist whose good relations with the Shiites had enabled him to score several scoops during the crisis, said, "This ordeal is not over until the last Shiite prisoner in Israel is freed." Host Ted Koppel, with obvious embarrassment, hurriedly added "and of course the seven American hostages still in captivity in Lebanon...."

***

The tragic irony of this story is that the Lebanese Shiites do indeed have legitimate grievances, grievances that have nothing to do with Israel or the U.S. They have been savaged, raped and murdered by the PLO (the erstwhile darling of the media), exploited by Sunni Moslems, patronized by Christian Arabs and oppressed by Syrians. Unfortunately, they have not chosen an association with the West and a democratic solution for their salvation. Since they are the largest sect in Lebanon, that would have worked

410

in their favor, but they chose instead to align themselves with medieval, fundamentalist Khomeini and radical, terrorism-prone Assad. Perhaps their perception that the West is in decline had something to do with it. But the media's glamorization of Shiites' anti-Western terrorism can only reinforce their contempt for the West, and help doom them to the darkness of fundamentalism and the oppression of radicalism.

It is difficult if not impossible to fathom why journalists side with fanatics and terrorists. Perhaps the abysmal, encyclopedic ignorance that afflicts many of them is partly to blame. (ABC-TV correspondent Michael Lee, reporting from Israel, once said, "I am standing here in what used to be independent Palestine.") There is also a palpable ideological bias among many journalists who grew up in the sixties and who still mindlessly believe that every self-styled "liberation movement," especially if it is anti-American, must be good, no matter how fascistic, totalitarian and anti-democratic it may be. But there is probably some truth, too, in what President Carter's press secretary Jody Powell has written, "The mistakes and excesses of journalists are not primarily a product of ideological or partisan bias. . .the root of the evil is the love of money which translates into competition for ratings." In this particular hostage crisis there was also the phenomenon Norman Podhoretz persuasively diagnosed, in a New York Post column, as a case in which the whole government rather than just

411

the hostages suffered from the "Stockholm syndrome"—the feeling of gratitude and sympathy for the terrorists for not committing *worse* atrocities. It undoubtedly affected the newsmen in Beirut and New York as well. Perhaps the special situation in Beirut provides an explanation, too. Two weeks before the hijacking David Blundy, correspondent for the London *Sunday Times*, described the atmosphere of fear and intimidation in Beirut: "Many reporters have been withdrawn because of the risk of being kidnapped or killed. Those who remain find it increasingly difficult and dangerous to work." A reporter in Beirut told Blundy, "If we print atrocity stories, we will get a bomb through our window."

Whatever the reasons for the media's conduct in the Beirut TWA hijacking and hostage crisis of 1985, there is no doubt that the tragic spectacle of an impotent, bewildered and helpless America, venting its frustration and rage on Israel instead of on the terrorists, was largely brought about by journalists, particularly those in American television.

I

CODE OF ETHICS OF THE AMERICAN SOCIETY OF PROFESSIONAL JOURNALISTS

The Society of Professional Journalists, Sigma Delta Chi, was founded in 1909. Headquartered in Chicago, it now has 28,000 members. Its Code of Ethics, first adopted in 1926 and revised in 1973, is presented here in full:

The Society of Professional Journalists, Sigma Delta Chi, believes the duty of journalists is to serve the truth.

We believe the agencies of mass communication are carriers of public discussion and information, acting on their Constitutional mandate and freedom to learn and report the facts.

We believe in public enlightenment as the forerunner of justice, and in our Constitutional role to seek the truth as part of the public's right to know the truth.

We believe those responsibilities carry obligations that require journalists to perform with intelligence, objectivity, accuracy, and fairness.

To these ends, we declare acceptance of the standards of practice here set forth:

I. RESPONSIBILITY: The public's right to know of events of public importance and interest is the overriding mission of the mass media. The purpose of distributing

413

news and enlightened opinion is to serve the general welfare. Journalists who use their professional status as representatives of the public for selfish or other unworthy motives violate a high trust.

II. FREEDOM OF THE PRESS: Freedom of the press is to be guarded as an inalienable right of people in a free society. It carries with it the freedom and the responsibility to discuss, question, and challenge actions and utterances of our government and of our public and private institutions. Journalists uphold the right to speak unpopular opinions and the privilege to agree with the majority.

III. ETHICS: Journalists must be free of obligation to any interest other than the public's right to know the truth.

1. Gifts, favors, free travel, special treatment or privileges can compromise the integrity of journalists and their employers. Nothing of value should be accepted.

2. Secondary employment, political involvement, holding public office, and service in community organizations should be avoided if it compromises the integrity of journalists and their employers. Journalists and their employers should conduct their personal lives in a manner which protects them from conflict of interest, real or apparent. Their responsibilities to the public are paramount. That is the nature of their profession.

3. So-called news communications from private sources should not be published or broadcast without substantiation of their claims to news value.

4. Journalists will seek news that serves the public interest, despite the obstacles. They will make constant efforts to assure that the public's business is conducted in

public and that public records are open to public inspection.

5. Journalists acknowledge the newsmen's ethic of protecting confidential sources of information.

IV. ACCURACY AND OBJECTIVITY: Good faith with the public is the foundation of all worthy journalism.

1. Truth is our ultimate goal.

2. Objectivity in reporting the news is another goal, which serves as the mark of an experienced professional. It is a standard of performance toward which we strive. We honor those who achieve it.

3. There is no excuse for inaccuracies or lack of thoroughness.

4. Newspaper headlines should be fully warranted by the contents of the articles they accompany. Photographs and telecasts should give an accurate picture of an event and not highlight a minor incident out of context.

5. Sound practice makes clear distinction between news reports and expressions of opinion. News reports should be free of opinion or bias and represent all sides of an issue.

6. Partisanship in editorial comment which knowingly departs from the truth violates the spirit of American journalism.

7. Journalists recognize their responsibility for offering informed analysis, comment, and editorial opinion on public events and issues. They accept the obligation to present such material by individuals whose competence, experience, and judgment qualify them for it.

8. Special articles or presentations devoted to ad-

vocacy or the writer's own conclusions and interpretations should be labeled as such.

V. FAIR PLAY: Journalists at all times will show respect for the dignity, privacy, rights, and well-being of people encountered in the course of gathering and presenting the news.

1. The news media should not communicate unofficial charges affecting reputation or moral character without giving the accused a chance to reply.

2. The news media must guard against invading a person's right to privacy.

3. The media should not pander to morbid curiosity about details of vice and crime.

4. It is the duty of news media to make prompt and complete correction of their errors.

5. Journalists should be accountable to the public for their reports and the public should be encouraged to voice its grievances against the media. Open dialogue with our readers, viewers, and listeners should be fostered.

VI. PLEDGE: Journalists should actively censure and try to prevent violations of these standards, and they should encourage their observance by all newspeople. Adherence to this code of ethics is intended to preserve the bond of mutual trust and respect between American journalists and the American people.

II

Maps

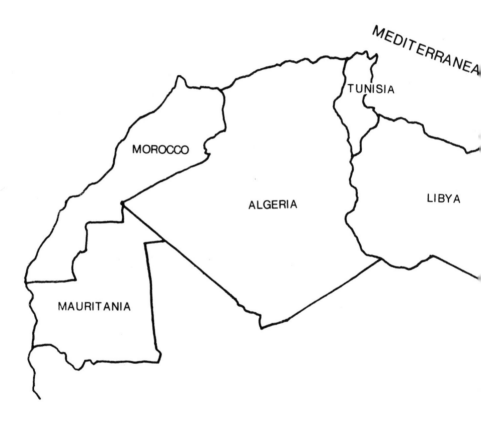

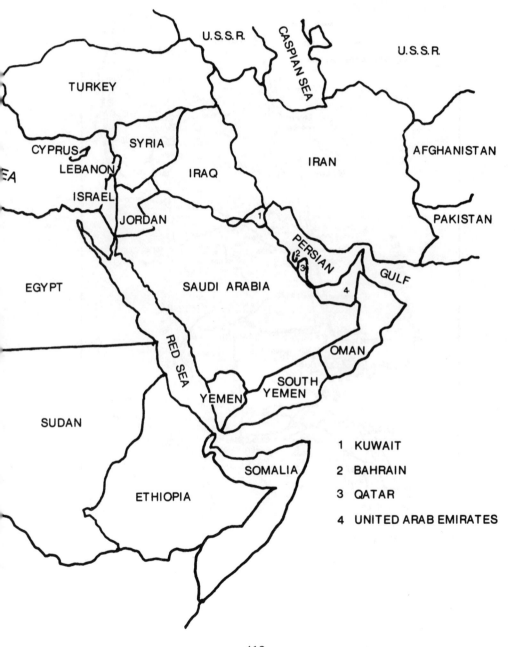

1 KUWAIT

2 BAHRAIN

3 QATAR

4 UNITED ARAB EMIRATES

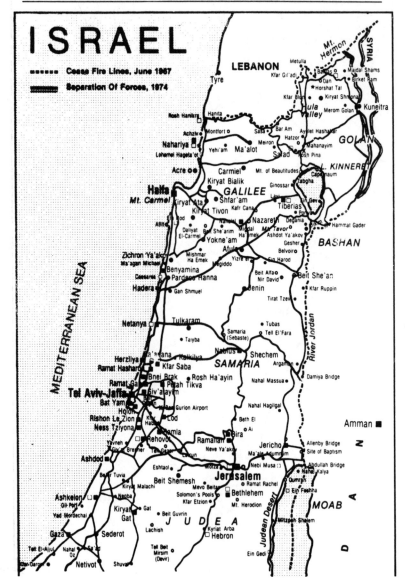

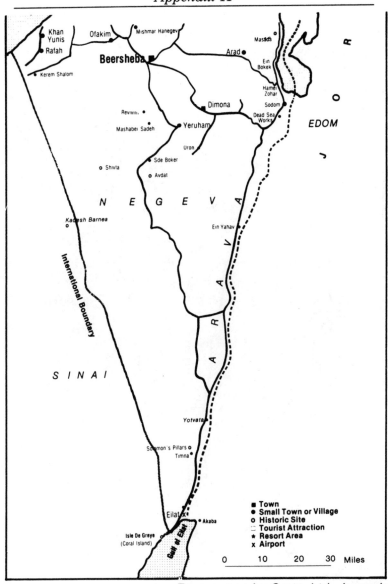

Town
Small Town or Village
Historic Site
Tourist Attraction
Resort Area
Airport

0   10   20   30   Miles

From a map by Carta, Ltd., Jerusalem

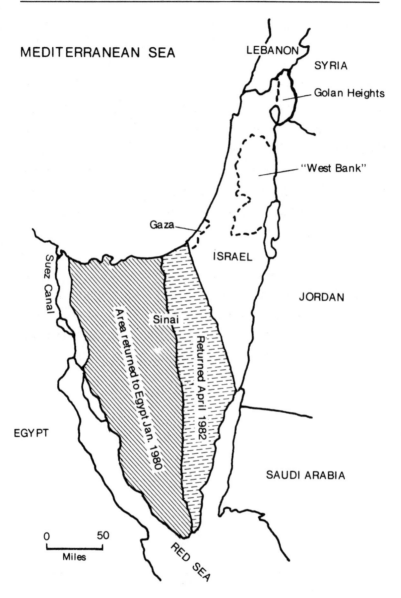

A Note About the Editors

Stephen Karetzky received his doctorate from Columbia University School of Library Service. He has taught mass communications and library science at San Jose State University, the University of Haifa (Israel), and the State University of New York at Buffalo. He is also the editor of the newsletter of the International Society of Jewish Librarians and has written for *Midstream*.

Peter Goldman is Director of Americans for a Safe Israel. He is also the author of numerous articles on the role the media plays in Middle East politics and the writer/director of the movie documentary *NBC in Lebanon: A Study of Media Misrepresentation*.

Steimatzky/Shapolsky Books of Related Interest

Available Wherever Fine Books Are Sold

Steimatzky Publishing of North America, Inc.
56 E. 11th St., N.Y., N.Y., 10003
(212) 505-2505

The Media's War Against Israel   by Stephen Karetzky $16.95

Battleground: *Fact and Fantasy in Palestine*   by Shmuel Katz $4.95

After Bitburg: *The Destiny of World Jewry*   by Illya Levkov $19.95

Breaking From the KGB   by Maurice Shainberg $16.95

General Sharon's War Against Time Magazine   by Dov Aharoni $4.95

Atlas of the Holocaust   by Martin Gilbert $14.95

The Diaspora Story   by Joan Comay $18.95

The Arab Israeli Conflict: *Its History in Maps*   by Martin Gilbert $14.95

Days of Fire: *The Secret Story of the Making of Israel*   by Shmuel Katz $9.95

Jerusalem: *Sacred City of Mankind*   by Teddy Kollek $29.95

Masada: *Herod's Fortress and the Zealots' Last Stand*   by Yigael Yadin $29.95

STEIMATZKY SHAPOLSKY
NEW YORK • JERUSALEM • TEL AVIV

Steimatzky Publishing of North America, Inc.
56 E. 11th St.
N.Y., N.Y., 10003
(212) 505-2505

Steimatzky/Shapolsky Books of Related Interest

Available Where Fine Books Are Sold

Steimatzky Publishing of North America, Inc.
56 East 11th Street., N.Y., N.Y., 10003
(212) 505-2505

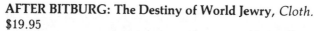

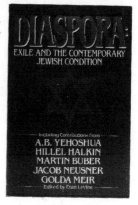

AFTER BITBURG: The Destiny of World Jewry, *Cloth.* $19.95

Was the day Ronald Reagan visited the German military cemetery at Bitburg a pivotal turning point for world Jewry? Why did the controversy over the President's visit stir up latent anti-Semitism in Germany and the United States? Which key figures in the Administration moved him toward this crucial act? What foreign and domestic political considerations figured most critically in the President's final decision to proceed with the visit? Did Bitburg create a new world-wide awareness of the Holocaust and its meanings? Or did it assist those wishing to exonerate the memory and crimes of the Waffen SS?

AFTER BITBURG will answer all of these urgent questions...and many more. In a series of candid and provocative essays and in interviews with high-level officials in the American government and in the international Jewish community, AFTER BITBURG will explore the impact for Jews throughout the world of this now historic event.

DIASPORA: Exile and the Contemporary Jewish Condition, *by Etan Levine. Cloth. $16.95*

For two thousand years, exile has been the quintessential, normative Jewish condition. However since 1948 diaspora is no longer an inevitability but an option. Jews now have the choice to continue to reside in the lands of the diaspora or to settle in the State of Israel. Thus it is in our own day, that the issue of the diaspora appears in a new perspective and takes on heightened importance for Jews both in Israel and around the world.

This collection combines, in one rich volume, an interdisciplinary spectrum of ideas and opinions concerning this basic Jewish condition. The academic experts, rabbis and political leaders who contributed to DIASPORA include: A.B. Yehoshua, Hillel Halkin, Martin Buber, Jacob Neusner, Salo Baron and Golda Meir. Their diverse experiences and insights shed light on various aspects of diaspora as a deeply rooted Jewish reality.

Steimatzky/Shapolsky Books of Related Interest

Available Where Fine Books Are Sold

Steimatzky Publishing of North America, Inc.
56 East 11th Street., N.Y., N.Y., 10003
(212) 505-2505

Battleground: *Fact and Fantasy in Palestine, by Samuel Katz. Paper. $4.95*

BATTLEGROUND: *Fact and Fantasy in Palestine* is an absorbing exploration into the origins of the Arab-Jewish conflict: How it began, why it continues. BATTLEGROUND effectively challenges the myths and half-truths that cloud the facts behind Arab-Israeli tensions.

Congressman Jack Kemp says, "BATTLEGROUND is one of the best written and most informative histories of the Arab-Israeli conflict...I advise everyone to read it."

Samuel Katz, a member of the first Israeli Knesset, has been a publisher for 25 years and a regular columnist of Israel's national daily *Maariv* and the *Jerusalem Post*. During Israel's struggle for independence Katz was a member of the Irgun High Command. He is the author of *Days of Fire, Battletruth* and *The Hollow Peace*.

General Sharon's War Against Time Magazine, *by Dov Aharoni. Paperback. Featuring original courtroom sketches and photographs. 335 pp. $4.95.*

The story of one of the most dramatic, tense courtroom wars ever fought in the name of civil liberties. This is the trial that shook Time, Inc. to its very foundations and elevated Ariel Sharon to contender status for Israel's highest office. Not since America's General Patton has the world seen a warrior for freedom like General Sharon. Find out why Time became Israel's and Sharon's most vicious and persistent enemy in the world press.